Subjects Not-(

Forms of the

in the Contemporary French Novel

FAUX TITRE

347

Etudes de langue et littérature françaises
publiées sous la direction de

Keith Busby, †M.J. Freeman,
Sjef Houppermans et Paul Pelckmans

Subjects Not-at-home:
Forms of the Uncanny
in the Contemporary French Novel

Emmanuel Carrère, Marie NDiaye, Eugène Savitzkaya

Daisy Connon

AMSTERDAM - NEW YORK, NY 2010

Cover photography: Sara Bouskela, Sevan, 2007.

Design cover: Sara Bouskela.

The paper on which this book is printed meets the requirements of
'ISO 9706: 1994, Information and documentation - Paper for documents -
Requirements for permanence'.

Le papier sur lequel le présent ouvrage est imprimé remplit les prescriptions
de 'ISO 9706: 1994, Information et documentation - Papier pour documents -
Prescriptions pour la permanence'.

ISBN: 978-90-420-3005-3
E-Book ISBN: 978-90-420-3006-0
© Editions Rodopi B.V., Amsterdam - New York, NY 2010
Printed in The Netherlands

Contents

List of Abbreviations

A - *L'Adversaire*, Emmanuel Carrère
AV - *Autoportrait en vert*, Marie NDiaye
CN - *La Classe de neige*, Emmanuel Carrère
EN - *Étrangers à nous-mêmes*, Julia Kristeva
EV - *En vie*, Eugène Savitzkaya
FF - 'La Fiction et ses fantômes', Hélène Cixous
FTP - *Fou trop poli*, Eugène Savitzkaya
LFP - *La Littérature française au présent: héritage, modernité, mutations*, Bruno Vercier and Dominique Viart
M - *La Moustache*, Emmanuel Carrère
ME - *Mentir*, Eugène Savitzkaya
MMC - *Marin mon cœur*, Eugène Savitzkaya
PH - *Pouvoirs de l'horreur*, Julia Kristeva
PP - *Prénoms de personne*, Hélène Cixous
RC - *Rosie Carpe*, Marie NDiaye
S - *La Sorcière*, Marie NDiaye
U - 'The Uncanny', Sigmund Freud
UN- *The Uncanny*, Nicolas Royle

Introduction

The uncanny familiar

The uncanny is currently assuming a new form within the contemporary French novel. While this literary term has traditionally been associated with imagery of the fantastic, such as vampires, doubles, zombies and Gothic mansions, today the uncanny also qualifies an unthematizable element in day-to-day life and in the subject's relationship to the most familiar environments: the home, the family and the self. The novels of Marie NDiaye, Emmanuel Carrère and Eugène Savitzkaya exemplify this aesthetic shift in the representation of strangeness. All three authors share a fascination with the *chez soi*.[1] As well as situating their narratives primarily in the domain of the everyday and the family home, they each explore the notion of selfhood as it relates to these environments, interrogating the subject's relationship to her familiar, domestic surroundings or to her family members.

The fictional realms generated by all three writers are at first strikingly familiar. The reader identifies a re-creation of her own everyday world and recognizes the commonplace landscape of contemporary suburban and urban France (or Belgium in the case of Savitzkaya). The action unfolds in familiar locations such as family homes, shopping centres, fast-food restaurants, administrative offices or public transport. In the work of all three writers we find close attention to the minutiae of everyday experience. The reader sympathizes to a large degree with the protagonists, who are generally ordinary, un-heroic individuals, simply carrying out their day-to-day lives and facing the minor challenges that confront anyone living in today's society: sustaining marriages and family relationships, keeping up with finances or fulfilling career-related responsibilities, maintaining the home intact. However, despite its familiarity and ordi-

---

[1] I have decided to use the term *chez soi* in this book, rather than simply saying 'home'. This French term is preferable for the purposes of this study, as it evokes not only the physical and emotional elements of home, but also the connection between home and self. A feeling of being *chez soi* may be undertood as a feeling of comfort and reassurance in one's home, but also in oneself. The uncanny suggests an unsettling of both these domains. This choice is further explained on pages 82-4 below.

nariness, the *chez soi* as represented in these narratives harbours a
certain strangeness. In the texts studied in this book, the home and the
'familiar' world shed their reassuring, anchoring and identity-
affirming connotations. Rather, we encounter subjects who are ill at
ease, threatened or otherwise estranged from everyday spaces and
phenomena.

Despite its surface banality, the depicted world often strays
from a familiar delineation by undergoing a series of subtle distortions. Familiar objects and individuals are endowed with strange
characteristics. Family homes are portrayed as domains of secrecy or
hostility. Although we are not quite within a world of fantasy or
magical realism[2], the moral, realist and natural laws that govern
common reality are often strangely absent or misshapen. Fantastic
themes such as metamorphosis, ghosts or doubles are more subtly
dispersed within a highly realist textual fabric and seem to emerge
from within the everyday, the home, the family and self, rather than
from the external world. The ordinary itself appears *extra-ordinary*.

While the protagonists of each of the selected novels turn
frequently to their homes, families and everyday objects in search of a
sense of reassurance, these domains present, in different ways, an
obstacle to subjective stability. We will see that unlike the Cartesian or
realist subject who maintains stable affinities with her surroundings[3],

---

[2] As we shall see, NDiaye's use of figures of the fantastic in *La Sorcière* is an
exception to this statement, as some of her narrative techniques do resemble those
employed within magic realism.

[3] By 'realist' subject, I mean a subject who is represented as maintaining an
objectifying gaze on the outside world. In his article 'Le Réalisme et la peur du désir',
Leo Bersani criticizes nineteenth-century realist writers, such as Stendhal and
Flaubert, for the feigned transparency of their representations of the external world
and the unity and stability which characterize their portrayals of subjectivity. For
Bersani, the appeal realism makes to linearity and its representation of the cohesion
and legibility of the external world are in contrast with its own agenda, since this
literary genre seeks to reveal the fragmentation and irrationality of social order. See
Leo Bersani, 'Le Réalisme et la peur du désir', in *Littérature et réalité*, ed. by Gérard
Genette and Tzvetan Todorov (Paris: Éditions du Seuil, 1982), pp. 47-80. In contrast,
the uncanny might be understood as the unsettling of such a realist gaze. For example,
in his analysis of the uncanniness of a painting by Hans Holbein, Jacques Lacan
understands the uncanny as a moment where the Cartesian subject-object gaze, which
generates the principles for the *camera obscura* and techniques of perspective in
painting, is reversed so that the subject experiences himself or herself as a strange
object, rather than maintaining a comfortable, domesticating subject position. See
Jacques Lacan, *Le Séminaire XI, Les Quatre concepts fondamentaux de la psycha-*

these subjects are slightly out of place, unable fully to grasp or merge with their environments, to maintain a firm footing in reality or to feel 'at home'. They appear to dwell in a relationship of *décalage* with the ordinary world.

Through reference to the uncanny, this book sets out to explore the nature of this perturbed relationship between the subject and her familiar world as represented within the selected novels. Associated with the breakdown of the boundaries between strange and familiar, the uncanny is an elusive literary and colloquial term which expresses the disturbance of the *chez soi*, both as location or environment and as an instance of selfhood. As well as being applied rather loosely in association with fantastic literature, the concept is often evoked in the context of a number of strange phenomena and experiences, all of which trouble a sense of home or self-certainty, or otherwise uproot the individual from her familiar environment or way of thinking: the double, déjà-vu, intellectual uncertainty, repetition of the same, images of being buried alive, the haunted house, the omnipotence of thoughts, dancing dolls, metamorphosis, the inability to distinguish animate from inanimate, the fragmented body, or the supplement.

As Freud's etymological study of the German term *unheimlich* reveals, the uncanny might be understood as a feeling of not-being-at-home in the world. For him, the uncanny is a form of mild anxiety, connected with certain fantastic imagery and real-life experiences. It designates a moment in which the porosity of strange and familiar is revealed, threatening the stability and comfort of the ego. The uncanny is thus the experience of something strange, but which harks back to something familiar or inseparable from the self, something repressed. In his landmark 1919 essay 'Das Unheimliche' (which will be discussed at length in the following chapter), Freud links uncanniness to castration anxiety and to the return of the repressed and views the concept as a side-effect of infantile psychosexual development or unsurmounted archaic human beliefs.

Yet despite Freud's rigorous scientific investigation, in which he seeks to domesticate this term according to the tenets of his theory of the psyche, the uncanny remains obscure. It is not simply a psycho-

---

nalyse, ed. by Jacques-Alain Miller (Paris: Éditions du Seuil, 1973), p. 121. For a more in-depth discussion of the Lacanian uncanny, see below, pages 54-5.

analytic principle, a phenomenon or even an experience. It is rather a moment which gestures to a place *outside* experience. It is a sidelong glance at the ordinary world, a feeling of separation from the collective real, a suggestion of the disintegration of familiar spaces and communal signification. Yet in the uncanny we are not entirely removed from reality, not entirely in a world of fantasy. As Nicolas Royle tells us, 'the uncanny involves a flickering sense (but not conviction) of something supernatural'.[4] In uncanniness we maintain a close connection with the familiar world and solicit its codes to explain the strangeness we encounter. The uncanny thus suggests a state of suspension between the world as comforting or re-assuring and terrifying or absurd, because it involves a striving to regain a sense of coherence and harmony. As Lucie Armitt suggests:

> In order for us to feel something to be uncanny, it must derive from a situation, object or incident that ought to feel (and usually has felt) familiar and reassuring, but which has undergone some form of slight shift that results in [...] a form of *dis-ease*.[5]

The uncanny is often a feeling of reassurance denied. It is an uncomfortable strangeness that emerges in a context where we would expect familiarity, an interruption of routine and daily life by something inexplicable.

This evolution in the literary representation of strangeness, which appears to move from the fantastic to the familiar, reflects, but also challenges, much of the post-Freudian reflection on the concept of the uncanny within cultural theory, psychoanalysis and deconstruction. The uncanny in fantastic literature and film studies is often figured as an otherwordly form, such as a monster, or a spectre, which imposes itself on the ordinary, familiar world.[6] The uncanny involves

---

[4] Nicolas Royle, *The Uncanny* (Manchester: Manchester University Press, 2003), p. 1. All other references are given in the text, following the abbreviation UN.

[5] Lucie Armitt, *Theorising the Fantastic* (London, New York, Sydney, Auckland: Arnold, 1996), p. 49.

[6] I am thinking here of fantastic or Gothic texts such as Shelley's *Frankenstein* or horror films. Of course there are examples throughout French literature, and particularly in nineteenth-century fantastic writing, of narratives in which uncanniness emerges within everyday spaces. In Gautier's *La Cafetière* (1831) and *Le Pied de momie* (1840), for example, ordinary objects such as coffee pots and paperweights 'come to life' as it were. However, in the case of Gautier, this defamiliarization of the everyday does not appear to be performed for the sake of interrogating the subject's

the perception of foreignness, something to be contrasted with the self, and which threatens its integrity. As we shall see, Freud's understanding of the concept as a 'return of the repressed' exemplifies this logic.[7] While the psychoanalyst affirms the 'familiar' component of uncanniness by connecting it to selfhood and the unconscious, he also portrays it as a threat to the ego, something to be rejected in the interests of preserving subjective stability.

However, contemporary psychoanalytic, deconstructionist, political and literary thought has reconfigured the uncanny to stress the familiar component of this duplicitous term. These reinterpretations of the uncanny tend to bring the concept into proximity with the ordinary, with ideology, with ethics and with the question of knowledge itself, exploring its implications for the familiar and the self-same. From Julia Kristeva's point of view, the embracing of the strangeness of the *chez soi* is a starting point for an ethics of perceiving the other. An encounter with the foreign is what reveals the vulnerability and alterity already present within the self. Hélène Cixous appeals to the concept of the uncanny to articulate her politics of literary creation, which is founded on a letting go of the myth of the unified *chez soi*, which she views as a totalizing refuge that might contribute to the marginalization and oppression of the other by designating 'other' as strange. For many contemporary thinkers, the uncanny should not be viewed simply as a moment of dissipation of reality, but as playing a role in every rational, epistemological and representational structure. However, while theorists have indicated the value of such a form of thinking, they have only just begun to suggest how such a perspective might be embraced within social, political or discursive practices.

---

relationship to the domestic or the *quotidien* itself. Rather, the significance of the coffee pot and the paperweight is subjugated to the socio-critical agenda of the author. In her Marxist reading of *Le Pied de momie*, Jutta Fortin suggests that the paperweight symbolizes the endowment of objects with a life of their own when they become commodities in consumer culture. According to this view, Gautier's use of the fantastic is akin to some of his realist literary ambitions, which involve a critique of certain social realities. See Jutta Fortin, 'Brides of the Fantastic: Gautier's *Le Pied de momie* and Hoffmann's *Der Sandmann*', *Comparative Literature Studies* 41, No. 2 (2004), 257-75. However, Gautier's fantastic foreshadows the desciptions of the *quotidien* that will be studied in the second chapter of this book.

[7] A detailed description of Freud's analysis of the uncanny begins on page 34 below.

As a concept which is metaphorically and performatively connected to unhomeliness[8] in all possible forms, the uncanny will thus
provide a fertile theoretical context to guide a reading of NDiaye's,
Carrère's and Savitzkaya's texts as *unheimlich* stories. Rather than
appearing simply as a collection of strange imagery with the potential
to rekindle repressed fears, the uncanny within the novels of NDiaye,
Savitzkaya and Carrère can be viewed as a revelation of the
strangeness inherent in the subject's ordinary rapport with the familiar
world. The uncanny is not simply a breakdown, a symptom or a form
of *dis-ease*. It is not only an intrusion on the norm, but rather an
inherent, creative possibility within each everyday moment, retriev-
able within all the comfortable and familiar structures that surround
the subject. Furthermore, by generating a strange or renewed glance
on habitual ideas and spaces, the uncanny is inextricably linked to
literary creation. In this book I would like to suggest that, within these
texts, the uncanny moves beyond a repertoire of fantasy or a
phenomenology of reading and becomes a renewed vision of the
familiar and the everyday and an approach to representation.

A literary context for the uncanny?
While contemporary critics often insist upon the current vitality of the
French novel, they nonetheless frequently evoke today's literary
trends as a series of 'returns' to past themes and preoccupations.
Specific works are often classified as participating in the return of the
subject, of realism or of the novelistic.[9] Of course, it is often pointed
out that these returns are far from wholehearted, and are better
understood as contemporary re-appropriations of past approaches in
the wake of the suspicion of representation generated by the *Nouveau
Roman*. Can the recent manifesttations of the uncanny within the

---

[8] The word 'unhomeliness' as employed in this book is not entirely synonymous with
'homelessness'. While 'homelessness' implies uprootedness or a loss of home,
'unhomeliness' suggests a sense of estrangement from one's home.

[9] See, for example, the series of papers published on the idea of the 'retour du
romanesque' in *Christian Oster et cie, retour du romanesque*, ed. by Aline Mura-
Brunel (Amsterdam, NewYork: Rodopi, 2006), or Johnnie Gratton's discussion of the
tendency to view certain contemporary autobiographical writings as participating in a
'retour du sujet'. See Johnnie Gratton, 'Postmodern French Fiction: Practice and
Theory', in *The Cambridge Companion to the French Novel, From 1800 to the
Present*, ed. by Timothy Unwin (Cambridge: Cambridge University Press, 1997), pp.
242-60 (pp. 245-6).

French novel be seen to constitute yet another 'return'? Perhaps so, if the uncanny is understood in a loose sense as being synonymous with fantastic imagery such as vampirism or the double. One might view the traces of fantasy found in Marie NDiaye, René Belletto or Marie Darrieussecq as contributing to a contemporary revival of the forms of the fantastic manifested in Maupassant's *contes*, Balzac's or Gautier's departures from the narrative codes of realism, or the tales of Cazotte and Nerval, perhaps forming a French version of the 'Modern Gothic' or magical realism.

One reason for hesitating to adopt the hypothesis that the contemporary uncanny is best understood as a 'return' is that it appears to emerge not from a desire to retrieve past forms of the fantastic as an expression of alterity, but from the opposite direction. The uncanny as incarnated within current French writing in fact takes on a unique form when it becomes intertwined with another contemporary literary tendency, the representation of familiar spaces, what I refer to in this book as the *chez soi*: the self, the home, the family and the everyday. It is possible to observe a strong interest in these domains within today's writing. In the post-Freudian era the intimate spaces of self and home have come to the forefront.[10] This tendency is visible in the recent interest in family narrative and *récits de filiation* (Ernaux, Nobécourt, Bergounioux, Vigouroux, Nimier, Boyer, Alféri), new autobiographical forms (Modiano, Duras, Ernaux) and in the representation of domestic spaces (Oster, Chevillard, Toussaint). While the three authors studied in this book do sometimes have recourse to fantasy in their texts, the more striking similarity among them is perhaps their tendency to focus on the most ordinary, 'familiar' domains of human experience. It seems that their uncanny narratives participate in this literary trend towards the representation of the *chez soi*, a theme which, for these writers, can best be understood, paradoxically, as an experience of the strange. The uncanny must thus be viewed as the response of NDiaye, Carrère and

---

[10] Dominique Viart comments on the prevalence of the representation of family and kinship in the French novel, which focuses on the failures and weakness of the family and home and is often written from a place of lack, featuring 'parents absents, figures mal assurées, transmissions imparfaites, valeurs caduques'. Dominique Viart and Bruno Vercier, *La Littérature française au présent: héritage, modernité, mutations* (Paris: Bordas, 2005), p. 91. All other references are given in the text, following the abbreviation LFP.

Savitzkaya to the 'repli sur l'intime'[11] found in contemporary French writing.

A cultural context for the uncanny?

Without wishing to reduce the uncanniness of the novels studied to a simple product of an unhomely era, it may be pertinent briefly to explore the broader context in which NDiaye, Savitzkaya and Carrère are writing. In a general way, their tendency to problematize the site of the *chez soi* is aligned with the fascination for home found in much contemporary thought and displayed in certain cultural and social phenomena.[12]

Within current reflection, the concept of home as a natural, organic place of comfort is often challenged. The profusion of recent thought on concepts such as nomadism, uprootedness, exile and dislocation reflects current debates concerning national borders, colonialism and immigration. The themes of the home and family have received significant attention since the beginning of the twenty-first century, and their uncertainty and mythical nature are being affirmed. This trend is not confined to literary practice and theory, but also appears within the discourses of feminism, anthropology and sociology. This surge of recognition for the home as a conceptual domain is perhaps related to identity politics, which have thus far been ubiquitous in contemporary reflection. It might also echo more tangible evolutions of the home and family within modern society and the haziness of the boundaries of home and other which are challenged through globalization and the expansion of Europe. Homi Bhabha asks this question with regard to immigrant writing:

> As the migrant and the refugee become the 'unhomely' inhabitants of the contemporary world, how do we rethink collective, communal concepts like homeland, the people, cultural exile, national cultures and interpretative communities?[13]

---

[11] Christian Michel, '"Le Réel dort aussi": un panorama du jeune roman français', *Esprit* 225 (October 1996), 43-67 (p. 14).

[12] It is also possible that this sense of homelessness has a personal significance for NDiaye and Savitzkaya. They perhaps both experience certain feelings of uprootedness, given their partially non-French origins. NDiaye's father is Senegalese and Savitzkaya's parents are Russian and Polish, although these writers were raised in France and Belgium respectively.

[13] Homi Bhahba, *The Location of Culture* (London: Routledge, 1994), p. 271.

Along with national and sexual identities, the location and significance of home as the derivation and core of the subject and as a primordial value-ascribing institution have been thrown into doubt. No longer viewed as an institution in and of itself, the nuclear family is explored as a symbolic discursive structure, a myth of the collective imagination and a regulatory ideal, which maintains minimal connection to reality, since the family is currently becoming more disparate, its definition incessantly evolving with its malleable contemporary incarnations. For Élisabeth Roudinesco, the deviation of the contemporary Western family from its previous nuclear ideal has repercussions for prevailing ideologies, which find themselves without a concrete, foundational substance in which to embed their discourse:

> Monoparentale, homoparentale, recomposée, déconstruite, clonée, générée artificiellement, attaquée de l'intérieur par de prétendus négateurs de la différence des sexes, elle ne serait plus capable de transmettre ses propres valeurs. En conséquence, l'Occident judéo-chrétien, et pis encore la démocratie républicaine, seraient menacés de décomposition.[14]

Much reflection on home has been directed towards upsetting the stability of the terms 'family' and 'home' as transcendental signifiers that could operate in favour of a particular ideological framework.[15] Many have stressed the duality of the family as a site of contradiction, revealing its uneasy conceptual status. It is represented as a natural, universal and inevitable form, while also being constructed as a fragile, threatened entity in need of maintenance. It is viewed as a private sanctuary from the real world, while also being a field for public enquiry and investigation and a site of violence and tension. It is a place of protection, but also of abuse.

Such reflections on the equivocal and evolving nature of home and family might be relevant to the work of these writers. However,

---

[14] Élisabeth Roudinesco, *La Famille en désordre* (Paris: Fayard, 2002), p. 11.

[15] In her book *Representing the Family*, for example, Deborah Chambers employs a Foucauldian perspective to examine the family as a culturally constructed sign, which is the product of discursive power relations. She looks at the representational construct of the family in media, film and political structures and the ways in which these frameworks reinforce or subvert the stability of the notion of the functional, white, nuclear family. See Deborah Chambers, *Representing the Family* (London, Thousand Oaks, New Delhi: Sage Publications, 2001).

the uncanny as explored in this book is not political or social, but more personal. For the purposes of this study, the *chez soi* is being primarily addressed as a subjective and aesthetic experience; the cultural dynamics of unhomeliness lie beyond the reach of this analysis.

Choice of corpus

Diverse forms, or at least, traces of what may be seen as a contemporary configuration of the uncanny, can be found in the work of several current French writers. Marie Darrieussecq, René Belletto and Linda Lê, for example, all employ figures of the fantastic or the grotesque within descriptions of ordinary family relations and day-to-day experience. Frédéric Boyer, François Vigouroux and Pierre Alféri share a fascination for the hidden corners, secrets and strangeness of family life. The novels of Christian Oster and Éric Chevillard depict the everyday world as one of obstacle and resistance and display a unique attention to the banal details of everyday life, drawing our attention to a certain strangeness within it.

However, because it is necessary for the purposes of this book to delimit the corpus, it might be argued that NDiaye, Savitzkaya and Carrère are three authors whose similarities and differences with respect to their representation of uncanniness complement one another in an illuminating way and offer a rich selection of novels in which the *Unheimliche* is significant not only on one, but on a number of levels. The narrative projects of NDiaye, Carrère and Savitzkaya are characterized by the destabilization and estrangement of the *chez soi,* which includes the problematization of the subject's relation to familiar spaces. As well as exploiting the leitmotifs of the uncanny and telling stories of the vulnerabilities and anxieties of home, all three authors elaborate visions of the ordinary which invite the reader to rethink the familiar as inherently strange. The uncanny evokes an experience of selfhood, a possible quality of the home and, as we shall see in the final chapter, an integral part of the writing experience. This multi-layered configuration of uncanniness, which comes across quite differently in all three writers, provides a rich foundation for a comparative discussion.

Marie NDiaye

Marie NDiaye published her first novel, *Quant au riche avenir* (1985) with Éditions de Minuit at the young age of eighteen. She then went on to write numerous works of fiction and theatre, including nine novels, four plays, three children's works and one collection of short stories. Her second novel, *Comédie classique* (published by P.O.L.) was composed during her studies in linguistics at the Sorbonne and took the form of a stylistic exercise, narrated in a single sentence. With *La Femme changée en bûche* (1989), the novelist found her unique narrative voice, which is characterized by a distortion of the realist pact to expose disconcerting dimensions of contemporary life, with a particular emphasis on the home and family relations.

Over the past decade NDiaye's work has become increasingly renowned in the Anglophone world; her plays have been translated and performed outside France.[16] Within both the French and Anglo-Saxon academic milieus, NDiaye's writing has recently been the object of international conferences and book-length publications, and her status as one of the twenty-first century's great writers has been formally recognised by a number of literary prizes and achievements.[17] Her 2001 novel *Rosie Carpe* earned her the *Prix Fémina*, while her play *Papa doit manger* was performed at the *Comédie Française* in 2003. NDiaye's most recent novel, *Trois femmes puissantes*, was honoured with the prestigious *Prix Goncourt* in 2009.

NDiaye is not easily situated within any particular literary framework.[18] Because of her tendency to privilege the themes of foreignness and identity, her writing has been appropriated within various critical contexts and quite specific past and present literary trends. Due to her Senegalese heritage on her father's side, NDiaye is sometimes considered in the context of African writing and the litera-

---

[16] *Hilda* (1999), for example, was performed during the 'Act French' festival in New York at the American Conservatory Theater in December 2005.

[17] For example, the conference 'Autour de Marie NDiaye' held at the London Institute of Germanic and Romance Studies (April 2007) or Dominique Rabaté's book, *Marie NDiaye* (Paris: Textuel, Culturesfrance, 2008).

[18] Véronique Bonnet stresses the difficulties encountered in trying to situate NDiaye's work within contemporary French literature. She concludes that: 'Marie NDiaye ne s'inscrit dans aucun courant littéraire constitué ou en voix *(sic)* de constitution'. Véronique Bonnet, 'Où situer Marie NDiaye', *Africultures* 45 (February 2002) http ://www.africultures.com/index.asp?menu=revue_affiche_article&no=2102 (accessed on 9 January 2008).

ture of *négritude*.[19] Her consistent choice of female protagonists and
the challenges she poses to conventional family roles and relationships
within the domestic sphere have led feminist criticism to view her
work as an exploration of feminine identity.[20] On purely aesthetic
grounds, within French criticism NDiaye's writing is often associated
with a renewal of the novelistic, given her taste for more traditional
elements of the novel, such as linear plots, unified point of view and
in-depth character development.[21]

Although her writing is very diverse, NDiaye's novels all
display certain common attributes and a distinct tone resonates
throughout her work. Her narratives are largely set within the family
home. Yet she evokes this space in such a way as to emphasize its
strangeness and discomfort, rather than its familiarity and reassuring
qualities. A theme that resurfaces in nearly all of NDiaye's texts is
that of the impossibility of the *rentrée chez soi*. The protagonists of
her stories share a desire to 'go home' and to retrieve their family
origins, yet this pursuit of a sense of rootedness and comfort is often
met with hostility and results in a feeling of dislocation. For example,
in *En famille* (1991), Fanny arrives at her grandmother's home where
all her relatives have gathered, only to discover that none of them
recognize her or accept her as a family member.

This return *chez soi* is often tied up with the identity quest of
the central protagonist and understood as an attempt to return to the
self, to know the self and feel at home with oneself. Furthermore, the
perturbation of the *chez soi* appears to describe the way in which
NDiaye's characters dwell in the ordinary and the familiar space of the
everyday. They are often at odds with their environments, both physically and emotionally, and experience ordinary scenarios and circumstances as foreign or disconcerting. This portrayal of subjectivity will
be discussed at length in the final chapter of this book through a
reading of *Autoportrait en vert* (2005). This text constitutes NDiaye's

---

[19] See, for example, Ambroise Têko-Agbo's article, '*En famille* de Marie NDiaye ou
l'insupportable étrangeté de "l'étrangère"', in *Littératures et sociétés africaines:
regards comparatistes et perspectives interculturelles: mélanges offerts à János Riesz
à l'occasion de son soixantième anniversaire* (Tübingen: G. Narr, 2001), pp. 533-43.
[20] See, for example, Colette Sarrey-Strack, *Fictions contemporaines au féminin:
Marie Darrieussecq, Marie NDiaye, Marie Nimier, Marie Redonnet* (Paris: L'Harmattan, 2002).
[21] See, for example, A. Thomas, 'Marie NDiaye. Renaissance de la littérature française', *Amina* 253 (May 1991), p. 81.

first and only autobiographical endeavour and makes use of photography by Julie Ganzin.

Critics often cannot help but evoke Kafka when describing NDiaye's writing because of the absurd scenarios that underlie the experience of her protagonists.[22] Characters are pursued by their doubles; inter-subjective relations are illogical; children are abandoned or mistreated by their parents. While her earlier novels were characterized by the intrusion of fantastic occurrences on an otherwise banal, cynical description of contemporary suburban life, her more recent works generate an uncanny atmosphere without direct recourse to fantasy. The reader has the sense of perceiving the ordinary world though an estranging lens, and strangeness is conveyed more through the impressions and inner ramblings of the characters than explicitly through event and plot. These distortions of the codes of realism are at the base of what often appears to be a critique of the mercantile, superficial nature of contemporary society. They also contribute to NDiaye's unique portrayal of subjective experience as over-abundant, disjointed and at odds with the collective real. NDiaye's prose is characterized by her unique use of syntax, sinuous sentences, a tendency towards strange repetitions and heavy use of the subjunctive mood.

Emmanuel Carrère

Emmanuel Carrère is a French writer, journalist, screenwriter and director. Unlike NDiaye and Savitzkaya, who tend to evade publicity and lead more marginal existences in small rural communities, Carrère is a prominent and polyvalent public figure in contemporary French film, literature and media. He is perhaps more accessible, both in terms of his writing and his character, to the general public. To date he is the author of seven novels, several of which have been awarded literary prizes, including the *Prix Fémina* for his 1995 novel, *La Classe de neige*.[23] He has also written three non-fictional texts,

---

[22] In *Un temps de saison* (1994), for example, a man goes on holiday with his family to a small village and decides to stay on past the end of the tourist season. Strangely, his wife and son disappear and his quest to relocate them is intertwined with a Kafkaesque administrative struggle at the local *Mairie* when he tries to solicit the help of the local village inhabitants.

[23] His 1984 novel *Bravoure* earned him the *Prix Passion* and the *Prix de la Vocation*, and in 1988 he was awarded the *Prix Kléber Haedens* for *Hors d'atteinte*.

including a monograph on the German film director Werner Herzog (1982) and a biography of the American science-fiction writer Philip K. Dick (*Je suis vivant et vous êtes morts*, 1993). He was awarded the *Grand Prix de la science-fiction* in 1987 for his essay on the concept of *Uchronie*, entitled *Le Détroit de Behring*. Two of his novels, *L'Adversaire* and *La Classe de neige*, have been adapted for cinema by other directors (Nicole Garcia and Claude Miller respectively), and were both official selections at Cannes. In 2003 Carrère directed a documentary entitled *Retour à Kotelnitch*[24] and in 2005, a film version of his own 1986 novel, *La Moustache*. He has also composed a number of film scripts for television.

Like NDiaye's work, Carrère's novels often seek to interrogate and challenge the certainty and comfort of the *chez soi*. Set largely within the landscape of the everyday, Carrère paints an estranged, amplified portrait of ordinary relationships and experience within the home and family, evoking the hidden traps that underlie and destabilize the terrain of the domestic sphere and family life. Often, this background of unhomeliness becomes intertwined with the uncertainties of subjectivity. Carrère's characters are, as Dominique Rabaté suggests, 'toujours prêts à basculer dans la folie'.[25] For example, both *L'Adversaire* and *La Moustache* generate scenarios in which a seemingly harmonious family existence is destroyed by a form of strangeness that emerges from within the family home. *L'Adversaire*, a generically indeterminate work based on a *fait divers*, is centred on the image of the Romand family home, burned to the ground by a father in an attempt to spare his family from discovering the truth about his false existence as a doctor. In *La Moustache*, a man's paranoia causes him to lose connection with reality, and devastates his relationship with his wife, when he shaves off his moustache and his friends, family members and colleagues refuse to acknowledge its previous existence. For the protagonists of both novels, the instability of self has repercussions for the representation of home; these two aspects of the *chez soi* are always interrelated.

---

[24] This project began as an endeavor to represent a small Russian village, home of one of the last prisoners of the Second World War, and became entangled with the plot of a *fait divers*, which occurred during the filming.

[25] Dominique Rabaté, 'Résistances et disparitions', in *Le Roman français contemporain*, ed. by Thierry Guichard, Christine Jérusalem, Boniface Mongo-Mboussa, Delphine Peras and Dominique Rabaté (Paris: Panoramas, 2007), pp. 9-46 (p. 28).

These experiences of subjective turmoil are related in a lucid, descriptive, contemporary narrative style, which has led some critics to view Carrère's writing as participating in a contemporary 'return to realism'.

However, the unifying characteristic of Carrère's œuvre is not simply thematic, but also conceptual. Nearly all of Carrère's novels are rooted in some form of intellectual uncertainty.[26] As is evident from the plots of *L'Adversaire* and *La Moustache*, the writer is fascinated with the boundary between fiction and non-fiction, realism and fantasy. This idea comes across in his book-length essay *Le Détroit de Behring* in which he develops the concept of *Uchronie*, defined as 'l'histoire si elle s'était déroulée autrement'.[27]

The uncanny overtones of Carrère's work appear to stem in part from a long-standing fascination with science fiction. Indeed, in *La Moustache* the protagonist appears to have slipped into a parallel universe which resembles his own, but which has undergone a slight glitch in the ordinary. This small detail proves to be just enough to throw reality off kilter. The novelist's fascination for this gap that he perceives between the real and the imaginary is a driving force behind his writing.

Another uncanny element in Carrère's work is his attraction for the gruesome. In *La Classe de neige*, for example, we are exposed to the grisly childhood fantasies of the young hero Nicolas, involving murders and fragmented body parts. Yet it seems that while the chilling atmosphere of the science fiction story envelops nearly all of the writer's novels, the material for these texts comes from reality itself: the banal, the concrete, the *fait divers*. Carrère often appears to be telling us that it is unnecessary to resort to pure fantasy to find the macabre and the strange, because this is what reality itself is made of. This is why Dominique Rabaté describes Carrère's style as an attempt to 'attir[er] le réalisme vers une sorte de fantastique insidieux'.[28]

---

[26] The notion of 'intellectual uncertainty' will be crucial to the discussion of the uncanny in the following chapter.

[27] The French philosopher, Charles Renouvier, who coined the term in the late nineteenth-century, views it as an 'esquisse apocryphe du développement de la civilisation européenne, tel qu'il n'a pas été, tel qu'il aurait pu être'. See Emmanuel Carrère, *Le Détroit de Behring* (Paris: P.O.L.,1987), p. 8.

[28] Dominique Rabaté, *Le Roman français depuis 1900*, coll. 'Que sais-je' (Paris: PUF, 1998), p. 115.

Carrère himself admits to being 'habité par l'horreur et par la folie'.[29] In what is perhaps a conscious attempt actively to steer his writing away from the themes of madness and gore, he has recently written an autobiographical text, *Un roman russe*. Quite different from his previous works, this text takes the form of an exploration of the author's family roots and secrets and childhood memories.

Eugène Savitzkaya

Eugène Savitzkaya is a Belgian novelist, playwright and poet with Russian and Polish origins. Despite these non-French roots, the fact that Savitzkaya publishes his texts with Éditions de Minuit means that his writing has its place within the context of French literature and can therefore be included in this study.[30]

Savitzkaya's early works were predominantly poetic. He published his first collection of poetry, entitled *Mongolie, plaine sale*, with Seghers in 1976. The poetry composed during the early stages of his writing career is dense and syntactically complex; thematically it is often very physical and organic, based on experiences of the human body. This is a style the author adopts again later in novelistic form in the very corporeal, animalistic, fantasy-driven work *Sang de chien* (1989), which is centred on the theme of the *corps morcelé*. In his novels, thoughts, memories and body parts are often portrayed as having a status that is indistinguishable from that of plants, animals, objects, natural elements and particles. All entities behave like characters, moving, evolving and interacting with one another.

Savitzkaya's first novel, *Mentir*, was published in 1977 with Éditions de Minuit and is based on a description of a series of photographs of the narrator's mother. Written in a sparser, straightforward language than his poems, this work marks the beginning of certain distinctive features that traverse Savitzkaya's œuvre: a fascination with childhood and parenthood, the expression of desire for an absent mother, a renunciation of the distinction between the poetic and the novelistic and between the fictional and the autobiographical.[31] His

---

[29] Florence Noiville, 'Emmanuel Carrère, "J'avais l'impression d'être enfermé"', *Le Monde des livres* (2 March 2007), p. 12.

[30] For Dominique Viart, when Belgian authors publish their books in France, 'ils écrivent à l'intérieur de la littérature française' (LFP 8).

[31] Although they almost always bear the subtitle 'roman', many of his works are largely autobiographical.

stories very often feature lived moments and contain references to existing figures and restorations of events and characters from his own past. In 1982, Savitzkaya published *La Disparition de Maman*, a work which earned significant critical acclaim.[32] In 1991 Savitzkaya wrote his first play, *La Folie originelle*, at the instigation of the director Dominique Pitoiset. This work plays with spatio-temporal codes and is centered on the dialogue of the inhabitants of a village threatened by an impending catastrophe. In 1992 Savitzkaya was awarded the Prix Point for his novel *Marin mon cœur*. More accessible than some of his earlier novels, this text appears to mark the beginning of a new phase in Savitzkaya's writing. One of the characteristics of this transition is an increased fascination with the strange and familiar nature of everyday life within the home, a tendency which is again observable in such works as his play *Aux prises avec la vie* (1992) and *En vie* (1995). Savitzkaya's more recent novels are characterized by a style that oscillates between lyricism and simplicity, in which he elaborates paradoxically colourful descriptions of commonplace occurrences and objects. In these more recent texts, such as *Fou trop poli* (2005), we begin to observe a paradoxical fluctuation in the author's style between a naïve, child-like language and heavy use of obscure, archaic, scientific and botanical language.[33]

In his later work especially, Savitzkaya's portrayal of the everyday, although equally defamiliarizing, does not convey the sense of anxiety that we observe in NDiaye and Carrère. The quest for home and the loss of the *chez soi* take a unique form in Savitzkaya's texts in that they are often divorced from the negative affects that we have come to associate with uncanniness. Given this difference, Savitzkaya figures in this study as a kind of *cas limite*. While many elements associated with the uncanny are present – the loss of home, the dissolution or problematization of the boundaries between strange and familiar, the strangeness of the family and the everyday – these phenomena, while destabilizing, are not experienced as fearsome, but

---

[32] This text is viewed by critics as Savitzkaya's first masterpiece. See Laurent Demoulin, 'Eugène Savitzkaya à la croisée des chemins', *Écritures contemporaines* 2 (1999), 41-56 (p. 44). The novel resembles *Mentir* in its exploration of the relationship between mother and son and the desire for union with the maternal, but these themes are articulated in a more complex and opaque language.

[33] Meticulous descriptions of plants and insects in the author's garden often feature in his novels.

are rather sought and celebrated. Often, as exemplified in his novel *En vie*, Savitzkaya's narratives set out to locate and rejoice in the strangeness the writer perceives within everyday spaces.

In a comprehensive way, Savitzkaya's entire narrative project is often interpreted as an enactment of the subject's quest for the union with the object of his desire, a search for a more primitive home.[34] Savitzkaya's subjects are desirous, organic, and often appear to be seeking to return to the point where the distinction between subject and object, self and other disintegrates.[35] Perhaps this is why certain critics stress the maternal aspect of Savitzkaya's writing, not only on a thematic level, but also in terms of the textual world that he evokes, which is fluid, and exempt from, or not yet subject to, the descriptive codes and subject-object distinctions of collective reality. For Laurent Demoulin, Savitzkaya's texts seem to 's'originer dans un ventre maternel'.[36]

Structure of the book

This book is divided into four main chapters. The first chapter takes the form of a theoretical discussion of the concept of the uncanny and explores the term's evolution from its origins in pre-Freudian psychology to its most recent forms within contemporary cultural theory. The aim of this chapter is to introduce the uncanny as a guiding theoretical framework and to emphasize its construction in the thought of certain thinkers who view it as a productive conceptual or ethical space. The subsequent chapters will be dedicated to readings of the individual novels, with three per chapter. Each chapter corresponds to a particular facet of the *chez soi* – the everyday, the family or the self – and will address the ways in which the unresolved tension between the codes of strangeness and familiarity lead these writers to recover a fruitful narrative space in which ordinary locations and phenomena are re-thought through codes of the strange. However, because these different elements of the *chez soi* are inextricably linked

---

[34] See, for example, Henri Scepi's discussion of the role of the primitive in Savitzkaya's work. Henry Scepi, 'Eugène Savitzkaya et le souci de l'origine', *Critique* 550-551 (March-April 1993), 140-66.

[35] Henri Scepi describes Savitzkaya's writing as a search for a reunion with 'un vaste monde tumultueux de pulsions étranglées, de cris et de bonheurs ensevelis'. Ibid, p. 143.

[36] Laurent Demoulin, 'Eugène Savitzkaya à la croisée des chemins', p. 43.

for all three writers, they will each resurface in every chapter. Chapter two is a discussion of the representation of the subject within everyday life and the home. Through a portrayal of the everyday as a place of inherent strangeness, the individual is represented in these texts as not 'master in her own house'. Chapter three will focus on the depiction of subjectivity within the family, by examining the ways in which stories of the most familiar people become stories of the strange. In interpreting relations of kinship and subjectivity within the contemporary home, all three authors draw upon language and motifs of alterity. Finally, in chapter four, I hope to show that the uncanny might be understood not only as an array of images and a literary device for the articulation of the strangeness of home and self, but also as a narrative ethos or stance of writing. In the three narratives that feature in this chapter, each author figuratively destabilizes his or her own authorial *chez soi* in order to represent the other or the self, exposing the anxieties and plurality of the narrative voice as it seeks to locate a point of view from which to narrate. The place from which the writing occurs is itself portrayed as *unheimlich*, located at a point of primary uncertainty.

Das Unheimliche

'Le dépaysement ne signifie pas seulement la perte du pays, mais une manière plus authentique de résider, d'habiter sans habitude'.

– Maurice Blanchot, *L'Entretien Infini*[1]

An Elusive Term

Paradoxically, the scholarly value of the concept of the uncanny arises from its indefinable nature. As a theoretical notion, the uncanny has constituted a rich topic for academic debate precisely by resisting 'domestication' by any particular interpretative grid. Like the sublime, uncanniness is primarily understood as something that defies description, and so any discussion surrounding it is destined to fall into certain traps. While countless attempts have been made to isolate contexts, triggers or symptoms of the uncanny, and to explain its phenolmenology, new interpretations inevitably emerge to point out the blind spots or dogmatism of the preceding ones. Of course, in this respect the uncanny simply resembles many other scholarly terms upon which theorists cannot agree.

This indefinable quality is apparent both within the term's most common usage and in relation to its adoption as a theoretical tool. We can often only speak of the uncanny in rambling, mystifying terms. We know that it has something to do with a loss of home and with the blurring of strange and familiar. It both *is* something in itself and may be an adjective, qualifying something else, an attribute ascribed to something formerly familiar. It has been described both as an absence (a lack or a hole) in discourse and reality and as a surplus (a supplement or a repetition).[2] The concept may be constructed with

---

[1] Maurice Blanchot, 'Parole de fragment', in *L'Entretien infini* (Paris: Gallimard, 1969), pp. 451-5, p. 452.

[2] In Jacques Lacan's version of the uncanny, which is often assimilated to his concept of the *objet a*, anxiety is constructed as the 'lack of lack', or when lack itself comes to be lacking. For Lacan, then, it is not uncertainty that generates uncanny experience,

regard to subjectivity, as an aspect of the psyche,[3] a symptom,[4] or structurally, as something present in the text or the exterior world.[5] While definitions of the uncanny inevitably vary according to differences in language use and visions of subjectivity, any attempt to speak about the uncanny itself seems to have the effect of generating chaos and discombobulating reality. A certain sense of bewilderment before the concept is apparent in Nicolas Royle's description of the term in his 2004 book-length study. Royle dedicates the first few pages to a seemingly miscellaneous brainstorm of uncanny imagery. He later elucidates this approach through meta-textual incentive:

> To write about the uncanny, as Freud's essay makes admirably clear, is to lose one's bearings, to find oneself immersed in the maddening logic of the supplement, to engage with a hydra. This is no reason to give up trying: examples of the uncanny get tangled up with one another, critical distinctions and conclusions become vertiginously difficult, but they are still necessary. (UN 8)

However, attempts to define the uncanny always evoke something of the feeling of uncanniness itself. To pursue a lexical definition, which requires the reduction of a term or idea to a specific set of semantic and contextual circumstances, is an instance of the kind of act rendered unworkable by the uncanny, that is, the filtration of the foreign from the familiar, the attempt to familiarize oneself with a concept or 'feel at home' with a particular vocabulary. The conceptual 'homes' that thinkers forge in an effort to define uncanniness inevitably reveal themselves to be haunted by presuppositions, distortions, reductions, confusions and repetitions. Yet each attempt to define the concept also lends more force to the uncanny, generating a performative exemplification of what is at stake in uncanny experience.

---

but too much certainty or proximity with the *objet a*. For an explanation of the Lacanian uncanny, see Mladan Dolar, 'I Shall be with you on your Wedding Night, Lacan and the Uncanny', *October* 58 (1991), 5-23.

[3] Julia Kristeva, for example, links the uncanny to the unconscious and explores its role as a universal element in the construction of subjectivity. Her account will be addressed later in this chapter.

[4] Freud and Lacan both link the uncanny to forms of anxiety.

[5] For Tzvetan Todorov, for example, the uncanny is a literary mechanism, and a subgenre of the fantastic. Todorov's understanding of the uncanny will be discussed further on. See pages 41-2 below.

Given this indefinable quality, rather than focusing on elucidating the uncanny, this chapter will trace some of the forms and bifurcations of the evolution of the concept, beginning with Freud's etymological confusions of *heimlich/unheimlich*, then exploring its scholarly and psychoanalytical meanings and applications, the most frequent contexts of its appearance, and emphasizing the movement of the uncanny away from a privileging of the strange towards its potential to provide grounds for a reinterpretation of the ordinary world. In the late twentieth and early twenty-first centuries, the uncanny teaches the re-assessment of the familiar, including familiar ways of thinking. In particular, I will focus on two analyses of the uncanny, those of Hélène Cixous and Julia Kristeva. Both thinkers have proposed rich and complex descriptions of possible forms of uncanny thinking, which have greatly influenced recent constructions of the uncanny and which suggest the pertinence of the concept for a politics of representation.

In discussions of the uncanny, our attention is inevitably drawn to the German word, *das Unheimliche*, which contains the root *heim* meaning 'home'. The puzzling semantics of the adjective *heimlich* (which, as Freud demonstrates, can also at times denote the same content as its opposite, *unheimlich*) have been a long-standing enigma in reflection on the uncanny and highlight the duplicity and inscrutability of the concept. Although the significance of the term's etymology has been interpreted differently by various thinkers, we could advance a preliminary understanding of the uncanny as an unhomely experience, a moment of uprooting, of losing one's firm footing in reality. Or alternatively, we could view the uncanny as a contamination of home, as a moment when we suddenly perceive the strangeness of familiar, previously comfortable environments.

This *heimlich/unheimlich* ambiguity and the difficulty of tracing the borders between these two ideas also expose an important conceptual dimension of the uncanny. The value of the concept arises from its hesitation between the unfamiliar and the familiar. Or, according to some interpretations, the anxiety of the uncanny is produced rather by a melding of these terms, by the dissipation of the binary oppositions of the strange and the intimate, inside and outside, proper and improper. Discussions of the uncanny have consisted of aesthetic, philosophical and political explorations of the strange/

familiar dialectic and attempts to account for the oxymoronic fusion of
these terms in uncanny experience.

Before evoking the cross-disciplinary legacy of this problematic, we might first note the connotative uncertainty relative to the
non-academic use of the word 'uncanny' in common parlance. Since
the vulgarization of Freudian doctrine, numerous psychoanalytic terms
have infiltrated day-to-day language (Freudian slips, the death drive,
phallic symbols). The uncanny, however, is an example of a term
which in fact began within colloquial speech and was later appropriated by a clinical framework. In ordinary English usage, the term
'uncanny' refers somewhat indiscriminately to a class of anxiety-
provoking experiences, in which the familiarity and security of
common reality appear to slide momentarily out of joint, but it is
difficult to specify what it is that makes a moment uncanny.

Uncanny experience is only integrated with difficulty into the
collective sphere. Although a given theme or occurrence may produce
uncanny feelings in more than one individual, the process of
translating the subjective experience of uncanniness into common
terms, or describing its aesthetic impact, often produces convoluted
speech. The discomfort of uncanny experience is often the result of
one's incapacity to explain, of a fracture in the collective pact of
communication. We speak of two people 'bearing an uncanny resemblance' to one another or of 'uncanny coincidences'. We may describe
a disconcerting phenomenon, image, person, film or book as
'uncanny' for lack of a more precise descriptive term because it is
something which leaves us with a feeling of irresolution, which
imposes a limit on our ability to interpret it. *Déjà-vu*, bizarre
coincidences, strange forms which appear to emerge from the dark-
ness, and confrontations with insanity are among commonly cited
uncanny experiences. The uncanny often occurs within the heart of the
familiar: A pile of laundry on a chair, for example, viewed in the dark
may be perceived as a person or an animal. In an uncanny moment we
feel confronted by a frightful disorder which intrudes on the discourse
of the logical, the rational, the comfortably ordinary. It is a feeling
which arises in an instance of hesitation and imminence, generated by
an occurrence which cannot be inscribed or accounted for in inter-
subjective space. It is a moment which constitutes a strange surplus to
what may be rationally explained through the language and logic of
the everyday.

The non-transparency of the uncanny is apparent in the intricacies of its translation into various languages. The English 'uncanny' does not account for the notion of home suggested by the German *das Unheimliche,* but presents its own fascinations. In the earliest recorded usages cited in the Oxford English Dictionary, the root 'canny' denotes sagacity and is synonymous with adjectives such as prudent, knowing, judicious, cautious or clever. However, the term then comes to mean skilful, artful or cunning and in the eighteenth century a 'canny wife' is a midwife. 'Canny' then begins to qualify someone who is 'supernaturally wise', assuming similar connotations to its opposite, since 'uncanny' describes something 'strange or mysterious' or a person possessing 'supernatural arts or powers'.[6] The English canny/uncanny dichotomy thus embodies an ambiguity similar to that noted by Freud concerning the German term.

The French *inquiétante étrangeté* is less performative in this respect, making no allusion to the aspect of familiarity we have come to associate with the uncanny. It is an odd and cumbersome design-nation, which is not easily incorporated into discourse. The expression designates first and foremost a literary notion and it is interesting to note that it does not feature in everyday language. In a psychoanalytic context the term is often translated simply by *l'étrange* or is left in the original German. The awkward rendering of *das Unheimliche* by *l'inquiétante étrangeté* is commented on by Hélène Cixous, who finds the translation itself disconcerting and attributes it to a French reluctance to abandon a Cartesian structure of thought:

> Nous n'aimons pas, très généralement, l'inquiétude, le trouble, le décentrement [...] Il n'y a pas pour la pensée française, d'exté-riorité à la raison que la raison ne puisse pas se réapproprier.[7]

Cixous's comment about the French translation raises a point which will resurface throughout this analysis. It seems that despite its ety-mology and longstanding association with familiarity and the home, the uncanny has been systematically moved as far away from home as

---

[6] *Oxford English Dictionary Online,* Oxford University Press, 2006, http://www.oed.com/ (accessed 7 October 2005).
[7] Hélène Cixous, 'La Fiction et ses fantômes: une lecture de *l'Unheimliche* de Freud', in *Prénoms de personne* (Paris: Éditions du Seuil, 1974), pp. 13-38, p. 37. All other references are given in the text, following the abbreviation FF.

possible and viewed as synonymous with terror, otherness and monstrosity.

Freud's dictionary
It was Freud's 1919 essay 'Das Unheimliche' which sensitized the
scholarly domain to the quandary of characterizing uncanniness. As
numerous readings of the essay have highlighted – Hélène Cixous's
'La Fiction et ses fantômes' being the most noteworthy in this respect
– Freud's analysis is itself rather uncanny as it reveals the strangeness
and vulnerability of Freud's familiar psychoanalytic tools, which
appear unable to account for the uncanny. The psychoanalyst also
appears to feel slightly ill at ease in the foreign realm of literature. He
begins his essay by announcing his own discomfort in a zone which
the psychoanalyst rarely 'feels impelled to investigate' (U 219), one
which he says he drifted into 'half-involuntarily' (U 251). Despite this
claim, Freud's literary intervention is quite prolific and he has turned
to the works of Shakespeare, Jensen, Dostoyevsky, Sophocles, Moli-
ère, Rabelais, Diderot, Goethe, Swift and others with a view to
illuminating or exemplifying the tenets of his science.

    The purpose of Freud's essay is to appeal to the domain of the
arts to resolve the mysterious workings of the uncanny, which he sees
as a form of mild anxiety provoked by certain literary texts and real-
life occurrences. He designates the uncanny as primarily an aesthetic
concept, associated with themes such as the double, strange
repetitions, omnipotence of thought, confusion of animate and inanimate, expressions of madness, the living dead, severed limbs, dancing
dolls, superstition, ghosts, vampires and representations of death.

    It is often pointed out that 'Das Unheimliche' was composed
concomitantly with his essay 'Beyond the Pleasure Principle', in
which Freud elaborates his concept of the death drive. In the latter he
pursues the idea of a force within the psyche and within the biological
organism propelling the subject towards her own death, a theory
which undercuts the pleasure principle, previously viewed by Freud as
the dominating influence in the constitution and motivation of the
subject.[8] Linked to the death drive, the uncanny is for Freud the dark

---

[8] See Sigmund Freud, 'Beyond the Pleasure Principle', in *The Complete Psycho-
logical Works of Sigmund Freud*, Vol. XVIII, 'Beyond the Pleasure Principle, Group
Psychology and Other Works', trans. and ed. by James Strachey (London: Hogarth
Press, 1955), pp. 7-64.

side of art, ignored by aesthetic theory, which is mainly concerned with the beautiful and the sublime. Elsewhere, in his studies on literature and fantasy, he explored the pacifying effects of the aesthetic and the identification of the reading subject with the hero of a literary text through a 'heroic feeling'.[9] The pleasure of reading is portrayed as entirely narcissistic and self-affirming. The uncanny, however, is the resurgence in life and literature of what was repressed to make narcissism possible.

In 'The Uncanny', Freud takes as a starting point the psychologist Ernst Jentsch's phenomenological explanation of the concept in his 1906 essay, 'On the Psychology of the Uncanny'. In this paper, Jentsch treats E.T.A. Hoffmann's narrative 'The Sandman' and attributes the uncanny quality of the writing to the 'intellectual uncertainty' experienced by the reader of the text.[10] The notion of intellectual uncertainty has since become central to discussions of the uncanny. For Jentsch, the uncertainty provoked by the tale is relative to the character of Olympia, the automaton with whom the main character falls in love after perceiving her through a telescope from his bedroom window and whose ontological status as a doll rather than a living woman is not revealed until near the end of the narrative. In virtually all passages in Hoffmann's text featuring Olympia, the reader is invited to believe both in her reality and her inanimateness. Hoffmann unceasingly sends mixed messages, employing in a single description words which evoke life and death, warmth and coldness, presence and absence, exemplifying literature's privileged capacity for uncertainty, for maintaining strangeness as a limit to interpretation:

> Olympia was, as usual, sitting before the little table, her arms lying upon it and her hands folded. Only now did Nathaniel behold Olympia's beautiful face. The eyes alone seemed to him

---

[9] Sigmund Freud, 'Creative Writers and Day-dreaming', in *The Standard Edition of the Complete Psychological Works of Sigmund Freud*, Volume IX (1906-1908): 'Jensen's "Gradiva" and Other Works', trans. and ed. by James Strachey (London: Hogarth Press, 1959), pp. 141-53, p. 150.

[10] Kathy Justice Gentile proposes a re-reading of Jentsch's text which has been largely ignored in studies on the uncanny. She stresses the ambiguities in many translations of his text. The term he employs throughout the text is *Unsicherheit* which, although often translated as 'uncertainty', would be perhaps more accurately translated as 'insecurity'. What Jentsch is evoking is closer to a feeling of doubt and insecurity than to a purely phenomenological experience. See Kathy Justice Gentile, 'An Analytic of the Uncanny', *Gothic Studies* 2, 1 (April 2000), 23-38 (pp. 24-5).

> strangely fixed and dead, yet as the image on the glass grew
> sharper it seemed as though beams of moonlight began to rise
> within them; it was as if they were at that moment acquiring the
> power of sight, and their glance grew ever warmer and more
> lively.[11]

Nathaniel later has the opportunity to dance with Olympia at a ball
hosted by the man we presume to be her father:

> The music and the dancing had long since ceased. 'Parting,
> parting!' he cried in wild despair; he kissed Olympia's hand, bent
> down to her mouth and his passionate lips encountered lips that
> were icy-cold! As he touched Olympia's cold hand, he was seized
> by an inner feeling of horror, and he suddenly recalled the legend
> of the dead bride, but Olympia had pressed him closer to her; as
> they kissed, her lips seemed to warm into life.[12]

While admitting that there is a certain degree of anxiety provoked by
Olympia, Freud rejects the hypothesis of intellectual uncertainty as
generative of the uncanny. He deems Jentsch's investigation to be
'fertile but not exhaustive' and elaborates his own analysis, positing
the psychoanalytic principles of repression and castration as a more
accurate account of uncanny experience. For Freud, the uncanny is not
simply the strange sentiment of hesitation and confusion. It is rather
'that class of the frightening which leads us back to what is known of
old and long familiar' (U 220). He concludes that uncanniness is thus
a form of ego-disturbance resulting from the revival of phenomena or
ideas that the subject needs to repress in order to constitute reality and
her subjectivity. As he states near the end of the essay: 'an uncanny
experience occurs either when infantile complexes which have been
repressed are once more revived by some impression, or when
primitive beliefs which have been surmounted seem once more to be
confirmed' (U 249).

  After positing the uncanny as a strange return to the familiar,
Freud appeals to the dictionary and conducts a lengthy and complex
etymological investigation into the semantics of the German word
unheimlich. He discovers that the positive form of the word, *heimlich*,
embodies a certain degree of ambiguity in that it has come to desig-

---

[11] E.T.A. Hoffmann, 'The Sandman' in *The Best Tales of Hoffmann*, ed. by E.F
Bleiler (New York: Dover Publications, 1967), p. 110.
[12] Ibid, p.115.

nate both what is familiar, pleasant and belongs to the home but also, or even, what is threatening. Heimlich or 'homey' can thus denote the same content as 'unheimlich', 'unhomely'.[13] Freud cites several examples of German sentences which display this inconsistency. For example, in Klinger's *Theatre:* 'At times I feel like a man who walks in the night and believes in ghosts; every corner is *heimlich* and full of terrors for him' (U 226).

The strange semantic haziness highlighted by Freud's inquiry lays the groundwork for his theory of the uncanny. He claims that the duality of the term *heimlich* reflects the workings of repression, since familiar experiences or thoughts may later re-emerge in the form of strangeness. The repression he is referring to here is that of the fear of castration, the underlying principle of his psychoanalytic theory, the key which allows him simultaneously to domesticate and render strange the human psyche. For Freud, the anxiety of Hoffmann's tale is linked primarily to the menacing figure of the Sandman himself, a character from the childhood fantasies of the main character, Nathaniel. According to the stories told to Nathaniel by his nanny, the Sandman is an evil man who burns out the eyes of children who refuse to go to bed. In the mind of the young boy, the Sandman comes to be associated with two other figures in the tale: firstly, a lawyer who doesn't like children, who visits Nathaniel's father late at night. This is also the person the boy holds responsible for his own father's death following an explosion in that man's company. Secondly, a figure named Coppola, a vendor of optical instruments who resurfaces throughout the story. Freud theorizes that the threatening ocular leitmotifs and the horrifying thought of losing one's eyes induce a fear of castration, a hypothesis he connects to the dual affliction of Œdipus, for whom self-blinding was a 'mitigated form of castration' (U 231). In Hoffmann's narrative, the anxiety surrounding the eyes is brought into proximity with the death of the father.[14]

Freud then presents a bizarre synopsis of Hoffmann's story, according to which the action appears to be centred entirely on the character of the Sandman and the theme of castration. Since in

---

[13] Freud is jumping to conclusions here, since he seems to equate 'secrecy' with foreignness and fright.

[14] When Nathaniel is hiding in his father's office, he hears the terrifying lawyer muttering about eyes. Then there is an explosion which is supposed to have killed Nathaniel's father.

psychoanalytic terms this is a fear repressed by the young child as his ego develops and he adapts to society, Freud is able to account for both the strange and familiar components of the uncanny through the castration hypothesis. He quotes Schelling's definition of the uncanny as what 'ought to have remained secret and hidden but has come to light' (U 224). The feeling experienced by the reader of Hoffmann's text is foreign, yet reminiscent of the past in that it returns the subject to the experiences he has repressed in his development. The remaining part of Freud's essay is an attempt to reduce other real-life examples of the uncanny, such as seeing one's double and strange repetitions, to the castration hypothesis.

In one way, Freud performs a deconstructionist analysis of the German term *Unheimliche,* which becomes a kind of 'pharmakon' in the Derridean sense, an unstable term which resonates polyseman-tically and which can be seen to subvert the transparency of the signifier. However, in another sense, Freud assumes a certain stability of language and meaning by employing the dictionary definition as a justification for his castration theory. He repeatedly returns to the idea that somewhere within Hoffmann's text is the answer to the question of the uncanny, that the term itself can be defined, and assimilated to a scientific methodology. This is also true of the identities of the characters, which Hoffmann leaves vague and unsettling. Each figure in the tale is uncanny, untrustworthy, hovering between sane and in-sane, good and evil, living and dead. In many ways, Freud's essay is a battle against the notion of uncertainty. Freud assumes that it is possible, in a fantastic tale, to determine which elements are real and which are the fictitious construction of Nathaniel's madness:

> There is no question therefore, of any intellectual uncertainty here: we know now that we are supposed to be looking on at the products of a madman's imagination, behind which we, with the superiority of rational minds, are able to detect the sober truth; and yet this knowledge does not lessen the impression of uncan-niness in the least degree. The theory of intellectual uncertainty is thus incapable of explaining that impression. (U 230-1)

As Cixous's reading of Freud's essay suggests, there is a certain degree of repression at work in Freud's attempt to thematize the uncanny. What Freud seems unaware of, and what makes his essay so curious, is the irony of his effort to localize the term, his revelation of the uncanny as the impossibility of boundaries of proper and improper which comes across performatively both in his own sense of not-being-at-home in the literary domain and in the strangeness that is revealed at the heart of Freud's own psychoanalytic theory, which appears incapable of accounting for uncanniness.[15] At the end of his essay he all but confesses the limits of his theory of the uncanny, considering his analysis to have produced only 'preliminary results (U 247)' which, while satisfying psycho-analytic interest in the problem of the uncanny, leave a need for an aesthetic enquiry (U 247). Freud appears somewhat aware that his scientific analysis does not produce the tight-knit conclusion he might have hoped for, but in fact renders the uncanny more and more elusive. Although early in his essay he clings steadfastly to the theory that the uncanny is always tied up with repression, the conclusions he advances at the end of the study appear less certain. What Freud finishes with is not so much a theory of the uncanny as a strange, random list of uncanny phenomena, which much resembles that which forms the introduction to Nicolas Royle's 2004 study of the same concept. Freud tells us that, 'animism, magic and sorcery, the omnipotence of thoughts, man's attitude to death, involuntary repetition and the castration complex comprise practically all the factors which turn something frightening into something uncanny' (U 243). To make things stranger, he tags on to the end of his analysis the example of the general uncanniness of the female genital organs, which has been related to him by patients (U 245).

Perhaps what Freud's essay does convey is something of the vulnerability and homelessness of uncanny experience. Freud sets out on a search to carve out a comfortable space in a strange land, that of literary criticism. He cites various forms of fantastic imagery and supernatural occurrences as uncanny, but what is strange is right there in his own approach. Ultimately his domesticating tools turn against

---

[15] Anneleen Masschelein explores the presence of metaphor in Freud's text. She says that, when Freud states possible explanations of the uncanny, it is often unclear whether or not he is speaking in literal or metaphorical terms. This is the case, for example, with the example of the phrase: 'Something that should have remained hidden but has come to light', as used by Freud. As Masschelein points out, this could be a definition referring to the actual experience of uncanniness or may be simply used as a metaphor for the return of repressed. See Anneleen Masschelein, 'A Homeless Concept: Shapes of the Uncanny in the Twentieth Century', *Online Magazine of the Visual Narrative* 5, 'The Uncanny' (January 2003), http://www.imageand narrative.be/uncanny/anneleenmasschelein.htm (accessed 20 November 2006).

him. The principles of repression and castration cannot possibly
explain away the uncanny. Freud begins to realize this, and his
familiar psychoanalytic territory begins to assume strange characteristics. What is striking in Freud's text is the very vivid *mise-en-
scène* of this quest for familiarization and domestication. Defining a
term or concept by trying to make it one's own might reveal the
strangeness or fragility of one's own assumptions and hypotheses.

In the twentieth century there was a marked curiosity about
the uncanny and Freud's essay became an object of great fascination
among scholars from wide-ranging aesthetic disciplines. Freud's
reading of the Hoffmann tale generated a significant body of criticism
composed of diverse reinterpretations of the uncanny, which take the
form of close readings, disparagements and analyses of Freud's own
methodological approach. Numerous thinkers have returned both to
Freud's essay and to the Hoffmann text in order to redirect or
transpose the uncanniness into various alternative forms, rejecting or
accepting elements of Freud's commentary and presenting their own
theories of the uncanny.[16] As an object of incessant analysis and trans-
position, what the Hoffmann text has shown is the multiplicity of
interpretations that are possible for a single tale, the uncertainty of the
literary text and the autobiographical or personal nature of uncanny
experience. No two readings of either Hoffmann's text or Freud's
essay attribute the uncanny to the same textual or theoretical element.

In their readings of the essay, many have pointed out the
absurdity of Freud's attempt to pin down uncanniness. Yet, many of
these critiques repeat Freud's mistakes by simply re-locating uncanniness, explaining it according to their own feminist, psychoanalytic
or scientific explanations. All scholars appear to find themselves
equally lost in the uncanny. As Royle tells us: 'There is no reading
that's not uncannily blind to its own presuppositions, procedures,
effects or discoveries' (UN 40).

---

[16] See, for example, Samuel Weber, Hélène Cixous, David Ellison, Sara Kofman and
Neil Hertz, whose analyses all criticize Freud's methodological approach and stress
the fictional undertones which are to be found in Freud's essay.

The Uncanny and Aesthetics

Freud distinguishes between the uncanny in real life and that which is present in literature (U 249). One divergence is that certain literary phenomena are not uncanny, yet would be were they to be present in ordinary life. Fairy tales, for instance, do not evoke any feelings of disconcertedness, yet in real life, suspecting that a frog had turned into a prince would be extremely strange. Freud concludes that when the reader assumes that the writer is basing his narrative world on 'real life' (collective reality or realism), the triggers for uncanniness in real life are applicable to the literary text. In terms of uncanniness then, the literary text offers something richer and more complex than the strangeness of real life, since it can encompass all the strangeness of the latter and, further, that created by fantasy.

The role of the uncanny in literature has been widely studied according to diverse methodologies. Literary critics have often spoken of the uncanny with regard to such authors as Kafka, Poe and Hoffmann, whose texts privilege the distortion and breaking down of realist codes, and who employ narrative tactics or present images which threaten the intellectual stability of the reader or characters, or arouse fear. The literary genre or mechanism that specializes in the uncanny is the fantastic, as it exploits the insecurity of the frontiers between the real and the unreal, the I and the not-I, the strange and the ordinary. The word 'uncanny' itself often appears in eighteenth and nineteenth-century Gothic literature, in writers such as Hoffmann and Shelley.

Among the best-known literary investigations into the uncanny is Tzvetan Todorov's structuralist study on the fantastic, *Introduction à la littérature fantastique*. The uncanny for Todorov, which he calls simply 'l'étrange', is a sub-genre of the fantastic. Todorov unites uncanny texts around the common denominator of the hesitation experienced by the reader when faced with an implausible or frightening event.[17] For him, this must be a temporary, unsettling ambiguity, which disconcerts the reader before being ultimately resolved in the narrative and explained through the laws of common reality. The uncanny effect lasts for the duration of this hesitation. Todorov

---

[17] Tzvetan Todorov, *Introduction à la littérature fantastique*, coll. 'Poétique' (Paris: Éditions du Seuil, Paris, 1970), p. 165.

examines, then, the textual mechanisms of uncertainty and attributes uncanniness primarily to the composition and form of the text. His structural analysis is not a phenomenology of reading but concerns the implicit reader who is inscribed in the text. Many have taken Todorov to task for his unclear use of his own terminology and questioned the pertinence and consistency of his construction of the concept.[18] His insistence on the formal structure of the uncanny differentiates his approach from other critical positions in fantastic literature, which base uncanniness on images, incidents or emotional responses. Like Freud, Todorov falls into the trap of trying to harness the concept and force it to adhere to a theoretical model. His analysis of the uncanny is performed in the interests of delineating the various forms of the fantastic genre and not for the sake of revealing or describing the strangeness of uncanny experience.

One limitation of Todorov's theory of the uncanny is that it is divorced from the *experience* of uncanniness. The uncanny in his account is reduced to an after-effect of the fantastic, which he defines as 'l'hésitation éprouvée par un être qui ne connaît que les lois naturelles, face à un événement en apparence surnaturel'.[19] A fantastic phenomenon is not uncanny when first introduced to the reader, but becomes uncanny only if the uncertainty may be dispelled without recourse to the marvellous. This means that to experience something as uncanny, the reader must believe that within the fictional world the strange event may be accounted for by natural law – for example, the character was dreaming – and not by fantasy. The problem here is Todorov's denial of the individuality of uncanniness and the fact that it might also depend on the past experiences, psychology and other particularities of the reading subject. The concept is most often understood to imply a rupture in communal experience, rather than as a literary mechanism upon which we can all agree. The uncanny is thus in some ways the perfect challenge to structuralist methodology, which is criticized for disregarding the reader's unique subjectivity.

---

[18] See, for instance, the Lacanian theorist Mladan Dolar's article in which he claims that Todorov essentially assimilates the uncanny to the logic of suspense in the detective story. Mladan Dolar, 'I Shall be with you on your Wedding Night', p. 23. Lucie Armitt says that Todorov neglects the psychoanalytic dimension of the uncanny and that his categories of the 'fantastic' and the 'uncanny' end up being very similar. See Lucie Armitt, *Theorising the Fantastic* (London: Arnold, 1996), pp. 50-1.

[19] Tzvetan Todorov, *Introduction à la littérature fantastique*, p. 29.

Monsters and doubles

Within literary studies, the uncanny has often been connected with quite specific fantastic imagery. As a figure of complete otherness, the monster is the perfect example of the sort of strangeness we find in the fantastic texts of German or French Romanticism or the English Gothic.

Mary Shelley's *Frankenstein,* for example, may even be read as an allegory for the uncanny itself. Many have linked the birth of uncanniness to the rational subject produced by the Enlightenment.[20] Set within this period, Shelley's tale enacts a confrontation between the rational and domesticating aims of science and the supplement, the monstrous by-product who turns on his creator, the scientist, refusing to be subdued by reason. Chris Baldick sees the tale as exploring 'the godless world of specifically modern freedoms and responsibilities' in a time when humanity takes upon itself the task of 're-creating the world'.[21] Frankenstein's monster is also the perfect uncanny figure, much like Hoffmann's Olympia. He is of dubious ontological status, belonging to the realms of both the living and the dead. Composed of dead bits of corpses his creator obtained from charnel-houses and dissecting rooms, the monster in fact attains life through death. Another uncannily modern dimension to the Frankenstein story is the blurring of the distinction between fantasy and realism, fiction and fact. Recent analyses have pointed out the monster's proximity to the current state of scientific capability, turning Shelley's monster into what Baldick calls 'an uncanny prophecy of dangerous scientific inventions'.[22] Likewise, Ray Hammond indicates the relevance of the Frankenstein tale for our contemporary world, since, through genetic engineering, 'modern Frankensteins now have the ability to turn Mary's fiction into fact'.[23] This last interpretation implies both the contemporary relevance of such a story and the merging of real and

---

[20] For Terry Castle the Freudian uncanny is 'a function of *enlightenment*: it is that which confronts us, paradoxically, after a certain *light* has been cast'. Terry Castle, *The Female Thermometer: Eighteenth-century Culture and the Invention of the Uncanny* (New York and Oxford: Oxford University Press, 1995), p.7. Orginal italics.

[21] Chris Baldick, *In Frankenstein's Shadow: Myth, Monstrosity, and Nineteenth-century Writing* (Oxford: Clarendon Press, 1987), p. 5.

[22] Ibid, p. 7.

[23] Ray Hammond, *The Modern Frankenstein, Fiction Becomes Fact* (Poole, New York and Sydney: Blandford Press, 1986), p. 7.

unreal, the possibility of the fantastic becoming banal in a rapidly changing world.

It seems that, in Shelley's narrative, the threat of the uncanny takes the form of an external alterity distinct from the normality of the collective real and which intrudes upon its rationality and order. However, the monster is also emblematic or symptomatic of latent tensions in the individual, of social ills and unrest, which materialize through fear of the other. The monster is rejected by the community in the interest of its comfort and security.[24] Yet *Frankenstein* is a text that promotes a vision of strangeness as something which is insepa-rable from the familiar. Many interpretations of the story focus on the monster as another face of Frankenstein himself. The fiend is what comes from the doctor, although he is then cast as evil and rejected by his creator.[25] Shelley in fact portrays the monster as a product of our own creation, as something within us. Her lesson is not that reality is often temporarily unsettled by an outside disturbance and then resumes as normal. Rather, *Frankenstein* teaches the responsibility of recognizing otherness as inherent to humanity and reality itself.

In this respect, Shelley's novel may in fact be viewed as a starting point for much contemporary reflection on the uncanny, which tends to consider that the more we attempt to familiarize and domesticate the world through a repression of alterity, the greater the potential for uncanny experience. Such a vision of the uncanny as intrinsic in the most familiar spaces is consistent with the decon-structionist and psychoanalytic agendas discussed further on, which destabilize sites of familiarity in order to render problematic the most familiar phenomena.

Another uncanny image prominent in Romanticism is that of the double.[26] Although, like the monster, it takes a fantastic form, the double is again an image that challenges the possibility of separating

---

[24] As we will see, in Julia Kristeva's analysis of the role of the foreigner with respect to the national narrative, this logic entails the danger of an economy of rejection.

[25] David Collings, for example, suggests in his Lacanian reading that the monster embodies the repressed fantasies of the Maternal Thing and the object *a*. See his article 'The Monster and the Maternal Thing: Mary Shelley's Critique of Ideology,' in *Frankenstein: The Complete Text in Cultural Context*, 2nd Edition, ed. by Johanna M. Smith (Boston and New York: Bedford/St. Martin's, 2000), pp. 280-95.

[26] For an in-depth study of the evolution of the double as a literary theme see von Andrew Webber, *The Doppelganger: Double Visions in German Literature* (Oxford: Oxford University Press, 1996).

the strange from the familiar. The figure of the double contains both self and other. This is also an image which fascinated Freud. In a lengthy footnote to his text, he relates an anecdote: the disagreeable experience of seeing what he thought was his own double on a train, before recognizing this figure as his own reflection (U 248). For Freud, the double was an exemplary strange and familiar experience, which he linked to a regression to a primitive stage of development of the psyche. He cites Otto Rank's extensive study of the double, in which the notion is reminiscent of a primary narcissistic fear.[27] Although a child might frequently imagine herself to have a friendly double, an imaginary playful companion, for the more repressed adult psyche, the double is a reminder of mortality, which confirms our ultimate superfluity, triggering the dreadful notion that someone might one day be coming to take our place. In her analysis of Freud's essay, Kathy Justice Gentile stresses the idea of the double as one of the primary illuminators of uncanny experience, which is simultaneously self-affirming and ego-destroying:

> On the one hand our existence is confirmed by seeking reflections, versions of ourselves in mirrors, photographs, off-spring etc., yet if we are taken unawares by a double, we quail from it as a supernatural visitant. Thus the unsolicited sighting of a double, an embodiment of unsurmounted supernaturalism, marks the eruption of the uncanny into everyday life.[28]

The double displays the interchangeability of the strange and familiar and evokes both the need to protect the self from alien presences and the proximity and intimacy of uncanny experience, as a feeling which takes place within the self, but which can never be one's own. What is fear provoking about the double is in fact not its foreignness, but just how familiar and knowable this figure is; it is something which is strange, but which cannot be entirely 'othered', or rejected by the self. As Slavoj Žižek suggests, the double's sameness increases its uncanniness. The experience of the double evokes the fear of being watched, 'the invisible, unfathomable, panoptical gaze'. [29] For Žižek, this

---

[27] See Otto Rank, *The Double: A Psychoanalytic Study* (London: Karnac Books, 1971).

[28] Kathy Justice Gentile, 'An Analytic of the Uncanny', p. 24.

[29] See Slavoj Žižek, 'Grimaces of the Real, or when the Phallus Appears', *October* 58 (1991), 45-68 (p. 55.)

'someone-is-watching-me' feeling is all the more terrifying when one finds '*oneself* at this very point of pure gaze'.[30]

Defamiliarization and the Gothic

An uncanny aspect is perhaps to be found in the 'defamiliarization' techniques of Russian Formalism, an aesthetic shaped by the problematization of the strange/familiar dialectic. For Victor Shklovsky the term *ostraneniye* designates the process that all artistic endeavours should strive to achieve: rendering the familiar strange. Shklovsky criticizes a vision of art as the act of presenting the unknown in terms of the known. Literature should instead seek to draw our attention to what would otherwise go unnoticed.[31] While ordinary experience involves processes of habituation, which permit the greatest economy of perceptive effort, art must develop a set of techniques to slow or impede the discernment of the ordinary as comfortable and familiar.[32] The concept of defamiliarization is in fact extremely relevant to the projects of the authors discussed in this book since, for the formalists, it refers not only to a momentary effect on the reader or a general atmosphere of the text, but to the very purpose of all creative activity.

Anglophone and Latin American literary studies have also made ample use of both Todorov's study and Freud's essay in connection with the modern Gothic and magic realism.[33] In their book, *The Gothic,* for example, David Punter and Glennis Byron discuss leitmotifs of the uncanny in contemporary Anglophone literature in connection with a neo-gothic trend in postmodern writing. The presence of gothic imagery in the novels of Paul Auster or Iain Banks, for

---

[30] Ibid, p. 56. Original italics. Žižek describes uncanniness according to the Lacanian gaze, as an instance of the annihilation of the speaking subject.

[31] Victor Shklovsky, 'Art as Technique', in *Russian Formalist Criticism: Four Essays*, trans. by Lee T. Lemon and Marion J. Reiss, ed. by Paul A. Olson (Lincoln: University of Nebraska Press, 1965), pp. 3-57, pp. 3-4. For example, Shklovsky shows how, in *War and Peace,* Tolstoy employs techniques of defamiliarization to describe battles, generating the effect that battles are something entirely new (p. 15).

[32] Similar motivations underlie the 'alienation effect' in Brechtian theatre.

[33] Lucie Armitt describes one of the principal aims behind magic realism's combining of the narrative codes of the strange and the familiar: 'Magic realism foregrounds story-telling and, in the process, an enchantment encapsulating erotic allure with spell-binding fascination. In its negotiation of the extraordinariness of the everyday, magic realism endows the familiar with an exotic appeal'. Lucie Armitt, 'The Magical Realism of the Contemporary Gothic', in *A Companion to the Gothic,* ed. by David Punter (Oxford: Blackwell, 2000), pp. 305-16, p. 308.

example, reflects a more general understanding of postmodernism it-self as 'the site of a certain haunting'.[34]

The tendency to associate the uncanny with fantasy and horror is especially noteworthy in film studies. Since the 1980s, the uncanny has occupied an increasingly important place in film criticism. Most uncanny reflection in this field concerns themes such as the living dead, ghosts, vampires and representations of mortality.[35] However, these analyses often fail to distinguish between horror and uncan-niness. As a result, uncanniness becomes synonymous with alterity and terror, and is used rather loosely to describe disturbing imagery; the familiar component of uncanny experience is often ignored.[36]

To my knowledge, there have thus far been no studies on the uncanny in relation to contemporary French literature.

---

[34] David Punter and Glennis Byron, *The Gothic* (Oxford: Blackwell, 2004) p. 53.

[35] See, for example, Barbara Creed, *Phallic Panic: Film, Horror and the Primal Uncanny* (Melbourne: Melbourne University Press, 2005). Creed looks at were-wolves, vampires, cannibals and other monsters in an attempt to reveal some of the unsettling effects of the horror film and to explore the question of monstrosity in relation to gender. She asks, for example, whether female monstrosity and male monstrosity are different. Robert Spadoni examines the historical evolution of the horror genre, focusing on the uncanny figures of Dracula and Frankestein's monster. See Robert Spadoni, *Uncanny Bodies, The Coming of Sound Film and the Origins of the Horror Genre* (Berkeley: University of California Press, 2007). Other studies on film and the uncanny have tended to take the *Unheimliche* quite literally to refer to disconcerting representations of the home and family dynamics. See, for example, Emma Wilson's book, *Cinema's Missing Children* (London: Wallflower Press, 2003).

[36] Steven Schneider exploits Freud's theory of the uncanny to account for the horror genre. He suggests that all horror film monsters metaphorically embody surmounted beliefs. In his analysis, horror and uncanniness are essentially the same thing. See Steven Schneider, 'Monsters as (Uncanny) Metaphors: Freud, Lakoff, and the Representation of Monstrosity in Cinematic Horror', *Other Voices* 1, No. 3 (January 1999), http://www.othervoices.org /1.3/sschneider/monsters.htm (accessed 20 March 2007).

The Contemporary Uncanny

Deconstruction and psychoanalysis
Since the late twentieth century, the uncanny has been a multi-disciplinary term with a complex history influenced by numerous theorists and contexts. The varied heritage of the uncanny and its ghostly ability to intrude subversively on any discourse have been viewed both as a merit and a drawback. In one way, the significance and worth of the concept can be attributed to its indefinable, evasive nature and its tendency to transcend disciplinary boundaries; its wide-ranging relevance may open an innovative, non-reductive context for expressing otherness and heterogeneity in all domains. Conversely, because the term may be provisionally appropriated by any form of thinking, it is sometimes employed indiscriminately and interchange-ably with other deconstructive terminology, often assimilated to such notions as the sublime, the feminine and the other.[37] However, the nomadic, elusive tendencies of the uncanny only prove to be an obs-tacle when one attempts – as Freud did – to put the uncanny at the service of ideology or to reduce the concept to a rational set of circum-stances, in which case it ceases to evoke the discomfort and confusion we have come to associate with uncanny experience.[38]

Since its origin in pre-Freudian psychology, the concept of the uncanny has undergone a complex and interdisciplinary evolution into its varied contemporary applications in the fields of aesthetics and cultural studies. The term has now been widely reinterpreted by liter-

---

[37] Martin Jay states that in the 1990s the uncanny became 'a master trope available for appropriation by a wide variety of contexts'. He notes the widespread and non-rigorous appropriation of the uncanny within diverse disciplines. See Martin Jay, 'Forcefields: The Uncanny Nineties', *Salmagundi* 108, Saratoga Springs (Fall 1995), 20-29 (p. 20). In her functionalist-discursive analysis, Anneleen Masschelein sees this differently. Although the 'original' meaning of concepts like the uncanny may be for-gotten, there is value and subversive potential in the proliferation of the term and its constant recontextualization, which undermines theoretical positions and constantly renews reflection. See Anneleen Masschelein, 'The Concept as Ghost: Conceptu-alization of the Uncanny in Late-Twentieth-Century Theory', *Mosaic* 35 (March 2002), 53-68 (p. 63).

[38] David Ellison puts this well when he says: 'The uncanny is a hidden bomb which detonates each time an interpreter armed only with the defusing device of his theory [...] makes his naively unprotected entrance onto the mined territory'. David Ellison, *Ethics and Aesthetics in European Modernist Literature: From the Sublime to the Uncanny* (Cambrige: Cambridge University Press, 2001), p. 62.

ary, political, feminist, philosophical and psychoanalytic theorists and has provided a dynamic speculative framework for discussions of identity, meaning and representation in the twentieth and twenty-first centuries. While many aesthetic applications of the term in literary and film studies have associated it with imagery of haunting and figures of alterity such as vampirism, fiends and doubles, much recent reflection has stressed the familiar component of this dual concept, emphasizing its value as a destabilizing apparatus which conveys the impossibility of demarcating boundaries between inside and outside, self and other, familiar and strange and of conceptualizing the self-same.

One might argue that the manifestations and uses of the term 'uncanny' have shifted over recent years; the term has moved from a designator of incomprehensible exteriority to a way of understanding the vulnerability and strangeness of phenomena which are closer to home, such as the experience of selfhood, familiar ways of thinking and perceptions of reality. Horror and the supernatural are no longer a pre-requisite for speaking about uncanny experience. Certain thinkers have hinted at the presence of such a progressive shift in the representation and conception of strangeness. For example, Thierry Hoquet proposes mutancy as a more pertinent contemporary figure than monstrosity, which dominated in the nineteenth century:

> Car le mutant 'relève' de l'homme de deux manières. D'un point de vue darwinien, il nous conduit à nous interroger sur l'identité de l'espèce humaine et sur les transformations qui affecteraient cette forme au point de la perdre. Le mutant devient notre plus proche cousin; il apparaît comme une différentielle qui prolonge un peu plus loin la ligne qui mène à l'homme.[39]

Uncanniness is now a way to speak about human activity and familiar contemporary spaces. For example, in his historical and theoretical study *The Architectural Uncanny*, Anthony Vidler appeals to the Freudian uncanny and the image of the haunted house to characterize certain phenomena of contemporary architecture. Vidler compares the architectural fragmentation of neoconstructivism to 'dis-

---

[39] Thierry Hoquet, 'Adieu les monstres, vivent les mutants', *Critique* (June-July 2006), 479-481 (p. 481).

membered bodies'[40] and evokes the unhomeliness of modern urban spaces, which are often sites of alienation, anxiety and paranoia.

The relevance of uncanniness to our contemporary period and the new 'familiar' configuration it is currently embodying, are also reflected in Nicolas Royle's study of the uncanny. For example, Royle describes the September 11th attacks as uncanny, in the sense that they defamiliarized the familiar America that was taken for granted: 'On 11 September the familiar, so-called 'domestic' security of the United States was evidently wiped out for ever' (UN viii). Here Royle constructs the uncanny as a situation where the stability of something formerly familiar and comfortable is undermined from the inside. In Royle's words: 'the uncanniness of September 11th has to do with what was *already happening* as well as with the fear or dread of what may be to come' (UN viii). He is referring here to the fact that the person suspected of initiating the attack on the Twin Towers was not an intruder, but had previously received military training *within* the US. Thus, the uncanny no longer simply designates, as it did within Romanticism or within Freud's analysis, a foreign image or presence which is revealed to evoke or recall something familiar; it also suggests the vulnerability and strangeness of what we already know, of our present homes, theories, visions of the world and environments. It has become a way of looking back on the previously familiar and perceiving it as already haunted. While Royle's example of the attacks on the Twin Towers does evoke the strangeness that can be found within the familiar, some might criticize his extension of the term 'uncanny' to include this event as an example of 'uncanny-ism', that is, a case of using the term too readily to describe any destabilizing occurrence.

Yet, as Royle and others have indicated, the uncanny may also be a positive force. With the recognition of the proximity and intimacy of the uncanny comes a heightened awareness of its potential to create new meanings rather than dismantle them. More and more the ethical, poetic, political or even realist value of the uncanny is emphasized and many have indicated the fruitfulness of the concept for acknowledging and embracing otherness and rethinking notions of home in personal, national, literary, or epistemological contexts. While, as certain theo-

---

[40] Anthony Vidler, *The Architectural Uncanny. Esssays in the Modern Unhomely* (Cambridge and London: The M.I.T. Press, 1992), p. ix.

rists have shown, fear of the unknown and the logic of the scapegoat may often incite a repression of the uncanny and a need to conceive of strangeness as that which is in complete opposition to stable reality, thinkers such as Julia Kristeva and Hélène Cixous have advocated a reversal of this structure, positing the value of the uncanny as a call to reinterpret the ordinary and renew familiar forms of perception. The uncanny must bring about a relocation of alterity to the domains of the intimate and proper, and can induce innovative recreations of communal space and the self. In this section I shall appeal to comments and analyses by various thinkers that present a vision of the uncanny not simply as an instance of foreignness, but as a starting point for an alternative vision of the ordinary and an ethics of perceiving or addressing the other.[41]

The two main branches of cultural theory that dedicate significant attention to the uncanny are deconstruction and psychoanalysis. The uncanny assumes particular relevance with respect to American and French deconstruction, intellectual movements which aim precisely to destabilize previously familiar texts and structures of thought. The uncanny might in fact be viewed as a relatively localized exemplification of the more abstract and general schema applied by deconstruction. Analyses such as Paul de Man's *Allegories of Reading* re-read familiar texts like Rousseau's *Du contrat social* and 'Essai sur l'origine du langage' in an effort to render their familiar readings strange. For de Man, no text practices what it preaches or may be reduced to the signification consciously posited by its author. The text has a life of its own.[42] Derrida's *Spectres de Marx* introduces the notion of 'hantologie' as opposed to ontology, as the element that

---

[41] It should be noted at this point that within contemporary theory the use of the term uncanny has strayed significantly from the resonances that the word possesses in colloquial speech. In the context of ethics and politics, for example, the uncanny has been intellectualized and is used to describe phenomena or patterns of conceptualization, rather than spontaneous feelings or experiences. Part of the term's fascination, however, lies in its semantic shape-shifting and contextual flexibility. Yet this might also be a limitation of the uncanny. The fact that it metamorphoses into other concepts and adapts to such varying uses means that it becomes easy to lose sight of what one understands by 'uncanny'. Everything appears uncanny if perceived in a certain way and, of course, this is also the point.

[42] In his chapter on metaphor for instance, de Man locates areas in Rousseau's texts where literal and figurative meanings contradict each other or are interchangeable. See *Allegories of Reading* (London; New Haven: Yale University Press, 1979), pp. 147-8.

must be introduced into every concept and as a logic which is 'plus ample, plus puissante qu'une ontologie'.[43] This notion of haunting might be understood as relating to the deconstructionist breakdown of borders between opposing concepts. As Colin Davis suggests, 'haun-tology' implies the replacement of ontology (being and presence) by 'the figure of the ghost as that which is neither present nor absent, neither dead nor alive'.[44] Deconstruction highlights the paradox of the contemporary uncanny, the fact that its relevance is no longer reduced to the fantastic, but has begun to refer to a more familiar problem of representation and subjectivity.

Nowhere is the familiar component of the uncanny more far-reaching than in psychoanalysis. The uncanny parallels the defining feature of the psychoanalytic project itself: its dedication to exploring the strange depths of the psyche, to summoning the ghosts which haunt subjectivity, to maintaining strangeness open as a limit to inter-pretation, to generating a methodology which preserves a space for what is unthematizable, yet intimate in the subject.[45]

The idea of the home and the concept of 'defamiliarization' are of course extremely relevant in a literal sense to psychoanalytic models, since a great part of the Freudian project consists in bringing to light a certain strangeness which exceeds and problematizes tra-ditional perceptions of the family. Concepts such as the 'Œdipus complex' and the 'law of the father' reveal latent tensions that under-score the perceived peaceful, unified myth of family life. The in-creased infiltration of Freudian and post-Freudian psychoanalytic thought into literary studies has perhaps influenced aesthetic ap-plications of the uncanny.[46]

Modern psychoanalysis is one of the only applied disciplines to incorporate the uncanny into its very premise. If it were not for the strangeness of the familiar, psychoanalysis would not exist. However, despite the general relevance of the uncanny for the field and the fact that its impact as an instance of subjective dissipation is readily acknowledged by Lacanian and Freudian clinical analysts, the exploi-

---

[43] Jacques Derrida, *Spectres de Marx* (Paris: Éditions Galilée, 1993), p. 31.

[44] Colin Davis, 'Hauntology, Spectres and Phantoms', *French Studies* LIX, No. 3 (2005), 373-379 (p. 373). Davis links hauntology to the ethical turn in deconstruction, as a way of understanding the irreducible other to which we are responsible.

[45] As Nicolas Royle points out: 'Psychoanalysis is itself uncanny' (UN 53).

[46] This point will be raised in more detail in Chapter 3.

tation of the concept within psychoanalysis has been largely restricted to aesthetic and cultural contexts.[47] The uncanny was incorporated fairly minimally into clinical practice at the time of its appearance. In fact, Freud made only infrequent references to the term after composing his essay on the uncanny.

Psychoanalytic theory has provided perhaps the most rigorous account of the uncanny as an unhomely subjective position by evocatively connecting imagery of home to the description of the subject. We might recall the Freudian metaphor for the discovery of the unconscious: the ego is not 'master in its own house'. Within psychoanalysis, the strange/familiar dialectic may be viewed in terms of the unconscious. Conceptions of subjectivity within continental psychoanalytic thought are based on the idea that the most fundamental part of the self is what is foreign or inaccessible to consciousness, while the individual's ordinary inscription in collective reality is a kind of alienation from that intimacy.[48] Strangeness is relocated to the inside, since the subject is often viewed as being constructed around an internal alterity.

Within certain psychoanalytic models, the experience of the strange can even imply a return to an 'original home', to a prior point in the evolution of the individual subject, which precedes the development of the adult self, a linguistic being.[49] The foreignness of the

---

[47] There are, however, some examples of clinical psychoanalytic studies on the uncanny. In Martin Grotjahn's 1948 paper, he relies on the Freudian theory of the return of the repressed in order to analyse certain uncanny experiences related to him by patients. He notes the high frequency of uncanny experience in schizophrenic patients. See Martin Grotjahn, 'Some Clinical Illustrations of Freud's Analysis of the Uncanny', *Bulletin of the Menninger Clinic* 12 (1948), 57-60. Edmund Bergler relies on the principle of the castration complex and the omnipotent stage in child development to describe uncanniness as a feeling of 'inner danger from the aggressive instincts'. The uncanny is a protective mechanism of the ego. See Bergler, Edmond, 'The Psychoanalysis of the Uncanny', *International Journal of Psychoanalysis* 15 (1934), 215-44 (p. 218 and 221).

[48] In Jacques Lacan's construction of the subject, the appropriation of the 'I' is an exteriorisation of the subject's identity. It is thus the subject's linguistic and symbolic existence that takes place in the realm of the other. See Jacques Lacan, *Écrits I* (Paris: Éditions du Seuil, 1966), p. 279.

[49] This is perhaps what Freud meant when he suggested that the uncanny was a momentary return to a phase preceeding the full development of the ego. This idea will gain clarity in our discussion of Julia Kristeva.

uncanny is perceived as something already there, both in the unconscious and in the primitive, pre-linguistic existence of the subject.

Psychoanalytic thinkers such as Jacques Lacan, for example,
view the uncanny as a by-product of the construction of subjectivity.
The anxiety of the uncanny results from the illusion of self-mastery:

> Here we see the ego, in its essential resistance to the elusive
> process of Becoming, to the variations of Desire. This illusion of
> unity, in which a human being is always looking forward to self-
> mastery, entails a constant danger of sliding back again into the
> chaos from which he started; it hangs over the abyss of a dizzy
> Assent in which one can perhaps see the very essence of
> Anxiety.[50]

In Lacanian thought, the anxiety of the uncanny, understood above as
a descent into original chaos, can also be referred to as 'le regard'. In
order to teach this concept in one of his clinical seminars, he recounts
a personal anecdote to his students. Once, on a fishing trip, he
perceived an empty sardine tin, which floated past his boat. One of his
fellow fishermen said 'Tu vois, cette boîte? Tu la vois? Eh bien, elle,
elle ne te voit pas'! For Lacan, this man was mistaken. The sardine
box *did* see him, insofar as it presented itself to him while posing a
certain challenge to his stable subjective position. There was something inexplicable about the experience of perceiving this object, a
strange reminder of the fishing industry, outside its usual context, that
put the psychoanalyst ill at ease. This story of this strange feeling was
an introduction to what Lacan calls 'le regard', a counter-symbolic,
annihilating instance which replaces the speaking subject 'dans les
lacunes mêmes de ce dans quoi au premier abord il se présente comme
parlant', and which, for him, temporarily brings back to the surface
everything which is outside of language: the repressed.[51]

Lacan further illustrates the aesthetic implications of this
concept with reference to the well-known portrait by Hans Holbein,
'The Ambassadors', which displays the commonly employed Renaissance technique of anamorphosis. Holbein's painting features the
French diplomat Jean de Dinteville and the Bishop Georges de Selve,

---

[50] Jacques Lacan, 'Some Reflections on the Ego', *The International Journal of Psychoanalysis* XXXIV(1953), 11-17 (p. 15).
[51] Jacques Lacan, *Le Séminaire XI: les quatre concepts fondamentaux de la psychanalyse,* ed. by Jacques-Alain Miller (Paris: Éditions de Seuil, 1973), p. 96.

both sumptuously dressed and surrounded by objects of science and luxury. In the foreground of the painting is an initially unidentifiable, dark object, which appears to be suspended in the air in front of the two figures. If the viewer adopts a certain sidelong perspective, a *memento mori* appears. Lacan suggests that engaging with an aesthetic object most often reinforces our Cartesian gaze and sense of subjective stability, whereas in Holbein's painting there is something of the uncanny, in the sense that the painter 'nous reflète notre propre néant dans la tête de mort'.[52] However, for Lacan it is not only the skull of death that symbolizes the annihilation of self, but the dynamics of spectatorship. In order to attain a clear vision of this floating form, the viewer must temporarily lose contact with the figurative coherence of the rest of the picture. To perceive the symbol of death, the intelligible form of the original image must be renounced, since the sidelong view of the anamorphosis creates a perceptual distortion of the portrait of the two men. It seems that, for Lacan, the subject of an uncanny experience is, in a sense, not a subject. 'Le regard' is the possibility of the temporary 'death' of the subject, since it is the dissipation of the lack which, for Lacan, maintains the subject within symbolic, coherent, inter-subjective reality. Thus, in uncanniness, the subject perceives something of her own subjective lack, since the place from which she is looking, her own subjective position, begins to appear strange to her. Lacan considers this sense of uncanniness to be 'castrating', as it threatens a return to a pre-subjective, pre-linguistic phase of subjectivity.

Lacan's interpretation of the uncanniness of Holbein's tableau through the notion of subjective annihilation may at first seem problematic, in the sense that it could be applied to any occurrence of the technique of anamorphosis. However, reading Lacan's seminar it is unclear whether he understands the description of this experience of spectatorship to be an instance of the uncanny, or simply views it as an allegory for its functioning.

Within psychoanalysis, the uncanny is thus often connected to the return of the repressed. This may also apply to collective and societal dynamics of repression. The uncanny reveals itself not only in moments of destabilization or foreignness but within frameworks of organization, rationalization and economies of separation and re-

---

[52] Ibid, p. 107.

jection, which seek to expel strangeness. Lacanian thinkers such as
Slavoj Žižek, for instance, see the uncanny as what is always at stake
in ideology. Ideology is an attempt to account for uncanniness, to find
a scapegoat for the alterity that threatens hegemonic discourses and
rigid worldviews. The uncanny refers to a point of breakdown, an
entropic function of the law.[53]

Cixous and Kristeva - an ethics of the unhomely

Two contemporary thinkers in particular, Hélène Cixous and Julia
Kristeva, have re-interpreted Freud's essay to bring out the fertile
nature of the uncanny and propose rich and complex descriptions of
its ethical implications. In their respective works *Prénoms de personne* and *Étrangers à nous-mêmes*, Cixous and Kristeva address the
relevance of the concept as part of a politics of representation or
conceptualization; the problematization, re-assessment, or even abandonment of the *chez soi* is a pre-requisite for conscientious discourse
and a new basis for perception. They favour the challenge to subjectivity produced in uncanny experience and insist on writing
strategies or frameworks of thought which resist a dynamic of
repression with respect to alterity.

For both thinkers, commentary on the uncanny may be seen to
illuminate their more over-arching views of language and subjectivity.
The concept's potential to break down patriarchal or rational orders
points to an instance of authenticity. In Cixous's deconstructive
account, Hoffmann's tale is venerated as a text which dissolves the
unity of the subject and brings it into play, destabilizing the logic of
domestication with which we may tend to approach textual
interpretation and writing. Her analysis of Freud's readerly unhomeliness is the basis for a discussion of reading and writing which seeks
to dismantle the strange/familiar dichotomy and other binary structures of thought. The uncanny becomes a means to achieve a more
poetic, plural and truthful vision of the real. For Kristeva, the negative
affect of the uncanny is generative of a dislocated subject position,
which is a starting point for the relation to the other. Rather than

---

[53] The Jews, for instance, act as a scapegoat permitting the construction of reality
within Fascism. The functioning of the Nazi narrative depends on the attribution of
alterity to the Jewish people who guarantee the integrity of that narrative 'as a point at
which social negativity as such assumes positive existence'. Slavoj Žižek, *The Sublime Object of Ideology* (London and New York: Verso, 1989), p. 127.

provoking abjection and the repressive othering of the strange, uncanny experience should command the subject to perceive vulnerability within the self, to acknowledge her own foreignness. Such a model of alterity must be embraced as an ethics of approaching the unthematizable difference of the foreigner in the national community.

It should be noted that aside from a shared fascination with the Freudian uncanny, Hélène Cixous and Julia Kristeva have much in common and are often invoked side-by-side in discussions of identity, politics and literature. In Anglophone academic circles in particular, they form part of a triad of 'French feminists' alongside Luce Irigaray. They share an interest in some of the same writers, James Joyce, for example, who has received significant attention within their work. Both thinkers' theories have been taken up in feminist discourses, since Kristeva and Cixous generate powerful, engaged critiques of patriarchal order and propose innovative strategies for writing, speaking or reading otherwise. Their critiques have called for a revolutionary reconsideration of Western philosophical and literary traditions in light of a heightened awareness of the corporeal, the feminine and the irreducibility of the other in literature, politics and inter-subjective relations.

Both theorists are concerned with reading and writing but also with the social or political repercussions of representation and interpretation.[54] They also salvage fragments of some of the psychoanalytic and deconstructive tenets rejected by other feminists and elaborate complex reinterpretations of Lacanian and Freudian accounts of subjectivity in order to locate a place for the insertion of a feminine discourse.[55] However, both thinkers also occupy somewhat unhomely positions within feminist thought since they are often condemned for essentialism (in the case of Kristeva), or for subscribing too whole-heartedly to rigid accounts of the relationship between language and self. They have also been criticized for privileging literature by men in their textual analyses.[56]

---

[54] An example is Julia Kristeva's early work where she explores the subversive potential of poetic language and its ability for disruption through its connection to bodily drives. See Julia Kristéva *La Révolution du langage poétique*, coll. 'Tel Quel' (Paris: Éditions du Seuil, 1974).

[55] See, for instance, Cixous's critique of Freudian and Lacanian theories of the subject in *La Jeune née*, with Catherine B. Clément (Paris: Inédit, Union générale d'Éditions, 1975).

[56] For more details on these accusations see Susan Sellers, *The Hélène Cixous Reader*

For both women, a captivation with the unhomeliness of the
uncanny may also reflect their personal backgrounds since Kristeva
and Cixous have each experienced linguistic and cultural exile, having
abandoned to some extent their maternal languages in order to live
and teach in France.[57] Both women produce literary and theoretical
texts in French and make regular reference in their work to their own
unheimlich positions, acknowledging affinities between the prevalence of the themes of social and linguistic otherness in their own
reflection and their particular statuses as both women and foreigners.[58]

Although the importance they attribute to the feminine as a
tool of subversion is undeniable, and though complex elaborations of
this concept exist in their work, constituting a large part of the
theoretical production of both thinkers, Kristeva and Cixous may also
be seen to be speaking more generally about the human subject. In
exploring their theories of the uncanny, it may be relevant at times to
turn to their feminist theories in order to illuminate or contextualize
their ideas, but what interests us primarily is their theorization of the
intricacies of the concept of the *chez soi*, its incarnations in their views
on reading, writing and dwelling, and the ways in which the uncanny
as a renunciation of home has paradoxically provided a starting point
for ethical and narrative constructions.

Hélène Cixous - writing the 'pluréel'

Of the plethora of re-readings of Freud's essay, Hélène Cixous's
account in her book *Prénoms de personne* is perhaps the most
seminal. Virtually all subsequent discussions of the uncanny allude to
Cixous's analysis, which re-kindled interest in Freud's text while at
the same time rendering it vulnerable to a series of ideological attacks
by psychoanalysts and literary theorists. Cixous's interpretation re-

---

(New York, London: Routledge, 1994),
[57] Kristeva is Bulgarian and moved to Paris for her doctoral studies. Cixous's case is
more complex. Her father was a Sephardic Jew whose ancestors came from Spain.
Her family moved first to Morocco then Algeria, where she grew up, educated in
French and surrounded by Arabic. But her mother was an Ashkenazi Jew descended
from a family in the Austro-Hungarian Empire and spoke German to her daughter.
See Susan Sellers, *The Hélène Cixous Reader*, pp. xxvi-vii.
[58] In *La Venue à l'écriture,* for example, Cixous discusses the ways in which her own
unhomeliness unsettles and disturbs her use of language. Hélène Cixous, *La Venue à
l'écriture,* with Madeleine Gagnon and Annie Leclerc (Paris: Union Générale des
Éditions, 1977), pp. 52-3.

veals the complex interplay between the diverse facets of uncanny theory. She evokes its effects on subjectivity, the multilayered etymological resonances of the German *unheimlich*, the potential productivity of the uncanny as a destabilizing tool and its paradoxical connection to the real. Unlike Kristeva's investigation, which focuses on the precursory, pioneering quality of Freud's theory as the groundwork for further elaborations of the concept, Cixous's reading reveals the fragility and rigidity of Freud's text. She criticizes Freud's repressive reaction to his own uncanny experience, citing it as an example of how not to behave when confronted with the incomprehensible and foreignness. However, she also sees Freud's unhomeliness, which comes across with force in his essay, as a fascinating metaphorical enactment of the mysterious behaviour of the uncanny itself and his account of the uncanny as a fruitful source, since it opens up new avenues for interpretation and reveals the elusiveness of the literary text.

Cixous's remarks about Freud's essay are better illuminated when placed in the scheme of her broader vision of literary meaning and language, both as expounded in *Prénoms de personne* and with respect to the reflection on femininity which informs her convictions about writing. This contextualisation should reveal the motivations behind the positive value Cixous attributes to the problematization of the strange/familiar dichotomy as a starting place for textual practice and thought.

Although in her reading of Freud she demonstrates that a literary quality and disruptive potential may be extracted from the most rigorously realist or even scientific texts, Cixous privileges writing which consciously resists totality and absorption or appropriation by patriarchal structures of thought; usually this is through a dismantling of the binary structures which she believes inform subjectivity and knowledge. Such structures are condemned by the theorist for necessarily bolstering a dynamic of oppression, since one side of any dual concept is always preferential. Following a deconstructionist line of thought, Cixous affirms that within a Western, logocentric model of knowledge based on presence, and supported by the subject-object distinction, binary oppositions inevitably entail hierarchy, since one component stifles its counterpart in order to affirm its superiority. The two components of a binary pair cannot co-exist on equal terms. 'Woman', for example, falls on the oppressed

side of the man-woman dichotomy, and is cast as other. Man requires
her presence to guarantee his own identity but her voice is repressed
and marginal, since she threatens his presence. This logic supports a
way of thinking in which development and progress can only occur,
and alterity can only be tolerated, within an order of suppression,
which becomes the driving force of history.[59] In *La Jeune née*, Cixous
references the Hegelian master-slave dialectic to elucidate this point in
the context of the plight of Algerians under French colonial power,
which she compares to that of women within patriarchy:

> J'ai vu que les beaux grands pays 'avancés' s'érigeaient en
> expulsant l'*étrange*; en l'excluant mais pas trop loin: en
> l'asservissant. Geste banal de l'Histoire: il faut qu'il y ait deux
> races, celles des maîtres, celle des esclaves. Et on sait l'ironie
> impliquée dans la dialectique du maître et de l'esclave: il ne faut
> pas que le corps de l'étrange disparaisse, mais il faut que sa force
> soit domptée, qu'elle revienne au maître. Il faut qu'il y ait du
> propre et de l'impropre; du propre donc du sale; du riche donc du
> pauvre; etc.[60]

The repression of alterity both homogenizes the real and empowers
the oppressor, who depends on the existence of the other to guarantee
his or her status as master. As a writer very much engaged in an attack
on patriarchy, Cixous's literature and theory focus on destabilizing the
man-woman dichotomy through feminist readings of mythical or
literary texts to attack a phallocentric way of thinking and promote her
écriture féminine and what she calls 'bisexual writing'. In 'Le Rire de
la Méduse' and *La Jeune née*, she describes *écriture féminine* as a
form of expression which seeks to re-create the cultural sphere by
generating a textual place which is in-between and which
accommodates the unthematizable, surplus energy, *jouissance* and
plurality.[61] Ethically speaking, her *écriture féminine* also entails a
commitment to writing the other by refusing to annihilate her
difference. Such a form of writing requires the adoption of a marginalized position and is capable of being practiced by both sexes. It
encourages new engagements of subjectivity with otherness, a frag-

---

[59] For a good account of Cixous's criticism of phallocentrism in the light of the
Hegelian master-slave dialectic, see Morag Shiach's chapter, 'Politics and Writing', in
her book *Hélène Cixous, Politics and Writing* (London: Routlege, 1991), p. 6-37.
[60] Hélène Cixous, *La Jeune née*, pp. 128-9.
[61] Hélène Cixous, 'Le Rire de la Méduse', *L'Arc* 61 (1975), 39-54.

mentation of the 'I' and a strong attention to the body in textual practice.[62] The intricacies and possible applications of such a theory are discussed at length by many Cixous scholars.[63]

Since for Cixous, even the notion of the body as it is normally constituted in textual practice and collective reality is itself a cliché, her writing insists on challenging the unified inscription of the writer or character in the text by representing a plurality of subjective positions, varying pronouns, oscillation between male and female subjects within a single sentence, or the portrayal of bodily drives, sensory experience and desire or *jouissance*. Many of Cixous's critics stress the exceptional dislocating, bewildering quality of her texts, their commitment to a non-concrete vision of the real and their interpretive obscurity.[64]

Although the concept is not apparent throughout her work, the uncanny may be viewed as an important notion for Cixous because it implies de-egoization and incarnates a collapse of the logic at work in all oppositional pairs, encouraging a merging of the strange and the familiar. The dualism of the uncanny embodies the logic at work in many binary oppositions, since patriarchal culture and language for Cixous are what tend to privilege the familiar, rejecting the strange. The conceptualization of the familiar and definitions of home that are generated through an evacuation of alterity re-enact, at least figu-

---

[62] In both form and content, Cixous's own work envisages such an approach and her texts are dotted with glimpses into her views on writing as a refusal of the self-same and an embracing of the other. In *Souffles* she addresses the other through a dislocation of the self and movement towards the 'you': 'ce n'est pas à moi, c'est à toi que je suis menée par cette voix qui passe à travers moi et me disloque. C'est sur toi que je m'ouvre'. Hélène Cixous, *Souffles* (Paris: Des femmes, 1975), p. 23. In this text as well as in *La*, she evokes the maternal as a model for the non-objectifying rapport with the other and the re-birth of the self in order to embrace a more plural apprehension of the real. Hélène Cixous, *La* (Paris: Gallimard, Des femmes, 1979). In novels such as *Neutre*, the fragmentation of the point of view, and the renunciation of narrative conventions such as a coherent plot and syntax, are evocative of a 'feminine' voice. Hélène Cixous, *Neutre* (Paris: Grasset, 1972). Words are written upside down or are crossed out; two pronouns are employed simultaneously. In *Dedans*, a textual space is created where the boundary between inside and outside is blurred through a dissolution of the ego, a displaced and unconventional representation of subjective encounters with external phenomena. Hélène Cixous, *Dedans* (Paris: Grasset, 1969).
[63] See Susan Sellers, Mireille Calle-Gruber or Morag Shiach for example.
[64] See, for example, Susan Sellers, *Hélène Cixous: Authorship, Autobiography and Love* (Cambridge: Polity Publishers, 1996), p. 5.

ratively, the oppressive master-slave dialectic of domestication, which Cixous's writing seeks to undermine.

In her preface to *Prénoms de personne*, Cixous discusses what she sees as the main task of literature, to prohibit or problematize the comfort of the *chez soi* and forms of textual domestication. Writing must seek to attack:

> le front de la subjectivité, dans la mesure où il héberge et assure le leurre de l'unicité, de la totalisation, et par là, du conservatisme et du totalitarisme. Il ne s'agit pas de faire disparaître le sujet, mais de le rendre à sa divisibilité: s'attaquer au chez-soi, au pour-soi, au revenu; montrer la fragilité du centre et des cloisons du moi; c'est empêcher la complicité du moi en tant que maître avec l'autorité (et la notion d'auteur); avec la répression et ses feintes; avec la propriété sous toutes les formes.[65]

The imagery of abandoning the home or the *chez soi* is employed to suggest a counterforce to conservative and totalitarian discourses. Although the concept of femininity underscores many of the ideas she presents in *Prénoms de personne*, Cixous temporarily sets aside her discussion of the feminine in this text, to adopt a vocabulary of the uncanny. Hoffmann's 'The Sandman', as well as the texts of Poe and Joyce also analysed in her book, are commended for their shared tendency to lead the reader astray, for challenging simple iden-tifications and for favouring feelings of readerly unhomeliness by being written in a kind of 'non-lieu' of uncertainty (PP 5). These textual strategies of de-homing also appear within these texts in the form of content or metaphors. She cites Joyce's 'Ithaca', the 'point du non-retour chez soi', as one of the ideas in the text which are 'drôlement, impitoyablement déconstructrices' (PP 8).

As an uncanny text, the value of Hoffmann's tale is, for Cixous, its annihilation of the falsely coherent subjectivity of the reader and its capacity to debunk rational methodologies and pre-informed interpretative grids. This is well brought out in Freud's essay on the uncanny, although not in the way he intended. In her extremely intricate, painstaking analysis of Freud's essay, Cixous portrays the uncanny as an elusive, sublime force, an unthematizable excess which

---

[65] Hélène Cixous, *Prénoms de personne* (Paris: Seuil, 1974), p. 6. All other references are given in the text, following the abbreviation PP.

returns to threaten the familiar dimensions of the ordinary and the economy of representation.

For Cixous, Freud's lexical perplexities concerning *heimlich* and *unheimlich* are doubly telling. His investigation brings him to a contemplation of the dual identity of the uncanny, simultaneously strange and familiar, and foregrounds the question of indefinability. Definition is precisely an act of domesticating, mastering and othering which favours a homely stance from which we may dispel alterity, isolating a term, separating what it is from what it is not. While condemning the psychoanalyst's attitude towards the other and his faith in science and rational systems of thought, her reading of Freud's text praises the psychoanalyst for producing a rich metaphorical demonstration of the uncanny through his rambling attempt to define it. For Cixous there is nothing uncannier than Freud's confused analysis of the notion itself, which attempts to dispel the intellectual uncertainty of the literary text, but, in turn, falls prey to this uncertainty. If the reader comes away from Freud's analysis with a deeper sense of the uncanny, this is because she has herself become sensitive to Freud's own uncertainty:

> Freud pose *l'Unheimiche* au même moment comme un domaine et comme un concept dans une désignation élastique. C'est que le 'domaine' reste indéfini, le concept est sans noyau: *l'Unheimliche* ne se présente d'abord qu'*en marge* d'autre chose. Freud l'apparente par rapport à d'autres concepts qui lui ressemblent (effroi, peur, angoisse): il est dans la famille ce qui n'est pas cependant de la famille. (FF 16)

Her reading highlights the repressed anxieties and ghostly resonances shadowing the psychoanalyst's methodological endeavour. As Freud attempts to master the term, to separate it from its others, to define it through the castration hypothesis and to demarcate its boundaries, the more its irreducibility exceeds his grasp. This is because the uncanny would lose its *unheimlich* nature were it possible to integrate it seamlessly into Freud's psychoanalytic theory. It must necessarily remain outside the realm of the rational, only achieving construction in the form of an excess to meaning and a resistance to domestication.

In Cixous's account, Freud's entire text is premised on an act of repression, since he begins by condemning Jentsch's attribution of the uncanny to the doll Olympia as a figure that hesitates between life and death. Cixous concentrates on Freud's distortion of Hoffmann's narrative as he re-tells it. In order to posit the uncanny as a concept, says Cixous, and dispel the intellectual uncertainty at its core so that it revolves around the manageable, homely tenets of psychoanalysis, Freud has attempted to re-write Hoffmann's story to stress the elements which support his theory. This re-writing marks his own suppression of the *entre-deux* of the feminine incarnated by the doll, Olympia, as neither living nor non-living, but pure enigma (PP 63). Freud relegates the automaton, whose role was so central in Jentsch's account, to a simple footnote as a way of repressing the uncertainty and duplicity generated by the presence of 'un peu trop de femme dans l'automate, un peu trop d'automate dans la femme...' (PP 52). The uncanny allows for a space where 'folie' intertwines with 'raison', 'l'attirant' with the 'repoussant', where fiction is inseparable from the real, a dualism which is nonetheless present within all texts (PP 41). For Cixous, the ambiguity of Olympia expresses the triumph of the uncanny, the inevitable transformation of the familiar into the strange, the rendering unhomely of the intellectual home of the reader.[66]

The confused nature of Freud's psychoanalytic explanation is thus no different in some respects from Hoffmann's disquieting tale, and Cixous focuses on the mysterious tone and disorderly nature of his account, which resembles a literary text:

> Le texte de Freud fonctionne lui-même à la façon d'une fiction: le long travail sur les pulsions, la redistribution dramatique sur telle ou telle voie, les suspenses et surprises, les impasses...Tout ici tourne court. La lecture saute. On pense suivre une démonstration, ou on sent le terrain se fendiller. Le texte glisse quelques racines sous le sol, d'autres sont aériennes. Ce qui a ici figure de science ressemble plus loin à quelque façon de roman. Métaphore de lui-même ce texte s'avance. (FF 14-20)

To a certain extent, Cixous denies the difference between science and fiction, using Freud as an example. This insistence on viewing even

---

[66] In the style of Barthes's analysis of Balzac's 'Sarrasine' in *S/Z*, Cixous also points out a certain fragility in the collective real, since in Hoffmann's story the very fact that a confusion may exist between a real woman and a living doll points to simulacrum and its social effects. The idea of a perfect copy threatens the economy of representation and Olympia becomes a metaphor for this threat.

theoretical texts as fictional is also reproduced in Cixous's own writing style, a fusion of literature and criticism. Cixous is a writer whose discursive manner, even in her theoretical texts, is noncommittal and elusive. Her reading of Freud's text is sprawling, sinuous, with ever-changing perspectives and unanswered questions. Although she does present an argument of sorts, a criticism of Freud's sealing-off of the literary text and denial of its plurality, at no time does she herself attempt to reduce the uncanny to a single hypothesis.

Hoffmann's text invites Freud to look back with an unhomely glance upon his own psychoanalytic theories which, in the process, are not so much confirmed through the uncanny, as rendered problematic. However, for Cixous Freud is fearful of the implications of the uncanny for his science and overwhelmed by the intricacies of interpretation. He closes his eyes to the strangeness of 'The Sandman' and builds his analysis on repression and fear.

On the other hand, one might disagree with Cixous's criticism of Freud. Although he passes the responsibility of uncanniness over to the literary theorists, claiming that any remaining questions surrounding the concept should be addressed in an aesthetic enquiry, this may represent Freud's own surrendering to the uncanny, his admission that it escapes the reach of science. It seems that at the end of his convoluted account, Freud does acknowledge his own uncertainty and the vulnerability of this argument and attributes much credit to the powers of literature which seem to engulf his science: 'the story-teller has a *peculiarly* directive power over us; by means of the moods he can put us into, he is able to guide the current of our emotions, to dam it up in one direction and make it flow in another [...]' (U 251). The fact that the uncanny rarely re-emerges in Freud's writings after this point perhaps means that even for him it remains a marginal, inexplicable element that psychoanalysis will never truly understand, which corresponds to Cixous's interpretation of the uncanny.

For Cixous, then, the uncanny not only designates an unthematizable surplus to representation and meaning, but points to the abandonment of the *chez soi* as a position adopted by the creator or interpreter. Although the uncanny is not frequently cited by Cixous's critics as exemplary of her vision of literary creation, many of them tend to speak of her project as a deconstruction of the habitual 'home' from which we approach the text, employing imagery of edifice and deconstruction to elucidate her writing strategies.[67] The command to exile in order to create, read and interpret and to envision the real adjacent to the rigidity of closed systems, forms an ethics of writing for Cixous, or as her critics suggest, an 'aesthéthique' or 'poéthique'.[68] This is implicit in several of her texts and the author is often portrayed as she who leaves her home and parts with the *chez soi* in order to write: 'Elle part de moi et va où je ne veux aller. Souvent je sens qu'elle est mon ennemie. Non pas hostile, mais celle qui me déborde, me déconcerte [...]'.[69] Writing is here portrayed not simply as a departure from the stability of the self but as a movement towards the acceptance of a certain alterity within the self, something hidden, from which the linguistic 'I' is alienated. As a writer, I go 'où *je* ne veux aller'; the writing self '*me* déborde, *me* déconcerte'. For Cixous the writer must unhome herself, whether this be through textual practices that subvert grammatical, syntactical and semantic norms, or through the forging of innovative and eccentric ways of writing subjectivity.

Rather than viewing such literary practices as a distortion of reality, it would seem that Cixous sees them as a form of the real, which she has alluded to as the *pluréel*. For Cixous, the most natural way to write the *pluréel* is through poetry. Poetry is a pathway to a kind of real, which she refers to as the 'nu'. In an interview she states:

> Le plus vrai est poétique. Le plus vrai c'est la vie nue. Ce voir, je ne puis l'atteindre qu'à l'aide de l'écriture poétique. 'Voir' le monde nu, c'est-à-dire presque é-nu-mérer le monde, je m'y applique avec l'œil nu, obstiné, sans défense, de ma myopie. Et tout en regardant de très très proche, je copie. Le monde écrit nu est poétique.[70]

As she sought to express it by relying on Freud's essay, a rigid, coherent sense of the ordinary is in fact what Cixous sees as absurd or fictional, whereas the real for Cixous is in some sense brought into light in a moment of uncanniness. The term implies both an ethics of

---

[67] For Mireille Calle-Gruber, Cixous seeks to 'déconstruire aussi bien les prisons du moi que les prises de l'auteur. Les pièges de l'hypostasie narrative'. *Du café à l'éternité, Hélène Cixous à l'œuvre* (Paris: Galilée, 2002), p. 19.
[68] Mireille Calle-Gruber and Hélène Cixous, 'Entre Tiens', in *Hélène Cixous, photos de racines* (Paris: Des Femmes, 1994), pp. 13-121, p. 88.
[69] Hélène Cixous, *Jours de l'an* (Paris: Des femmes Antoinette Fouque, 1990), p. 153.
[70] Mireille Calle-Gruber and Hélène Cixous, 'Entre Tiens', p. 13.

writing and a possibility of authenticity, through an acknowledgement of unthematizable alterity within the ordinary. Cixous constantly reminds her reader that there is no knowable, homogenous, ordered real and that all representation must account for this: 'De même que l'un n'est pas sans l'autre, l'un ne peut être *pensé* sans l'autre'.[71] Cixous advances the idea that the renunciation of the *chez soi* inspires the representation of a more sincere and unaffected experience of the subject in the world through a recognition and embracing of her own alterity.

Yet there are certain ways in which Cixous herself gets tangled in a quest to distinguish the familiar from the strange. By claiming to access an unaffected vision of the world and promoting this version of the real over others, Cixous risks reproducing the very dynamic she attacks. She asserts her own feminine forms of writing as more 'truthful' compared with others which tend to contaminate the real by portraying experience from an inferior viewpoint, premised on the stability of home and self. On the one hand, Cixous appears to be affirming the dangerous, totalizing qualities of the *chez soi*, but she also brings out its mythical and ultimately fragile nature, since the uncanny always triumphs, destroying the patriarchal gestures of hegemonic discourses such as psychoanalysis. Since she claims that even scientific languages such as Freud's can be performatively subversive and that such discourses naturally undo themselves, as was the case with Freud's text, it would appear that they too must embody the vulnerability that she advocates in writing and intellectual practice. Yet her own writing is presented as more ethical, which seems a problematically sharp distinction to draw, given her suspicion of binary oppositions and reductiveness.

Cixous also invokes a reciprocal readerly position, a disarming of the reader who does not so much read as 'se laisser lire', which is what Freud's scientific approach refused.[72] This suggests that she invites the reader to abandon her 'home' in order to welcome the strangeness of hesitation. The reader no longer reads the text but in some sense allows herself to be *read by* the text.[73] This analysis

---

[71] Hélène Cixous, *Neutre*, p. 20.

[72] Cited by Mireille Calle-Gruber in *Du café à l'éternité, Hélène Cixous à l'œuvre*, p. 19.

[73] When speaking of the difficulties in interpreting Cixous's writing, one of her critics says: 'C'est la position de la lecture qui fait obstacle, pas le livre. Parce qu'elle est,

implies a responsibility of the reader to open her interpretation to otherness, liberating herself from certain prejudices and representational norms. Of course this may be an unrealistic or difficult position to adopt and it is unclear exactly what Cixous might mean by this. Some critics have suggested that in practice this vision of reading is utopian.[74] Cixous's texts are in fact so plural and dispersed that they may appear incoherent when contrasted with the sense of the ordinary through which we inhabit and know the world. In wishing her project to be a politics or ethics of writing, Cixous encounters the irony of attempting to change the way people think through a form of writing which appears extremely detached from collective significance.

It seems that for Cixous, the *chez soi* always implies a danger. Rather than suggesting that the uncanny reveals the fragility of home or the need to re-write the familiar, she chooses the route of abandoning the concept of home entirely. This is reflected in her own writing, which seems to be a constant project of uprooting both writer and reader. Cixous's tendency to affirm the mythical nature of home corresponds to the writing strategies of the authors studied here, for whom the home always eludes its supposed comfort and harmony, never functioning in the ways one might expect. However, as we will see, these writers do not always reject the home completely, but maintain it as an ambiguous space, which can be constantly regenerated, interrogated and perceived from multiple angles.

Julia Kristeva - the uncanny foreigner
Anchored in a psychoanalytic discourse, Julia Kristeva's analysis is centred on the repercussions of uncanniness for the subject and re-affirms the concept's associations with the mechanism of repression and the unconscious. However, this psychological, subject-oriented understanding is also broadened to incorporate social and political consciousness in her critique of nationalism. Her work *Étrangers à nous-mêmes* presents the ego-disturbance produced by the uncanny as

---

avant même d'ouvrir l'ouvrage, armée de grilles à déchiffrer et revêtue de prêt-à-penser, la lecture souvent n'est pas en état d'accueillir les libertés qu'offre l'écriture'. Mireille Calle-Gruber, *Du café à l'éternité*, p.19.

[74] Susan Sellers evokes the experience of reading her texts as being 'disappointing'. Cixous's writing can 'produce a bewildered retreat to more conventional textual pleasures with a feeling nothing short of relief', rather than enabling the reader and bringing her into contact with new realities. Susan Sellers, *Hélène Cixous: Authorship, Autobiography and Love*, p. 5.

a social device, a guarantor of responsibility and openness to the other. Kristeva turns the Freudian notion into a model for the logic of the affective negotiation of the foreigner within the national community. She claims that uncanny experience could potentially favour non-violent being with the other, by generating new forms of self-awareness, which interfere with rigid assertions of homogeneity upon which national identity depends. Inflexible visions of the national 'home' lead to a rejection of the foreigner, who is viewed as a threat to the integrity of the community. For Kristeva the uncanny experience of the foreigner should cause the subject to experience herself and her own familiar world as foreign, rather than drive her to ostracize the foreigner for the sake of preserving and defining home through the exclusion of difference. In Kristeva's essay, the uncanny moves from a predominantly aesthetic concept to a political one, becoming a tool which reveals the mythical nature of unbending visions of the *chez soi* on a collective level. The uncanny may also provide a resistance to abjection, which Kristeva views as a violent form of rejection.

Although, like Cixous, Kristeva celebrates the destabilizing value of the uncanny, her negotiation of the concept is very different. She appears to inherit the uncanny directly from Freud as an applicable psychoanalytic principle and she then attempts to link it to concrete societal circumstances. This apparently methodological approach enables her to suggest a context and social value for the uncanny; however, her psychoanalytic harnessing of the term may appear reductive given our previous claims about its elusiveness. Kristeva's essay is valuable for the present analysis in that it delves into the ambiguities of home and self and raises important questions about what may be at stake in the way we conceive of these terms. It is Kristeva's perception of the uncanny as productive, her relocation of uncanniness from externality to an unknown place inside the subject, and her vision of the uncanny as an experience which imposes a reverse dynamic of self-judgement rather than scapegoating, which might provide a framework to illuminate some of the textual practices of the writers under consideration in this book. Her comments about political and social models may be quite rich when considered in a more literary context and it is her general approach which will interest us in our textual analysis rather than the specificities of her description of the psychoanalytic mechanisms for negotiating alterity.

Like Cixous, Kristeva encounters difficulties in navigating a transition from personal to political space. From reading Kristeva's essay it is not easy to determine exactly how the author believes that aesthetic, personal or psychological experiences may found political structures. The reader is sometimes unsure if, when she makes this jump, she is using the uncanny in a more allegorical sense, or if she believes herself to be psychoanalysing social relations and collective experience.

Kristeva's elaboration of the concept also begins with a reading of Freud's 'Das Unheimliche'. However, she differs from Cixous in perceiving the psychoanalyst as an adventurer and a pioneer. Whereas for Cixous, Freud's appeal to the arts was an attempt to remain in the realm of the familiar, by reducing the literary to a scientific framework, for Kristeva, his willingness to overstep disciplinary boundaries and his embracing of the *heimlich/unheimlich* duality reveals a bold movement away from 'home'. She points out Freud's inclination for travel and the fact that, as a Jew, he himself identified with a marginalized position. This awareness perhaps helped kindle his interest in the uncanny and, more generally, in the unconscious and the permanence of otherness within the self, which becomes the basis for his 'éthique de l'inconciliable'.[75] For Kristeva, Freud's analysis of the uncanny may bring us to a vision of ourselves as vulnerable, so that we may better accept the other. Uncanniness has the potential to fragment the imaginary unity of the 'I', revealing the fragility of repression and the ultimate instability of the self, which harbours the foreignness of the unconscious.[76]

Just as Freudian thought teaches that the subject itself 'se révèle comme un étrange pays de frontières et d'altérités sans cesse construites et déconstruites' (EN 283), the uncanny reveals the same about collective social identity through the shattering of communal codes. In the temporary disintegration of common meaning which occurs when one is confronted with strangeness, a crucial point in conceptualization is opened up, where the subject may choose bet-

---

[75] Julia Kristeva, *Étrangers à nous-mêmes* (Paris: Fayard, 1988), p. 269. All other references are given in the text, following the abbreviation EN.

[76] Freud touched upon this in his essay when he spoke of uncanny experience as a return 'to particular phases in the evolution of the self-regarding feeling, a regression to a time when the ego had not yet marked itself off sharply from the external world and from other people' (U 358).

ween a suppression of alterity, through a forceful reaffirmation of the border separating self and other, or a reappraisal of the self and revision of attitudes, which turns the judgement inwards towards the foreignness we already carry within. From Kristeva's psychoanalytic perspective, this inner foreignness is the unknowable unconscious.

For Kristeva, there is always a choice involved in how we react to uncanny experience, and its repression entails risks for the psyche and the community:

> L'inquiétante étrangeté peut être aussi évacuée: 'Non, cela ne me trouble pas: je ris ou j'agis – je m'en vais, je ferme les yeux, je frappe, j'ordonne...' Une telle liquidation du psychique, laissant, au prix d'un appauvrissement mental, la voie libre au passage à l'acte, jusqu'à la paranoïa et au meurtre. (EN 281)

She appropriates Freud's terminology and exploits the configuration of the uncanny to illustrate the ways in which the dialectic of strange and familiar influences social relations and to show that it must be negotiated ethically. She is speaking particularly in relation to the plight of the foreigner in the national community. Kristeva begins this transition from psychological to political space by affirming the historical and circumstantial origins of the modern conception of the nation state, which she feels favours linguistic and cultural hegemony. The frameworks of Stoicism, Christianity and pre-Enlightenment humanism were able to accommodate otherness without indulging in the economy of rejection that founds the modern conception of the state. Whereas past discourses posited transcendental values promoting an acceptance of difference, in the Enlightenment, the nation assumed a totalizing form, which refused the other. To examine contemporary social and conceptual visions of foreignness, Kristeva traces the moral and philosophical evolution of the national sentiment through Cartesian rationalism, Kantian universalism and Rousseauean individualism and, finally, looks at the incarnation of this phenolmenon in the *Gemeinschaft*, or national community. It is in this German notion, she says, that community evolves from a purely rational and moral form into an organic, virtually metaphysical concept (EN 260-61). She compares the emotional attachment of citizens to the solidarity of the national community, to the feeling of belonging to a family, as a 'structure assurant une intégrité archaïque' (EN 261). With Romanticism, Herderian philology and the German

Bildung (the modern notion of culture), begins the assimilation of language to individualized societies and the 'accentuation du *parler national comme le petit dénominateur d'identité*' (EN 265). This facilitates an experience of the foreigner as a threat to the familiarity and imagined integrity of the native language and community. This, in turn, provokes either the taming of foreignness, its reduction to a model of similarity, or its expulsion, which is the logic at the centre of the hegemonic discourses of fascism and the Nazi ideology, which for Kristeva, effects a 'perversion nationaliste de l'idée cosmopolite' (EN 267).

National sentiment is thus founded on the illusion of an un-contaminated home, which cultivates an idea of symbolic unity and identification. The foreigner performs a parallel role in the national community to that of the uncanny in an aesthetic context, by troubling the order of the rational, the familiar or the expected. For Kristeva, the foreigner should be welcomed as an incitement to re-write the national narrative, perceiving *it* as foreign as she identifies with the perspective of the newcomer. This perception discourages the foreigner from being closed out of this narrative or viewed as contaminating. The fact that the foreigner undercuts the stability of the national narrative is positive for Kristeva if it results in an un-homing of the subject belonging to it, rather than the alienation of the newcomer. The disconnectedness from communal significance we experience in un-canniness reveals the possibility that we are in fact all foreigners, so that in a sense there are no foreigners.

Rather than reinforcing a vision of strangeness as a purely external form, the Freudian contribution entails an acknowledgement of the inherent incongruity which upsets subjectivity and coherence from the inside, and of ways of constructing difference in less categorical terms.[77] Freud's uncanny teaches that, like the subject as

---

[77] Although they are not explicitly revealed in this particular text, it is possible, using Kristeva's psychoanalytic discourse, to determine the psychic processes by which such a transformation may occur. These are discussed briefly by Ewa Ziarek in her article 'The Uncanny Style of Kristeva's Critique of Nationalism', *Postmodern Culture* 5 (January 1995), http://www3.iath.virginia.edu/pmc/textonly/issue.195/ziare k.195 (accessed 10 November 2004). In this same article, Ziarek discusses the ethical complexities that arise from Kristeva's very aesthetically-based ethical analysis and her reduction of the oppression of the other and the rejection of difference to an inevitable unchangeable aspect of the human psyche. It should be noted that, for the purposes of this book, what interests us is Kristeva's problematization of the home

constituted through repression (which for Freud was the act that founded individual belonging to a community), notions of the *chez soi* must be viewed as tenuous:

> Avec Freud, l'étrangeté, inquiétante, s'insinue dans la quiétude de la raison même, et, sans se borner à la folie, à la beauté ou à la foi, pas plus qu'à l'ethnie ou à la race, irrigue notre être-de-parole lui-même, étrange par d'autres logiques, y compris l'hétérogénéité de la biologie. Désormais, nous nous savons étrangers à nous-mêmes, et c'est à partir de ce seul appui que nous pouvons essayer de vivre avec les autres (EN 269).

Of course, one could argue here that Kristeva's mission to destabilize the polarities at work in the perception of foreignness is rather ineffective, since polarities continue to operate, but are simply turned around. Like Cixous, she advocates an awareness of the strangeness of the *chez soi*. For Kristeva, this entails a form of self-perception based on alterity, but it does not dissolve the binary logic at work in the strange and familiar dichotomy. If anything, it maintains active the boundaries between the two concepts, by simply transforming something familiar into something strange, since it presupposes the possibility of estranging perception.

The abject

In order to appreciate what Kristeva sees as the value of the uncanny, that is, the defamiliarization of the self and the *chez soi*, it is helpful to turn to her writings on the abject, which illuminate her perception of the ethical and psychological risks of structures of thought which are constructed upon a violent resistance to alterity. The value Kristeva places on uncanniness may perhaps be explained in part by its being a softer, less damaging version of abjection, which she sees as a brutal annihilation of the subject-object distinction, rather than simply its problematization. Through uncanniness, we can perhaps save the foreigner from the extreme rejection she might suffer in abjection, which is the most dangerous form of scapegoating.[78] Like the uncanny, the abject is what perturbs and reveals the failures of codes,

---

and her particular view of uncanniness as that which commands a reassessment of orders of the same. Her reinterpretation of national space through the Freudian psychology of the uncanny may be problematic when viewed in political terms.

[78] An in-depth dicussion of the concept of the abject begins on the following page.

order, the law and the home. But unlike the uncanny, the abject often entails a deeper form of rejection because approaching the abject would destroy the 'I'. Although it is not explicit in her analysis, it seems that Kristeva's distinction between the two allows her to privilege the uncanny as that which maintains a certain grip on reality, enabling change and innovation, while a moment of abjection destroys the other in a struggle to preserve the 'I'. The abject (in the context of a negative response to repulsive food or waste, for example) may only be captured in confrontation with the 'I' and otherwise contains no qualities of object:

> 'Je' n'en veux rien savoir, 'je' ne l'assimile pas, 'je' l'expulse. Mais puisque cette nourriture n'est pas un 'autre' pour 'moi' qui ne suis que dans leur désir, je *m*'expulse, je *me* crache, je *m*'abjecte dans le même mouvement par lequel 'je' prétends *me* poser.[79]

In her work *Pouvoirs de l'horreur*, Kristeva elaborates the concept of the abject as the experience of the subject when faced with revolting phenomena such as faeces, vomit, urine or death. Such entities provoke fascination and desire, which are subsequently re-placed by refusal, due to the subject's prevailing need for self-preservation, through maintaining her place in an integral symbolic order which precludes such fascination.[80] Faced with the threat of abjection, the subject undergoes a 'crise narcissique' and puts forth her resistance to the disintegration of meaning (PH 22). When confronted with the abject, the subject turns away in repulsion and the spasm of disgust or the expression of shock are the inscriptions of the abject in the symbolic. As is the case with the uncanny, Kristeva sees the abject not only as a principle at work locally in the subject, but as explanatory of larger-scale social, political and representational trends. She advances the view that it is the logic of abjection which founds the

---

[79] Julia Kristeva, *Pouvoirs de l'horreur: essai sur l'abjection*, coll. 'Tel Quel' (Paris: Éditions du Seuil, 1980), pp. 10-11. All other references are given in the text, following the abbreviation PH.

[80] The symbolic for Kristeva is borrowed from the Lacanian symbolic, as the societal order of language through which the subject is constituted. Kristeva's understanding differs from the Lacanian model since she also posits the existence of the 'semiotic', an insubordinate, plural domain within language, which does not exist in Lacanian thought. See Julia Kristeva, *La Révolution du langage poétique*, pp. 22-30.

signifying economy of Western culture. Processes of rejection and separation are constitutive of all cultural and intellectual activity involving boundaries. The repulsion expressed by the subject faced with that which threatens her positioning in an ordered reality, is in fact a sign of the 'proper' functioning of these orders.

This landscape of abjection gestures to a pre-symbolic stage, before the demarcation of the boundaries between self and other, before the constitution of the subject; like the uncanny for Freud, the abject harks back to the pre-subjective maternal.[81] The maternal is always in question when speaking about the abject since, for Kristeva, the foundation of the subject involves the abjection of the mother:

> L'abject nous confronte, d'une part, à ces états fragiles où l'homme erre dans les territoires de l'*animal* [...] L'abject nous confronte d'autre part, et cette fois dans notre archéologie personnelle, à nos tentatives les plus anciennes de nous démarquer de l'entité *maternelle* avant même que d'ex-ister en dehors d'elle grâce à l'autonomie du langage. (PH 20)

Although abjection is always more strange than familiar, it offers a hint of a time of amorphousness, choric unity[82] and absent boundaries, before the separation of the self from the maternal plenum and the mapping of the clean and proper body through the denunciation of urine, excrement and other 'unclean' materials.

In this way, the threat to subjectivity in abjection, and the risk it entails for the boundaries between self and other, contain something valuable if channelled positively towards 'un assouplissement du surmoi', rather than towards a preservation of a rigid sense of self (PH 23). The abject initiates a process by which the pre-symbolic may perhaps speak, unlegislated by the paternal order, retrieving remnants of this space prior to the subject-object distinction. In negotiating abjection, literature may be cathartic and provide a means to escape its violence by investing it in something productive. In *Pouvoirs de l'hor-*

---

[81] In 'Das Unheimliche', Freud attributes the uncanniness of the notion of being buried alive to the fantasy, both feared and desired, of returning to the maternal womb.

[82] For Kristeva, the 'chora', a term borrowed from Plato's *Timaeus*, refers to pre-symbolic libidinal drives and energy and precedes the semiotic stage of subjective development, in which the groundwork for subjectivity is laid through the mirror stage and maternal authority. Kristeva describes the chora's relationship to the subject as 'le lieu de sa négation'. Julia Kristeva, *La révolution du langage poétique*, p. 27.

reur, Kristeva studies texts by Céline and other writers which represent what to some readers could provoke abjection. In *Voyage au bout de la nuit* Kristeva sees that Céline approaches speaking the abject, but also that the poetics of his text perform a process of figurative abjection.[83]

The unhomely

Although in *Étrangers à nous-mêmes* Kristeva does not address the uncanny as a uniquely aesthetic phenomenon, her reflection on the arts in *Pouvoirs de l'horreur* and other texts has often brought her to reflect upon the unhoming capacities of literature. For Kristeva, art creates a relationship with a pre-linguistic subject position, a subject not yet inscribed in the symbolic order. She maintains that the work of art or the text generates a place where the subject-object distinction is equivocal and where regulatory orders are unsettled and expanded.[84] Language is both homing and unhoming: while ordinary language has the capacity to imprison us in banality, poetry is the means to liberate us from it. The unconscious and the influence of the pre-symbolic on subjectivity can be tools of 'intimate revolt' which affirm the singularity of a subject who exceeds linguistic and social norms.[85] Kristeva advocates an ethics of psychoanalysis in which radical alterity and the singularity of the subject are constantly stressed rather that repressed.

Intellectual displacement is, then, always promoted in Kristeva's thought both as part of the development of a healthy psyche and as an ethics of accepting difference. We should be, and in a sense already are, both strangers to language and strangers to ourselves. Art enables us to interact with our surroundings in such a way as to put

---

[83] For a detailed analysis of Kristeva's writings on Céline see Megan Becker-Leckrone, *Julia Kristeva and Literary Theory* (Basingstoke: Palgrave Macmillan, 2005).

[84] For Kristeva subjectivity is constituted through separation from the primary object, which is the mother. Innovative relationships with language can recreate pre-symbolic, semiotic pleasures and compensate for this loss. In her early work, Kristeva explores the poetry of Lautréamont and Mallarmé to explore the ways in which poetic production and reading playfully disrupt the subject and reveal her heterogeneity. See Julia Kristeva, *La Révolution du langage poétique*.

[85] Again, see Kristeva's concept of the semiotic chora, which relates to a pre-symbolic state, but continues to exercise an influence on the symbolic and may in some way be retrieved through creativity.

ourselves constantly in the position of foreigner.[86] While Cixous saw the need to abandon the *chez soi* entirely, in many of Kristeva's writings we find imagery of travel and displacement used to refer to the potential unsettling of the subject *within* the *chez soi*. The subject may always be estranged from her home and any identity may be dissolved or transformed through changing positions of perception and representation.

Kristeva's own literary endeavours often gesture to the importance of subjective un-homing, which is raised both thematically and through dialogue. In her most recent novel, *Meurtre à Byzance*, one of the main characters, Stéphanie Delacour, declares: 'Je me voyage', a statement which may be seen to encapsulate Kristeva's vision of the subject as one who is never entirely at home with herself.[87]

For Kristeva, the uncanny denotes the fragility of structural or conceptual systems which rely on an economy of rejecting the improper. It reveals the imminence of a certain breakdown or precariousness in such orders and the mythical nature of certain collective structures: it is also a means to prevent the violence of abjection. Her interest in processes of unhoming and in ways of thinking which trouble the *chez soi* marks a larger quest within her work for a reinterpretation of the subject and a commitment constantly to re-process and to unsettle visions of reality, to unfasten and regenerate the implicit ties of identification which connect the individual to her environment. However, as some of her critics have pointed out, a society which functions according to such an ethics is nearly inconceivable. While Cixous encounters the problem of cutting all ties with the *chez soi* to embrace the strange, Kristeva perhaps errs on the side of insisting on the applicability, the almost methodological value of the uncanny by suggesting a clear political or social role for it. However, the dynamic of the uncanny that she presents provides an interesting context in which to read the texts of the authors to be studied here.

The uncanny real

---

[86] Anna Smith studies the theme of estrangement in Kristeva as both a recurring motif in her reflection and a feeling produced in the reader of her texts. See Anna Smith, *Julia Kristeva: Readings of Exile and Estrangement* (Houndmills, Basingstoke, Hampshire, London: Macmillan Press, 1996).

[87] Julia Kristeva, *Meurtre à Byzance* (Paris: Fayard, 2004).

Twenty-first century theorists are seeking innovative ways to account for the uncanny while avoiding the pitfalls of attempting to define it rigidly. Some theorists do, however, assume relatively stable definitions of the uncanny or at least assert that the uncanny does possess a particular structure or set of criteria. Samuel Weber, for instance, stresses the importance of maintaining the uncanny as a phenomenon which is determined by a series of 'objective' factors.[88] But for Anneleen Masschelein, 'the uncanny has gradually come to signify the very problem or even impossibility of clearly defined concepts as such'.[89] Within cultural theory, at least, we are increasingly beginning to accept the uncanny as a concept which reveals the mythical nature of stable meaning and of the boundary between the proper and the improper. As it evolves away from the fantastic and towards a revision of the rational and the real, the uncanny begins to suggest that what is fantastical is to believe that there is a firm place upon which we might stand to constitute knowledge.[90] As Freud discovered in his own etymological investigation, the uncanny is not simply something we cannot define, but something strange that occurs when we attempt to familiarize ourselves with something. Much current reflection on the uncanny is well aware of the uncanny's performative value. For Nicolas Royle, the only way to speak of the concept is to allow one's own text to be seized by its exemplary illogic. The uncanny is inseparable from subjective, personal encounters. According to Royle:

> The uncanny is destined to elude mastery, it is what cannot be pinned down or controlled. The uncanny is never simply a question of a statement, description or definition, but always engages a performative dimension, a maddening supplement, something unpredictable and additionally strange happening in and to what is being stated, described or defined. (UN 15)

---

[88] Samuel Weber, *The Legend of Freud* (Stanford: Stanford University Press, 2000), p. 208.

[89] Anneleen Masschelein, 'A Homeless Concept: Shapes of the Uncanny in Twentieth-Century Theory and Culture', p. 1.

[90] Terry Castle suggests that the uncanny is a by-product of the Enlightenment attempt to schematize and totalize reality, to account for all phenomena and to produce a rational view of the subject. Such a quest for coherence produces what she calls a 'toxic side effect, a new human experience of strangeness, anxiety, bafflement, and intellectual impasse'. Terry Castle, *The Female Thermometer: Eighteenth-century Culture and the Invention of the Uncanny*, p. 8.

This performative dimension to the uncanny's intangible nature is also evident in the self-contradictory ways in which we are forced to speak about uncanniness. Most thinkers who engage with the concept provide provisional or 'working' definitions of the term which are often necessarily illogical or point to the obscuring or convoluting power of the concept. For David Ellison, for instance, 'das Unheimliche is the domain of death-in-life, a ghostly place or non-place'.[91] However, the intangibility of the term does not seem to impede our being able to use it. Masschelein raises this point in her article, 'The Concept as Ghost':

> As an 'unconcept,' the uncanny haunts conceptuality and infects it with the spectre of fiction, and at the same time it maintains enough solidity to travel among disciplines in the wake of the common frame of reference that psychoanalysis, no matter how modified, still provides.[92]

And for some, this 'unconcept' may itself have a certain value as we come to view the indefinable nature of the uncanny as fruitful. Many are today contemplating the uncanny as a mind-opening and de-stabilizing tool, which could open up new discursive spaces and revive perceptions of the ordinary. The questions raised by uncanniness imply a place within discourse for a non-place, which can always destroy that which is being affirmed. But this form of questioning may in turn enrich our perceptions of reality and invite an element of precariousness and tentativeness into rationalistic constructions. James Donald, for example, promotes a re-thinking of popular cinema in terms of the sublime to encourage sensitivity to 'the materiality and limits of representation' and the inadequacy of 'the idea of totality'.[93] He also indicates a certain truth-value for uncanniness and suggests its potential for informing descriptions of the self which 'present a version of subjectivity that is closer to the insistent, everyday reality of how we experience ourselves in the world than the

---

[91] David Ellison, *Ethics and Aesthetics in European Modernist Literature: From the Sublime to the Uncanny*, p. 133.

[92] Anneleen Masschelein, 'The Concept as Ghost: Conceptualization of the Uncanny in Late-Twentieth-Century Theory', p. 66.

[93] James Donald 'The Fantastic, the Sublime and the Popular, Or, What's at Stake in Vampire Films', in *Fantasy and the Cinema* (London: bfi publishing, 1989) pp. 248-9.

myth of autonomous, self-conscious agency'.[94] Here again we confront a view of the uncanny as that which could possibly provide a
new form of realism, but such claims are also problematic in that they
may simply re-locate the myth versus reality dichotomy. By alleging
that the fantastic imagery of vampire films provides a more accurate
'reality', a more faithful portrayal of individual experience, thinkers
like James Donald appear to be describing the uncanny as a positive,
reducible value or implement for achieving authenticity.

This position resembles that held by Nicolas Royle, for whom
'the uncanny can perhaps provide ways of beginning to think in less
dogmatic terms about the nature of the world, ourselves and a politics
of the future' (UN 3). For Royle, the uncanny points to a need for a
constant reassessment of theoretical and societal principles, what he
thinks of as a new thinking of origins, involving a vision of 'beginning
as already haunted' (UN 1).

It seems that Royle intends his book to be emblematic of the
uncanny since it presents an anarchic structure, with trailing fragments, disproportionate chapters, frequent ellipses and a strange
blending of uncanny images and text. Since this style does in some
way reflect the elusiveness of the uncanniness he is trying to address,
Royle's presentation of his theoretical text provides a clue as to how
scholarly practice might begin to incorporate an awareness of the
uncanny into its very functioning. His message appears to be that,
since uncanniness is unavoidable and the concept obscure, it is futile
to attempt to produce a coherent text in which an exploration of the
term is carried out. Here, however, we might raise the point that an
uncanny text was previously thought to be one which, like Freud's,
does not 'practice what it preaches'. Royle's text would seem to be
both claiming uncanny status and believing to practice what it
preaches. This is also the case for Cixous, whose meandering analysis
perhaps strives to re-enact uncanniness or to behave uncannily. Here
again, we risk re-locating the uncanny, by separating that which is
uncanny from that which is not, thereby recycling the binary process
supposedly undermined in uncanny experience.

In her functionalist-discursive examination of the history of
the conceptualization of the uncanny, Anneleen Masschelein tries to
avoid this trap by concentrating on the history of the concept's various

---

[94] Ibid, p. 235.

applications, instead of on the notion in and of itself. But she also appears to privilege the uncanny over other concepts by saying that our acknowledgement of its indefinable nature might incite a reinterpretation of reality in order to account for the unthematizable. For her, the heterogeneity of its applications and contexts constitutes the main purpose of the term. The uncanny is:

> lastingly loaded with new connotations and new kernels of meanings. The uncontrollable (unconscious) subversive potential thus undermines closed, self-contained theoretical and critical positions and forces the reader to contemplate or carefully consider the meaning and function of a concept in every new situation.[95]

Of course, Masschelein's tendency to use terms such as 'kernels' and to describe the uncanny as 'lastingly loaded' is relatively undeconstructive, despite her claims for the rebellious, non-totalizing nature of the concept. What her argument does point out is that, if the uncanny might be viewed as suggesting a certain vision of reality, it is one which expresses itself through rupture and fragmentation.

Surveying these theories and experiences of the uncanny as well as comments made by various thinkers, it becomes apparent that, for many, the uncanny is more than just a moment of fright or senselessness. It is an entire philosophy of the ordinary. Not only does it remind us that the familiar, coherent world is always vulnerable to the intrusion of alterity, but also suggests a responsibility figuratively to unsettle the space of the familiar and willingly to perceive and welcome such disorder. The uncanny imposes both a conceptual site of interrogation and an ethical incentive to reevaluate the ideological and affective underpinnings of normality and habit by assigning a status of precariousness to the previously familiar. It reminds us that the everyday world is not inherently ordinary, but in fact constitutes a delicate space of confrontation between the forces of the strange and the familiar.

In a sense, these contemporary interpretations hark back to the Heideggerian *Unheimliche*. Heidegger saw the anxiety of the uncanny as a pre-phenomenological moment which could rescue *Dasein* from the inauthenticity it suffers in the idleness of the everyday.[96] Bruce

---

[95] Anneleen Masschelein, 'The Concept as Ghost', p. 63.
[96] For Heidegger, the resurgence within the everyday of the anxiety of an original 'homelessness' is *Dasein*'s way of revealing the more primordial state of the

Bégout develops a similar idea in his philosophical study of the *quotidien*, suggesting that ontological insecurity and moments of intellectual uncertainty 'ne relèvent pas de la seule indécision de la pensée, mais de l'ambivalence même de la vie humaine dans le monde'.[97]

Reconstructing the chez soi

Metaphorically and performatively connected to feelings of unhomeliness, it seems that the uncanny is often understood as a disturbance of the *chez soi*. The French *chez soi* is a particularly useful and evocative phrase in discussions of the uncanny, since it allows us to speak simultaneously of a destabilization of the self and the home. Compared with 'home', however, this term leans more noticeably towards the element of self, reflecting a tendency to conceive of the self as a form of home. Viewing the uncanny in terms of the *chez soi*, we might describe a moment where the world no longer operates in continuity with the self, affirming its unity and stability. A place in which the individual previously felt comforted and affirmed assumes a menacing or incoherent quality.

For the purposes of this book I thus consider that the *chez soi*, or the home, might be viewed not only as a place, but as a contemplative or emotional positioning, a notion which comes across well in Kristeva's and Cixous's analyses of home. This understanding of a meaning for home which goes beyond its mere geographical location already underlies our vocabulary of home. Terms such as 'homesickness' or 'homeland', for example, suggest the affective quality that is always attached to home, the idea of a stable, comforting, beginning point, to which one might return. 'Home' typically calls up an *imaginaire* of intransience and sanctuary. For Gaston Bachelard, the home is a 'un corps d'images qui donnent à l'homme des raisons ou des illusions de stabilité'.[98] It relates both to feelings of stability with

---

individual in the world. Anxiety is produced when *Dasein* confronts the un-homely nature of its being. '[T]his individualization brings *Dasein* back from its falling, and makes manifest to it that authenticity and inauthenticity are possibilities of its Being'. Martin Heidegger, *Being and Time*, trans. by J. Macquarrie and E. Robinson (Oxford: Basil Blackwell, 1962), p. 235.

[97] Bruce Bégout, *La Découverte du quotidien* (Paris: Éditions Allia, 2005), p. 290. For Bégout, the uncanny is 'la manifestation seconde et redoublée de l'incertitude primitive'. Ibid, p. 449.

[98] Gaston Bachelard, *La Poétique de l'espace* (Paris: Presses Universitaires de France, 2001; first published in 1957), p. 34.

respect to one's physical environment and to the interiorization of that certainty in order to feel at ease with oneself.[99]

The notion of home may also be associated with ideas of normalcy, familiarity and with what is non-disruptive to the community, the self or our ways of thinking. For Pierre Bourdieu, home is not only geographical or spatial, but also an ideological, political and economic structure. As a motif, it evokes the solidity and harmony of community. To found a home is to create a collective space of identification and regularity and 'la capacité de résister à la désagrégation et à la dispersion'.[100] For J. MacGregor Wise, the designation of home is a process of territorialization through which spaces are invested with 'cultural and social norms'.[101]

We also do not hesitate to employ imagery of the home when describing processes of conceptualization. The very idea of a stable, transcendental subjectivity implies feeling at home with oneself, the ability to trace the frontiers of interior and exterior, self and other and to objectify the outside world. The home implies a firm intellectual ground to stand on. We speak of 'domesticating' an idea, or of 'familiarizing' ourselves with certain notions. Contemporary ethical and cultural studies often introduce the theme of the home into descriptions of the traditional Cartesian approach to knowledge, as one which reinforces the illusion of attaining mastery over an object of investigation. Feeling at home can imply the ability to generate certainty and to forge a comfortable place for reflection.

This idea of home as a *process*, rather than simply a domain of self-assuredness, comes across in the work of many thinkers, for whom home refers to a way of alloying unease.[102] For Emmanuel

---

[99] In his psychoanalytic exploration of the notion of home, Alberto Eiguer studies links of cohabitation among family members and introduces the concept of 'l'habitat intérieur', which he sees as a psychic representation which synthesizes the image of the subject's body and that of the family group which is projected onto the home. He compares the activities of the home to bodily functions such as eating, excretion, sleep and sexuality. See his book *L'Inconscient de la maison*, coll. 'Psychismes' (Paris: Dunod, 2004), pp. 2-8.

[100] Pierre Bourdieu, *Les Structures sociales de l'économie* (Paris: Éditions du Seuil, 2000), p. 35.

[101] J. MacGregor Wise, 'Home: Territory and Identity', *Cultural Studies* 14, No. 2, ed. by Andrea L. Press and Bruce A. Williams (April 2000), 295-310.
p. 300.

[102] J. Macgregor Wise takes as her starting point Deleuze and Guattari's story of a child in the dark comforting himself by singing. She elaborates an idea of home as a

Levinas, for example, home is a movement of labour and domestication, through which the subject exercises a 'saisie originelle', viewed by Levinas as a form of domestication. In this sense, the *chez soi* is what renders contemplation possible and is the process 'qui *suscite* les choses et transforme la nature en monde'.[103] Ontology and knowledge are in fact the product of a form of homing which involves separation, rejection, possession and interiorization.

By challenging the naturalness of structures of familiarity and our sense of comfort within the ordinary world, the uncanny suggests that these processes of homing are not infallible. Discussions of the uncanny and, as we will see, the writing of the novelists studied in this book, promote a profound questioning of the *chez soi* as an environment, as an intellectual, conceptual positioning and as a process of familiarization. As will be demonstrated throughout this study, the approaches to the representation of the *chez soi* found in the selected authors are somewhat aligned with trends in contemporary French writing which involve the revelation of the complexities of certain 'familiar' spaces. However, through their insistence on the uncanny nature of these domains, NDiaye, Carrère and Savitzkya generate a unique portrayal of the home, the family, the everyday and the self, characterized by a perpetual oscillation or tension between strange and familiar.

---

cultural and personal process of territorialization.
[103] Emmanuel Levinas, *Totalité et infini: essai sur l'extériorité* (Paris: Kluwer Academic, 1971), p. 168.

Extra-ordinary Homes

Le quotidien échappe. C'est en quoi il est étrange, le familier qui se découvre (mais déjà se dissipe) sous l'espace de l'étonnant. C'est l'inaperçu, en ce sens d'abord que le regard l'a toujours dépassé et ne peut non plus l'introduire dans un ensemble ou en faire la 'revue', c'est-à-dire l'enfermer dans une vision panoramique; car par un autre trait, le quotidien, c'est ce que nous ne voyons jamais une première fois, mais ne pouvons que revoir, l'ayant toujours déjà vu par une illusion qui est précisément constitutive du quotidien.

— Maurice Blanchot, *L'Entretien infini*[1]

Encounters with the banal

Although it was in the nineteenth century that the French novel first conferred a literary status on commonplace objects and everyday detail, the complexity of the self's relationship to the everyday was not under investigation in its own right. In realism, the representation of the ordinary was largely subjugated to other aesthetic or ideological agendas and participated in descriptive practices, symbolism, functionalism, plot and the economy of mimesis.[2] This evolved in the Proustian aesthetic, where everyday moments, such as the famous 'madeleine' episode, were invested with poetic importance and could illuminate reflections on self and memory. The *Nouveau Roman* often denied literature the capacity to account for the everyday world. As Robbe-Grillet tells us: 'Le monde n'est ni signifiant ni absurde. Il *est*, tout simplement'.[3] Within the *Nouveau Roman*, the description of objects and surroundings, however banal, is present, but often becomes constitutive of an interrogation of the act of writing itself.[4]

---

[1] Maurice Blanchot, 'La Parole quotidienne', in *L'Entretien infini* (Paris: Gallimard, 1969), pp. 355-66, pp. 357-58.

[2] See on this point Naomi Segal, *The Banal Object: Theme and Thematics in Proust, Rilke, Hofmannsthal and Sartre* (London: Institute of Germanic Studies, 1981), pp. 10-11.

[3] Alain Robbe-Grillet, *Pour un nouveau roman* (Paris: Éditions de Minuit, 1963), p. 18.

[4] Bernard Canal describes the role of the object in the *Nouveau Roman* as a rejection of the pananthropism of the realist novel: 'la description précise et essentiellement

In his study of the current status of the contemporary French
novel, Christian Michel suggests that 'si le roman contemporain n'a
pas de conscience *politique*, c'est qu'il n'a plus que des soucis *domestiques*'.[5] Michel was using the term 'domestique' in its broader sense,
proposing the idea that today's novelists privilege the representation
of the intimate, personal sphere over that of the political or social
world. However, Michel's observation of the abundance of 'soucis
domestiques', which, for him, preoccupy today's writers, may also be
taken in quite a literal sense, since current novelists often accord an
exceptional attention to day-to-day experience and phenolmena within
the home. The *quotidien*[6] is no longer relegated to the role of backdrop
for the plot or placed purely at the service of 'l'aventure d'une
écriture'.[7] It has emerged from its various subsidiary roles to become a
literary object in and of itself, which presents its own ecstasies and
obstacles. The narrativization and amplification of the *quotidien* and
the domestic environment is a trend found in novels by many
twentieth and twenty-first century writers, such as, of course, Georges
Perec, but also Éric Chevillard, Christian Oster, Eugène Savitzkaya or
Jean-Philippe Toussaint, and complements a more general cultural

---

visuelle s'arrête à la surface des objets, constate leur extériorité, leur indépendance,
leur absence de signification éternelle, cherche à couper court à la recherche de tout
au-delà métaphysique: on se contente d'enregistrer la distance (et non le divorce ou le
déchirement) entre l'homme et le monde'. Bernard Canal, *Paysage et Nouveau
Roman*, Le Français dans tous ses états 33, 'Le Paysage', http://www.crdp-montpel
lier.fr/ressources/frdtse/frdtse33e.html (accessed 25 November 2007).
[5] Christian Michel, '"Le Réel dort aussi": un panorama du jeune roman français', p.
44.
[6] For Blanchot the *quotidien* is: 'ce que nous sommes en premier lieu et le plus
souvent: dans le travail, le loisir, dans la veille, le sommeil, dans la rue, dans le privé
de l'existence'. Blanchot thus understands this domain as a branch of human activity
that escapes law and structure. For the purposes of this book I am primarily interested
in the domestic elements of the *quotidien* and its relationship to the subject's ability to
feel *chez lui*. See Maurice Blanchot, 'La Parole quotidienne', p. 355. I am following
Michael Sheringham's example in this book by using the terms 'everyday' and
'*quotidien*' in their 'neutral and indeterminate' sense, not to be confused with Henri
Lefebvre's understanding of 'everyday life', which, as Sheringham points out, has
political and sociological implications. See Michael Sheringham, *Everyday Life,
Theories and Practices from Surrealism to the Present* (Oxford: Oxford University
Press, 2006), p. 3.
[7] Jean Ricardou, *Problèmes du nouveau roman* (Paris: Éditions du Seuil, 1967), p.
111.

trend towards rendering the private sphere public.[8] Moreover, everyday spaces are now rarely portrayed as comforting locations. In much contemporary writing, phenomena of the everyday are portrayed as being in disharmony with the subject.[9]

This approach to the representation of familiar space is in contrast with the common tendency to view the *quotidien* as a stable, emotionally supportive realm. In his book *L'Inconscient de la maison*, psychoanalyst Alberto Eiguer suggests that the comfort of the *chez soi* depends on the collaboration and harmony of various forms of homing. One element of this phenomenon involves the material domestic environment. For Eiguer: 'La maison crée les conditions pour que l'on s'y sente à l'aise et étayé entre proches alors que les objets avec lesquels on meuble la maison [...] ordonnent ce territoire de l'intimité'.[10] His discussion of the family home as an emotionally and psychologically invested physical location is informed by his broader understanding of home, which includes the spatial, intellectual or subjective states generated by one's relationship with one's domestic environment. The notion of home may be extended to evoke the self-assurance of the individual in everyday space. For many, the *chez soi* is a location, a state of selfhood and also a positioning within the ordinary, one which is qualified by a sense of certainty with respect to the outside world. In his book *La Découverte du quotidien*, Bruce Bégout employs the image of a home, or a refuge, to describe the security of the individual's existence within the familiar space of the everyday, which for him provides defence against uncertainty:

> Afin d'échapper à la menace diffuse de la contingence du monde, à l'invraisemblable et à la démesure, le quotidien bâtit un refuge familier, réconfortant, auquel il accorde tout de suite la valeur

---

[8] Michael Sheringham notes that since the 1980s the *quotidien* has become an increasingly prominent topic within various media and genres in France and elsewhere. He links this trend with the decline of the novel which sparked the development of a series of hybrid genres, including biography, autobiography, the journal, travel writing, essays etc. See Michael Sheringham, *Everyday Life, Theories and Practices from Surrealism to the Present*, p. 3.

[9] See on this point Florence Bouchy, '"Mais au diable la peinture sociale": les objets quotidiens dans quelques romans de Christian Oster', in *Christian Oster et cie, retour du romanesque*, ed. by Aline Mura-Brunel (Amsterdam, NewYork: Rodopi, 2006), pp. 83-92.

[10] Alberto Eiguer, *L'Inconscient de la maison*, coll. 'Psychismes', ed. by Didier Anzieu (Paris: Dunod, 2004), p. 2.

> d'une nécessité à la fois irrécusable et commune. Grâce aux
> techniques de domestication et de climatisation, il se défend
> contre de nouvelles irruptions de l'indéterminé.[11]

In *La Poétique de l'espace,* Bachelard represents the domestic space of the family home as a site of comfort and stability, which assures the individual's identity and sense of subjective coherence when faced with the foreignness of the outside world. Bachelard emphasizes the imaginative topography of home as a physical space and a heartening site of memory: '[Tous] les abris, tous les refuges, toutes les chambres ont des valeurs d'onirisme consonnantes [...] Ainsi la maison ne se vit pas seulement au jour le jour, sur le fil d'une histoire, dans le récit de notre histoire. Par les songes, les diverses demeures de notre vie se compénètrent et gardent les trésors des jours anciens'.[12]

It is perhaps this familiar 'refuge' of the everyday that is per-turbed or contaminated in uncanny experience. Freud was aware of the fragility of this refuge and of the potential strangeness of formerly familiar, everyday environments. In the last pages of his essay on the uncanny, he relates a story he read in a magazine about a young couple who move into a furnished house in which there is a table with carvings of crocodiles. That evening they begin to notice a strange odour pervading their new home; in the dark they stumble over an object and then perceive an elusive form gliding over the stairs. There is a sense that the crocodile table has somehow 'come to life' (U 244). While this incident is indeed uncanny, Freud is unable to account for it with the aid of his theory. It is not explicitly a reminder of the re-pressed fear of castration, nor does it incite the resurgence of infantile or primitive beliefs. While most of Freud's uncanny examples constitute moments in which a fearsome alterity harks back to something familiar, the crocodile story is a case where the com-fortable, domestic environment in which we may expect to feel at home suddenly assumes a ghastly quality. It is also an instance where a familiar and seemingly lifeless entity, the table, appears to lose its status as object and take on a life of its own, in some way expressing itself.

Freud's crocodile story might serve as an introduction to the

---

[11] Bruce Bégout, *La Découverte du quotidien*, pp. 287-8.
[12] Gaston Bachelard, *La Poétique de l'espace*, p. 25.

multi-faceted configurations of unhomeliness which will arise in this chapter. In contrast to the comforting visions of domestic space presented by Eiguer, Bégout and Bachelard, writers such as NDiaye, Carrère and Savitzkaya depict domestic environments as sites of incongruity or anxiety, challenging the received imagery and myths of the home which emphasize its stability and comforting qualities. They present a defamiliarized vision of the everyday in which the subject cannot feel *chez elle*. The vicissitudes of the banal and the home are transfigured or exaggerated in an attempt to expose a strangeness which lurks within the commonplace.

The primary focus of this chapter will be the ways in which these writers exploit themes and dynamics of the uncanny to recover a fruitful narrative space in which the most ordinary landscapes, and the relationship of the subject to the *quotidien*, are re-thought through codes of the strange. Moments where the *chez soi* dissipates are not portrayed as exceptional, fleeting instances, to be repressed or overcome. These moments often in fact appear to represent the primary condition of the subject in the world and may be productive, capable of generating meaning and illuminating experience. The individual is never 'master in her own house'. Through a portrayal of the everyday as a place of inherent strangeness, NDiaye, Carrère and Savitzkaya express certain uncanny realities of subjective experience.

Marie NDiaye's *La Sorcière* and Emmanuel Carrère's *La Moustache* will be studied together in the context of uncanny realism. Both authors are associated with the contemporary 'retour du réalisme'[13] and cultivate anxiety and forms of the uncanny as a context which can enrich their critiques of contemporary society and their portrayals of the unsettled experience of the subject in the world. Eugène Savitzkaya's *En vie* will then be studied both in proximity with and in contrast to these texts. For Savitzkaya, the vulnerability and loss of the *chez soi* becomes primarily a *celebration* of the strangeness of the real and a means to revive the poetic elements hidden within the banal, so that one may dwell creatively in one's immediate surroundings. For all three writers, descriptions of a habitual, realistic domestic realm borrow from the alternative genres of poetry and of the fantastic in order to acknowledge, in the case of

---

[13] See Dominique Rabaté, *Le Roman français depuis 1900*, p. 112.

NDiaye, its potential violence, in that of Carrère, its absurdity and humour, and in that of Savitzkaya, its lyrical splendour.

Uncanny Realism in *La Sorcière* and *La Moustache*

The appropriation of the everyday in the nineteenth-century realist aesthetic is criticized for generating an excessively ordered recreation of reality, where the external world presents an illusion of coherence. This vision of the real is doubled by a subject who, while being at odds with the political and social environment, feels at home in the immediate, material world.[14] This homeliness is also shared by the author, who enjoys a comfortable stance of domestication over the object of representation. For Leo Bersani, the textual world of realism is suspiciously functional:

> Le roman réaliste nous présente une image de fragmentation sociale comprise dans l'ordonnancement de la forme signifiante – et suggère par là que ces fragments chaotiques sont, d'une certaine façon, socialement viables et moralement rachetables. Le roman se sert de l'anarchie sociale pour fabriquer du sens esthétique.[15]

Among recent trends observed by critics of the contemporary French novel is a paradoxical return to certain forms of realism.[16] Keen to retrieve some of the novel's more traditional 'romanesque' forms, French novelists are currently in search of a voice to express certain realities of the contemporary world, but no longer have at their disposal a knowable, stable subject or a faith in the text's ability to re-create reality or decode the social world. If the real is in any way repossessed in the contemporary period, this trend has little in common with the mimetic ambitions of the nineteenth-century novel. This new realism assumes a drastically modified, more modest appearance and embodies multiple paradoxes. Dominique Viart indicates the necessity for a revision of our expectations of narrative

---

[14] This was, of course, the vision of reality challenged by some of the practitioners of the *Nouveau Roman*.

[15] Leo Bersani, 'Le Réalisme et la peur du désir', p. 58.

[16] More and more, a realist intention is attributed to present-day writers such as François Bon, Éric Chevillard, Jean Échenoz or Marie Redonnet.

realism to accommodate these seemingly contradictory twenty-first century incarnations. Today's realism locates reality in the incomprehensible, the irrational and the *non-dit*:

> La recherche d'une langue non mimétique permet de toucher au plus intime du réel. Non pas en reproduisant quelque parole spontanée, surgie des flux de conscience ou de l'inconscient, mais en allant jusqu'au bout de la déraison et de son lyrisme brisé. Les brisures d'une langue défaillante s'aggravent des fulgurances de la littérature. (LFP 213)

In no way susceptible to Barthesian critiques of realism as a perpetual recycling of the same, the reproduction of 'l'ennui, le conformisme, le dégoût de la répétition',[17] the real now exists as a point of rupture and contravention. As Dominique Rabaté suggests, new realist discourses maintain a more ambiguous relationship with collective reality, inscribing themselves in a space of resistance, of 'décalage' and 'dégagement'.[18] The real no longer exists as a pre-established order, but requires various, self-conscious reconstructions of its fragmented bits and pieces.[19]

Emmanuel Carrère and Marie NDiaye are two novelists whose writing exemplifies this re-engagement with the real. They cultivate the literary potential of this space of *'décalage'* to generate sincere yet disconcerting descriptions of modern life. Although their texts might instinctively be classified as fantastic, both writers re-appropriate, yet also distort, some of the stylistic and thematic conventions of realism. Without aspiring towards transparency and coherence, their novels nevertheless manifest a desire to transcribe subjective experience, often opposing the desires of the individual to the norms of the collective sphere. There is, in their writing, a marked tendency towards in-depth character development and the portrayal of personality traits and social values as explanatory of the decline or the success of a given fictional individual. Both authors respect certain plot-related, descriptive and spatio-temporal norms of the novel, foreground undignified everyday detail and, particularly in the case of Carrère, display a lucid narrative voice, which is often absent from the *Nouveau Roman* and certain contemporary texts. However, we will

---

[17] Roland Barthes, *S/Z* (Paris: Éditions du Seuil, 1970), p. 145.
[18] Dominique Rabaté, *Le Roman français depuis 1900*, p. 112.
[19] Ibid, p. 117.

see that in both Carrère's *La Moustache* and NDiaye's *La Sorcière,*
textual 'realism' is susceptible to frequent invasions of the uncanny,
which are often felt in the form of atmospheres and themes of
realism's other: the fantastic.

'*Péril en la demeure*': Carrère's *La Moustache*

Although it avoids such a blatant appeal to motifs of the fantastic,
Emmanuel Carrère's *La Moustache* (1986) tells a contemporary
version of Freud's crocodile story. In *La Moustache*, the tranquil,
everyday 'bobo' existence of a young couple is gradually invaded by
the strangeness which emerges during the hero's ontological crisis.
One evening he spontaneously shaves off his moustache as a surprise
for his wife, but neither she nor any of his friends or colleagues notice
the slightest change in his appearance, and in fact insist that he has
never worn a moustache. This preposterous, yet mundane interruption
of the ordinary sets the intimate spaces of the self, the home and the
familiar world under an estranging, suspicious gaze, as the character
struggles to emerge from his uncanny disconnection from the collective real and to retrieve his sense of being *chez lui*. The sudden
precariousness of this person's assumptions about his own identity,
due to the other's misrecognition of his appearance, dissolves his
sense of continuity with his usual surroundings, acquaintances,
domestic rituals and objects, which are now approached against the
grain. This scenario permits the writer to submit the *chez soi* to a
process of symbolic reversal whereby the familiar becomes synonymous with the strange. Everything which should evoke banality,
comfort and self-assuredness instead appears opaque or hostile. This
progression may be observed in the evolving representation of the
self, the home and the character's rapport with his everyday
environment. Each of these familiar spaces is first established as
stable and hospitable, but in the wake of the moustache crisis they
assume a horrific quality and suggest the impossibility of home.
    Despite this aesthetic of resistance and the anxiety and
ultimately horror, which come to dominate the fictional world in *La
Moustache*, it is possible to observe fragments of a realist agenda,
perceptible both in terms of content and on a discursive level. Realism
and the fantastic work together to create a certain tension, and this

tension evolves according to various narrative techniques. In *La Moustache* the uncertain atmosphere of the fantastic is present with no direct recourse to imagery of fantasy. In fact, every frightening object and figure in the story belongs to the domain of the banal or familiar. The author foregrounds the everyday to the degree that it appears invested with strangeness. The uncanny is again an angle from which we might perceive the absurdity of certain formerly ordinary aspects of contemporary life. *La Moustache* may perhaps be read as an attack on contemporary middle class materialism and individualism, suggesting the superficiality of the social persona and reminding us that we should never allow ourselves to get too comfortable at home.

Chez lui

Both the domestic setting of the novel and the uncertainty which qualifies the character's rapport with the everyday are suggested in the first line. One evening, a man asks his wife from the bathroom: 'Que dirais-tu si je me rasais la moustache'? In retrospect, this seemingly innocuous proposal announces the Kafkaesque, conditional nature of reality which will emerge in the story. However, at this early stage in the plot we simply recognize the normality and ease of the lifestyle of a young, happily married couple, through their typical household comings and goings and haphazard conjugal conversation in an environment of material comfort. The anti-hero, a self-absorbed, thirty-something architect, who remains nameless throughout the novel, is engaged in the habitual activity of shaving in the bathtub. He views this nightly act as his 'exercise zen',[20] one which, through the comfort of routine, participates in guaranteeing his sense of stability: 'ce rite vespéral tenait sa place dans l'équilibre de la journée, tout comme l'unique cigarette qu'il s'accordait, depuis qu'il avait cessé de fumer, après le repas de midi' (M 10). This shaving ritual is portrayed here as a self-affirming, narcissistic rite which reinforces the *chez soi*. This is apparent as the character looks at himself in the mirror after performing this task:

> Il avait terminé, à présent. Les yeux mi-clos, tous les muscles au
> repos, il détaillait dans le miroir son propre visage, dont il

---

[20] Emmanuel Carrère, *La Moustache* (Paris: P.O.L, 1986), pp. 9-10. All other references are given in the text, following the abbreviation M.

> s'amusa à exagérer l'expression de béatitude humide puis,
> changeant à vue, de virilité efficiente et déterminée. (M 10)

This intimate, self-indulgent, moment of engagement with his own
reflection allows the character to assert his masculinity, reconfirm his
sense of self and take pleasure in his own image, controlling and
voluntarily altering his persona. However, the self is also portrayed as
split and transitory. The mirror scene sets out the possible opposition
of the character to his own reflexion and suggests the changeability
and diverse faces of the self, perhaps foreshadowing the ultimate
dispersion of the subject which will occur further on. When, a few
moments later, he decides to alter his daily routine and shave his
moustache as well, his self-confidence will gradually begin to
dissipate. The moustache is, at this point in the narrative, invested
with a certain symbolic significance. The affirmation of its initial existence becomes the prerequisite for the character's sense of self and
synonymous with his ability to control his image in the eye of the
other. He does not realize that this banal gesture is a self-sacrificing
act. This will be fully revealed in the final, gruesome scene of self-
mutilation where the everyday activity of shaving is transformed into
a nightmare: after fleeing his home and his wife for Hong Kong, he
brutally and entirely defaces himself with his razor in a hotel
bathroom.

      In the opening chapter, his wife Agnès is portrayed as lovable
and familiar, nourishing her husband's ego, reinforcing the comfort
and contentment of his domestic situation. When she steps out to go to
the supermarket, he enjoys her predictability as he foretells her movements, imagines her demeanour in this everyday environment and
contemplates her virtues:

> Il se représentait Agnès progressant vers le supermarché, talons
> claquant sur le trottoir, patientant dans la queue, devant la caisse,
> sans que ce piétinement entame sa bonne humeur ni la vivacité de
> son regard: elle remarquait toujours des petits détails bizarres, pas
> forcément drôles en soi mais qu'elle savait mettre en valeur dans
> les récits qu'elle en faisait. (M 11)

Just as the protagonist appears in control of the self, he also has a clear
grasp of his wife's typical manners and attributes. He does not
recognize the irony of his allusion to the 'petits détails bizarres' within
the ordinary brought out in Agnès's anecdotes, which will be pro-

gressively 'mis en valeur' in his own story.

This rapport of familiarity and even domination that the character at first appears to maintain with his home extends to his material surroundings. As a physical space, the home is a site composed of familiar people, sounds and objects, which often go unnoticed, only coming into visibility when they fail to function properly. In the novel, the home is initially depicted as a hospitable space in which the material world provides a reassuring backdrop of constancy. When Agnès leaves to do her shopping, the protagonist is in the bath, a familiar space where a predominant need to indulge in domestic comfort temporarily shrinks the world, distracting the individual from any superior philosophical or social responsibility:

> Il entendit un froissement d'étoffe, sa veste qu'elle enfilait, le cliquetis du trousseau de clés ramassé sur la table basse, la porte d'entrée ouverte, puis refermée. Elle aurait pu brancher le répondeur, pensa-t-il, m'éviter de sortir du bain tout ruisselant si le téléphone sonne. Il but une gorgée de whiskey, fit tourner le gros verre carré dans sa main, ravi par le tintement des glaçons – enfin, de ce qu'il en restait. Bientôt, il allait se redresser, s'essuyer, s'habiller…(M 11)

This description performs the dual function of setting out the tranquility of the character's home and establishing the realist pact. The passage evokes the passive domestic consciousness of the home-dweller, depicting the private sphere as a series of unthinking, familiar, yet singular moments in which the individual takes comfort: recognizing the sound of a door closing, the jingle of a set of keys as well as trivial pleasures such as the rattle of ice cubes in a glass. We note the character's resentment of any outside disturbance which might disrupt this space, such as a phone call. The common, universal quality of the verbs at the end of the passage suggests the automatism of the banal acts we perform, nearly involuntarily, everyday.

We also remark the abundance of commonplace objects: *veste, clés, table, porte, répondeur, téléphone, glaçons* and their participation in an economy of the familiar, the sense of normalcy acquired in their simple identification. Objects appear to be human-centred, objects of possession. These insignificant objects also serve to anchor the reader in the realist world, functioning as what Barthes referred to as 'détails superflus'.[21] This is a comfortable, transparent

---

[21] See Roland Barthes, 'L'Effet de réel', in *Littérature et réalité* (Paris: Éditions du

fictional world in which we may label and identify things. The familiarity of the objects suggests the continuity of the character and his environment.

However, in *La Moustache*, at an oblique angle to the framework of décor and recognition identified in the passage above, the everyday also emerges as a space of event in and of itself. Carrère's privileging of extremely banal domestic entities and circumstances is an example of the contemporary novel's fascination with the everyday. This is visible in the very premise of the novel, but also on a more understated level throughout the narrative. While many passages from *La Moustache,* such as the one addressed above, depict the functional, agreeable nature of the everyday, others portray this domain as being in disharmony with the individual. The objects and materials of the domestic sphere often appear in their non-functionality and specificity, brought to the forefront in the form of 'micro-récits'[22] such as: 'Le rasoir crissa, lui arrachant une grimace', or 'Dans sa nervosité, il tira trop fort sur un lacet de chaussure qui cassa' (M 15). In her analysis of the contemporary writer Christian Oster, Florence Bouchy, sums up this trend as a staging of 'l'embarras quotidien'.[23] For Carrère, such minor setbacks and accidents that form part of the texture of everyday experience both assert the possible resistance of the material world, and presage the rebellion of the familiar against the character, which will assert itself as the story unfolds. It is this alternative reality of the everyday as a place of struggle and event and of the banal object as something ungraspable or alien that will increasingly take priority.

Seuil,1982), pp. 81-90.

[22] This was the term employed by Florence Bouchy in her article 'Les objets quotidiens dans quelques romans de Christian Oster'.

[23] Bouchy views this trend as symptomatic of the current paradoxical return to traditional novelistic tendencies in which French writing is engaged. While the detailed description of the familiar world of everyday objects re-emerges in narrative, this space is no longer subjugated to the ideological constraints and ordered vision of reality which traditionally characterized the novel. See Florence Bouchy, 'Les objets quotidiens dans les romans de Christian Oster', p. 92. Blanchot evokes a similar idea using the term 'la tragédie de la nullité'. Maurice Blanchot, 'La Parole quotidienne', p. 357.

Un-homed

After shaving his moustache, the character progressively inhabits a world in which the familiar elements that first underpinned his sense of self turn around to challenge it. We can observe the beginning of this uncertainty and self-questioning when he examines himself in the mirror immediately after accomplishing this task:

> Il leva les yeux. Pas terrible. Le hâle des sports d'hiver, à Pâques, tenait encore un peu sur son visage, si bien que la place de la moustache y découpait un rectangle d'une pâleur déplaisante, qui paraissait même faux, plaqué: une fausse absence de moustache, pensa-t-il, et déjà, sans abdiquer complètement la bonne humeur malicieuse qui l'y avait poussé, il regrettait un peu son geste, se répétait mentalement qu'en dix jours le malheur serait réparé. (M 14)

When Agnès and others refuse to acknowledge the change in his appearance, when they imply that the moustache is 'falsely absent', his self-doubt increases and he finds himself suspended between three uncanny explanations: a rational account which would turn the protagonist's familiar acquaintances and loved ones into monsters for making him the victim of a malign joke initiated by his wife; a science-fictional scenario in which the ordinary world has undergone a nightmarish distortion, and has bifurcated into two parallel universes; or the possibility of madness.

In all three cases, he has lost the *chez soi*. In the subsequent representation of his domestic situation, we note a gradual loss of identification between the character and his wife. In a movement away from her amiable early portrait, Agnès's predictable and compassionate qualities are replaced by malevolence and she becomes an obstacle to the character's attempts to reclaim his sense of self. Her defamiliarization is fully realized when she advances a series of statements which contradict the protagonist's memories of events from the couple's past. Suddenly Agnès claims not to know Serge and Véronique, the couple at whose home they dined in the opening chapter. She maintains that on that particular evening they went to the cinema to view *Péril en la demeure*, a film the protagonist is sure he has never seen.[24] When he finally asks, 'Tu t'appelles bien Agnès?' (M 89) it is

---

[24] This film is based on René Belletto's novel *Sur la terre comme au ciel* (Paris:

clear she has become a complete stranger.

The familiar sounds of Agnès's movements about the home are no longer presented as reassuring. In a climactic scene where the protagonist fully accepts the prospect of his wife's involvement in a conspiracy against him, he phones a colleague to solicit advice. The protagonist strives to relate his story before Agnès catches him in the act: 'Il entendit la clé tourner dans la serrure de la porte d'entrée. Je crois qu'elle arrive, dit-il précipitamment. Je te rappelle' (M 96).

The loss of the *chez soi* also extends to the protagonist's dwelling within the home, which he ultimately decides to flee. Immediately preceding his escape, he begins to note the capacity of the most familiar activities to turn strange:

> Il gagna la chambre, referma la porte derrière lui. Sans qu'il puisse l'exprimer, le sentiment de la raréfaction des gestes possibles l'obsédait, il lui semblait avoir déjà fait ça ; bien sûr qu'il l'avait fait, passer du salon à la chambre, et des centaines, des milliers de fois, mais ce n'était pas pareil, il n'y avait pas alors ce tournis de manège détraqué, venant heurter un butoir, repartant dans l'autre sens sans qu'il puisse ni descendre ni souffler. (M 106)

In his state of paranoia, the home and the everyday no longer simply exist as a surrounding environment, but emerge as objects under scrutiny. The simple gestures so often repeated, such as the mechanical act of passing from one room to the next, assume an element of strangeness; the unthinking space of familiarity is destroyed, creating an environment in which the 'je' is detached from the *chez moi*.

The estranged depiction of the familiar transforms the usual environment of the home from a humdrum space of modest triteness into one which is reminiscent of Maurice Blanchot's vision of the everyday: the most elusive domain, 'ce qu'il y a de plus difficile à découvrir'.[25] For Blanchot, the familiar is in fact the strangest possible space, because the moment we seek to repossess it, to make it an object of inquiry, actively to experience it in its familiarity, it necessarily disappears. What this character seems to have lost is his passive, unthinking, dwelling in the everyday as 'l'homme quell-

---

Hachette, 1982).
[25] Maurice Blanchot, 'La Parole quotidienne', p. 355.

conque'. But the familiar is what can never intentionally be retrieved, or rediscovered.

Strangeness emerges from every attempt at familiarization. By the end of the novel, the once convivial household is represented as a menacing prison guarded by the monstrous, conspiring Agnès. When the protagonist suddenly decides he must escape, he is obliged to vacate the bedroom and cross the living room where Agnès is reading. The everyday act of dressing is now depicted not as a passive, routine moment, but as the task of a soldier suiting up for battle; the home is evoked in language that expresses the dread of the unknown:

> Slip, chaussettes, pantalon, chemise, veste, souliers enfin, par chance il s'était déshabillé dans la chambre. Il ferma les yeux un instant, pour se concentrer, avec l'impression d'être dans un film de guerre, sur le point de quitter l'abri pour s'élancer en terrain découvert, sous une rafale de balles. (M 116)

Here, the reference to the war film is pertinent insofar as it conveys the character's sense of being in a *representation*, or fictional world. This sense of 'péril en la demeure', seen in the evocation of the character's own living room as a hostile, foreign land extends to the representation of the protagonist's original family home. Hoping to seek refuge with his parents, he takes a taxi to their neighbourhood. When he reaches their street, he realizes, in a moment which evokes the sense of impotency that often occurs in nightmares, that he can no longer remember which apartment building is theirs.

The double
The protagonist's varying degrees of unhomeliness are emblematized in his rapport with his reflection in the mirror, a motif that runs throughout the narrative. In the first scene of the novel, the character's encounter with his own image in the mirror was ego-affirming, bringing out the dynamic of the double as an experience which asserts the permanence of the self. However, following the uncertainty concerning the moustache, the alternative story of the double is revealed. In subsequent scenes involving representations of the main character, they serve to disturb further or to challenge his vision of himself. Although he frequently turns to photographs as a means of confirming his prior appearance, the encounter with his own image only intensifies its ambiguity.

This emerges in the episode involving the couple's holiday photos from Java. Immediately following their initial disagreement over the moustache, the protagonist is able to locate these photographs and perceives the alleged moustache; however, the pictures later disappear mysteriously. When he questions Agnès concerning their whereabouts, her response only increases his insecurities: 'Mon amour, je te jure, il n'y pas de photos de Java. Nous ne sommes jamais allés à Java' (M 82). Not only does the photograph fail to appear as an effigy of his former appearance, perhaps due to Agnès's conspiracy, but its evocation renders more extreme the character's uncertainty about his past and perhaps in some way further undermines a former image of his social status, as a man who regularly takes luxury holidays. When he finally succeeds in locating another photograph in which he possesses the moustache, he presents it to Agnès, who forthrightly denies the presence of the facial hair in the image (M 99).

The role played by the image in the intensification of the character's anxiety is also exploited in an episode relating to his identity card. This time he appeals to an external party. Pretending to be blind, he presents his card to a young woman on the street and asks her to describe it. Her reaction creates a kind of double-bind scenario which renders the situation even more complex. While she immediately acknowledges the presence of the moustache in the photograph, she also claims that he has one at present, further unsettling his sense of self, by refuting his current self-image (M 68-70). When he returns home and triumphantly presents the card to Agnès at dinner, she accuses him of tampering with the image and proceeds to scratch the moustache off the card violently, in a symbolic repudiation of the character's identity. The identity card, a most familiar object, which normally serves to prove one's identity, thus comes to operate as an uncanny double, evoking mortality. In his use of the image, Carrère exploits the paradoxical nature of the double as both self-confirming and annihilating. The familiarity the character expects to find in his own image is repeatedly overridden by strangeness.

The extra-ordinary

The moustache problematic seems to represent a point of rupture in the stable image of the home. In light of the fragility that this uncertainty reveals within the couple's previously harmonious existence, the initial representation of their happy-go-lucky, everyday life elaborated in the first chapter beings to appear suspect. Their comfort in the home assumes an abnormally normal, almost fraudulent quality. While the strangeness of their familiar world might have been detectable, or at least, foreshadowed in the first pages of the narrative, its absurdity is amplified as the story continues. While the signposts of the familiar are not represented as disturbing or menacing, they are often portrayed as deceptive, counterfeit and bearing no rapport with reality, since they are able to exist in the absence of any feeling of normality on the part of the character. The writer often stages the unsuccessful imposition of the banal object or scenario as a form of concealment, to mask the turmoil within the home. As the couple strives to ignore the intrusion of the moustache episode on the harmony of their domestic space, they appeal to indicators of the commonplace as a form of reassurance. The more the domestic space is disrupted and the split between the couple is affirmed, the more we see an ironic multiplication and not a retraction of the symbols of tranquility and familiarity within the home. On the Saturday immediately following the couple's initial disagreement, the protagonist is careful to buy *Libération* and *Le Monde* as he does every weekend and to read them on the sofa, sharing comical personal ads with Agnès. Later, the couple take care to dine at one of their usual chic Parisian restaurants. Further on, just before the protagonist's final breakdown when he flees his home, the couple's relationship and the character's psychological state have reached a point of disaster, yet Agnès makes a point of buying croissants for their breakfast as usual and of talking about the weather as if all were well. It is the couple's comforting, ordinary bourgeois existence that begins to appear uncanny, insofar as these symbols of familiarity exist on their own, as if stating their own emptiness. There are resonances of the Heideggerian uncanny here. Ordinary, familiar life is *Da Sein's* mode of uncanniness, since the *Unheimliche*, for Heidegger, is the more primary phenomenon.[26]

As we witness the gradual deterioration of the self from narcissism to self-destruction, and the increasingly *unheimlich* representation of the home, the character's domestication of the material world also collapses. It emerges in the narrative as a domain which strangely possesses its own voice. This sense of discontinuity appears

---

[26] See pages 81-2 above.

to announce itself in one vivid scene. Desperate for concrete proof of the moustache's former existence, the character embarks on a mission to search for the lost hairs, which he remembers disposing of in the bathroom dustbin. When he realizes that Agnès has shrewdly removed the previous bag, he goes out to the apartment bin area to locate it and retrieve the remnants of his previous identity. The everyday reveals its duplicitous nature, its ability to oscillate between the strange and the familiar:

> Curieux comme il est facile de reconnaître sa poubelle, pensa-t-il en tombant sur des bouteilles de yaourt à boire, des emballages froissés de plats surgelés, ordures de nantis, et de nantis bohèmes qui mangent rarement chez eux. Ce constat lui procurait un vague sentiment de sécurité sociologique, celui d'être bien dans sa case, repérable, reconnaissable, et il vida le tout sur le trottoir, avec une sorte d'allégresse. Il trouva vite le sac, plus petit, qu'on plaçait dans la poubelle de la salle de bains, en retira des cotons-tiges, deux tampax, un vieux tube de dentifrice, un autre de tonique pour la peau, des lames de rasoir usagées. Et les poils étaient là. Pas tout à fait comme il l'avait espéré, nombreux mais dispersés alors qu'il avait imaginé une touffe bien compacte, quelque chose comme une moustache tenant toute seule. Il en ramassa le plus possible, qu'il recueillit dans le creux de la main. (M 53-4)

This scene, which occurs just after the couple's initial disagreement, marks a turning point in the representation of the everyday. Here again we have what is, in some sense, a nearly hyper-realist description, where the protagonist confronts his own everydayness. The objects in the description of the bathroom waste are perfectly banal, that is, significant in their insignificance. For the reader, the meticulous account of the materiality and inane ordinariness of the empty packages and leftovers confers on them a strange, even humorous quality and exemplifies this contemporary tendency to elevate and narrativize the commonplace. As items of waste, these entities are not supposed to be viewed again. The household remains from the dustbin initially appear to reinforce the hero's sense of self, symbolically affirming his social status ('ordures de nantis'), providing him with the certainty of being *chez lui*, or 'bien dans sa case'. However, this ontological certainty is also challenged by the manifestation of the moustache. Although the character does succeed in locating the lost hairs, they refuse to cooperate symbolically to form a moustache and appear not as a uni-fied, verifiable mass, reconfirming the character's sanity and unity, but as a dispersed collection of individual hairs, which he desperately strives to re-assemble. These detached hairs in the rubbish bin announce a fragmented self. It seems that the moustache, a former symbol of self-possession, has been reversed to signify just the opposite. However, the presence of verbs such as *ramasser* and *recueillir* in the passage also suggest the possibility of recomposing the self. For the reader, however, what is stranger than the dispersed manifestation of the moustache is the character's assumption that he would find a moustache in its entire form, implying his false sense of self-unity or his further descent into madness. What Carrère's novel playfully reveals is the abundance of such absurd moments in everyday life, and the general suspension and oscillation of the self between various states of egotism and vulnerability.

Following this encounter, objects that figure in the text appear to elude the protagonist's grasp, transforming themselves from items of possession into objects which oppose his sense of being *chez lui*. Like Freud's crocodile table, they appear to come to life in a disturbing manner, asserting themselves in confrontation with the character's sense of who he is. One example is the wall-hanging in the couple's living room, which he remembers purchasing during their holiday in Java. While this exotic object was previously an emblem of the couple's bohemian lifestyle and affluence, which permitted them to take extravagant holidays, Agnès now denies the reality of the trip to Java, and claims that this object is simply a gift from a friend.

The search for the moustache hairs is, in a sense, this man's search for his previous, passive existence in the ordinary and in the world of realism,[27] where objects are either invisible or symbolic, that is, either blend into the background, or are invested with some kind of human significance, imbued with meaning by a perceiving consciousness. For Leo Bersani, within realism, 'le monde s'accorde, structuralement au moins, avec le personnage de roman, en ceci qu'il

---

[27] Perhaps the world this character is searching for is one already modeled on a mode of representation. This would be a world evocative of Husserl's *Lebenswelt* or lifeworld, reality as coherently and harmoniously experienced. Lifeworld structures are those experienced for the most part without their being made the object of explicit reflection; they function in everyday experience anonymously, requiring radical reflection for their identification. See entry on Edmund Husserl, *The Stanford Encyclopedia of Philosophy*, http://plato.stanford.edu/ (Accessed 3 November 2007). The character's earlier allusion to feeling as though he were in a war film suggests the possibility of this world of realism undergoing a change of genre or mode.

propose constamment à notre intelligence des objets et des évé-
nements qui contiennent des désirs humains et leur confèrent une
forme intelligible'.[28] We are reminded of Balzac's description of
Madame Vauquer's pension in *Le Père Goriot*: 'toute sa personne
explique la pension, comme la pension implique sa personne'.[29] If
realism generates an aesthetic effect of commensurateness between
the individual and her environment, the uncanny perhaps implies just
the opposite: the resistance of the external world to the successful
positing of the self.

Relevant here are Kristeva's interpretations of the uncanny as
a privileged moment which should impose a re-assessment of self and
home and an acknowledgement of our own foreignness, rather than a
rejection of strangeness in an attempt to conserve intact the *chez soi*.
According to this view, the uncanny might provoke a revision of
familiar modes of perception, but one which is in some sense
incompatible with comfortable identifications and feelings of everyday harmony. However, the hero of *La Moustache* chooses not to undergo self re-evaluation, but instead insists upon retrieving the *chez
soi*, re-asserting his persona. And it is this, perhaps, which leads to his
demise.

The relief experienced by the character after his escape to
China sets up an ironic dynamic where the foreign appears to rescue
him from the terror of the familiar. The strange land of Hong Kong, a
place unfamiliar to the protagonist, where he is entirely alone, is
represented as a kind of refuge after the horror he has experienced in
his own home. As he says, returning to Paris would be tantamount to
'se jeter dans la gueule du loup' (M 138). He finds a kind of sanctuary
in travel, spending his days taking perpetual commuter ferry rides,
back and forth from Kowloon to Hong Kong. He constantly repeats
the need to disappear in order to escape the monstrous world 'qui était
le sien', telling himself that his place is no longer 'parmi les siens' (M
138). The realms of what is 'known' and what is 'his' are paradoxically what the character must flee in order to be saved from self-
annihilation.

The hazardous underside of the familiar is evocatively suggested in the final scene of the narrative, when he is, as it were,

---

[28] Leo Bersani, 'Le Réalisme et la peur du desir', p. 49.
[29] Honoré de Balzac, *Le Père Goriot*, ed. by Charles Gould (London: University of
London Press, 1967), p. 113.

'haunted' by the familiar in his hotel room in China. After spending the day at the beach, he returns to his room to find that elements of his home have strangely returned to plague him. Agnès has mysteriously appeared in Hong Kong and he finds her stretched out on the bed, in a chillingly familiar pose, reading her magazine and behaving as if everything were normal. When he enters the bathroom he is pained to discover that she has meticulously arranged all of the usual toiletry products which fill their bathroom at home: toothbrushes, cosmetic creams, make-up remover. The novel ends gruesomely as the character lacerates himself with his razor, all the while tortured by the sound of magazine pages turning and by the banal, spontaneous remarks made by Agnès from the other room. The familiar, comforting ritual of shaving has come full circle to destroy the self.

For Blanchot there is something in the everyday that evokes death, but also gestures towards a crucial element of human experience. He says:

> Le quotidien, c'est la platitude (ce qui retarde et ce qui retombe, la vie résiduelle dont se remplissent nos poubelles et nos cimetières, rebuts et détritus), mais cette banalité est pourtant aussi ce qu'il y a de plus important, si elle renvoie à l'existence dans sa spontanéité même et telle que celle-ci se vit, au moment où, vécue, elle se dérobe à toute mise en forme spéculative, peut-être à toute cohérence, toute régularité.[30]

Blanchot's everyday cannot be seized in thought, but when the individual stands back and looks at her own trivial activities, at her own everydayness, she is faced with a void, a feeling of nihilism.[31] In *La Moustache* the everyday is the site of an authentic subjective experience, one which is revealed in both subjective annihilation and self-confirmation. Although the novel reveals the uncanny, menacing nature of the everyday, a realm in which one can disappear, in which the self can dissolve in uncertainty, it also constantly re-affirms the security and comfort that the individual acquires in this domain.

---

[30] Maurice Blanchot, 'La Parole quotidienne', p. 357.

[31] Here we are reminded of the Lacanian uncanny, presented as a moment of subjective annihilation, in which we no longer see the material world, but the material world 'sees us' as it were, by posing a challenge to our subjective comfort. Jacques Lacan, *Le Séminaire XI, Les quatre concepts fondamentaux de la psychanalyse*, p.110.

It seems that much of the anxiety of the novel is generated by intellectual uncertainty – was there or was there not a moustache? It is interesting that the ambiguity is in some sense shared by the author. The narrative creates a three-way dynamic of irresolution. None of the figures involved – character, reader or creator – holds the key to this question. In an interview, Carrère explains that he views this un-certainty as the motor behind his narrative and as that which characterizes his particular approach as a writer.[32] It is essential that there be no pure objectivity in the voice of the narrator to which the reader may cling for answers and that Carrère himself, as author, has no idea what 'really happened'.

This conscious decision not to domesticate his own story at times obliges the writer to contradict himself. Occasionally, realities he affirms early in the text, through the perspective of the character, are later refuted. At the height of the couple's domestic turbulence, Agnès reminds her husband of their plan to have lunch the following day with his parents. She phones to cancel these plans and then informs him five minutes later that it was his mother she phoned, that his father is no longer living. As Dominique Rabaté points out in his analysis of the text, when Agnès refers to his 'parents' in the plural and it is later affirmed to his surprise that his father passed away a year earlier, the reader cannot help but re-read the previous passage to confirm that she did indeed say 'chez tes parents' and not 'chez ta mère'.[33] This is also the case with respect to the photos from Java. Since these photos were confirmed present at an early point in the narrative, the reader, like the character, witnesses the initial existence and subsequent disappearance of the holiday photographs, as well as Agnès's denial of the trip to Java. This uncertainty is put to a productive end, as it allows Carrère to adopt certain modes of realist

---

[32] This interview is included on the DVD of Carrère's *La Moustache*.

[33] Dominique Rabaté, 'L'Exaltation du quotidien', in *Modernités 16: Enchantements, mélanges offerts à Yves Vadé* (Bordeaux: Presses Universitaires de Bordeaux, 2003), pp. 229-37, p. 231. In this example, the film version of *La Moustache* generates a different kind of uncertainty than that experienced when reading the novel. Although it may be possible to rewind the film to review the passage in question, it is an unlikely gesture on the part of the viewer who must simply wonder if she heard correctly. The film creates the potential for a kind of torment in the spectator, which mimics that of the character, whereas the reader experiences a different kind of frustration due to the contradictory text.

representation, while simultaneously asserting the vulnerability of these representational tools as a mirror of the real.

At no time does the author appeal directly to imagery of the fantastic; the plot is in no way refracted or dissolved. The events that transpire possess a concreteness which prevents them from being categorized by the reader as projection, metaphor or daydream. The uncanny is the means by which the author re-appropriates some of the mechanisms and codes of the fantastic by putting them at the service of a form of exaggerated realism. The novelist encourages the reader's identification with a recognizable fictional world through the familiar portrayal of the domestic sphere and the self, constructing a readerly 'home', which is increasingly upset as the narrative unfolds.

By mobilizing the anxiety of the fantastic within a highly realist framework, the author unveils an alternative reality of the familiar, presenting our own ordinary world as an alien and disturbing realm. The novel is a humorous invitation to the reader to detach herself temporarily from the *chez soi* and re-assess her own place within the everyday. In *La Moustache* the uncanny contributes to a destabilized or less coherent vision of the everyday, but also constructs new meaning. Uncanniness appears to be at the service of a realist critique of contemporary values. The flawlessness of the *chez soi*, seen in the tranquility and comfort established at the beginning of the text, is revealed to be superficial, interrupted by a more primary uncertainty, which destroys the illusion of the ideal couple, the narcissistic self and the continuity between the individual and the world and between the author and his text. In *La Moustache* it is, in a sense, the world of realism that appears as an uncannily perfect realm where everything functions in an impossibly normal way.

The Suburban Gothic: NDiaye's *La Sorcière*

Critics often emphasize the uncanny nature of Marie NDiaye's writing, describing it as 'inquiétante, presque fantastique'[34], 'entre le désir et le réel'[35] or characterized by 'une sensation de malaise'.[36] Her novels frequently feature contemporary incarnations of classic supernatural themes such as ghosts, doubles, metamorphosis or sorcery. However, despite the disconcerting quality of her work and her reliance on imagery of the fantastic, we also tend to view her narrative project as participating in a contemporary 'return to realism'.[37] This realist classification can be justified in light of certain features of her novels. They are often set within the recognizable, banal, contemporary landscape of suburban France. The protagonists, often female, are generally ordinary individuals, living out their day-to-day lives and struggling with the complexities of family relationships within the home.

The dual classification of the author's work is not necessarily paradoxical, since as the majority of recent criticism on the fantastic tells us, realism and fantasy are not mutually exclusive forms, but rather, intertwined and often co-dependent. Nearly all fantastic texts depend on realist strategies to produce their aesthetic effects. For Gilbert Millet and Denis Labbé:

> Le fantastique ne peut fonctionner qu'avec l'assentiment du lecteur qui doit accepter de se laisser entraîner dans ce train fantôme, autorisant ainsi le narrateur à lui faire peur ou à le déstabiliser. Pour cela, il faut qu'il puisse y croire, qu'il y ait au moins l'impression de se retrouver face à un univers familier ou d'apparence familière.[38]

As Claire Whitehead puts it, '[b]efore a reader can be prompted to

---

[34] Dominique Rabaté, 'L'Éternelle tentation d'hébétude', *L'Atelier du roman* (September 2003), 48-55 (p. 49).

[35] Torfi H. Tulinius, 'Relations proches', *L'Atelier du roman 35* (September 2003), 68-75 (p. 69).

[36] Sara Bonomo, 'La Mise en œuvre de la peur dans le roman d'aujourd'hui: *Rosie Carpe* de Marie NDiaye', *Travaux de littérature* 17, 218-225 (p. 218).

[37] See, for example, Dominique Rabaté, *Le Roman Français depuis 1900*, p. 116, or Xavier Garnier, 'Métamorphoses réalistes dans les romans de Marie NDiaye' in *Itinéraires et contacts de cultures* (Paris: L'Harmattan, 1982), pp. 79-89.

[38] Gilbert Millet and Denis Labbé, *Le Fantastique* (Paris: Belin, 2005), p. 11.

hesitate, she must be encouraged to believe'.[39]

In Marie NDiaye's novels this interplay of the codes of strangeness and familiarity, which is always present to some degree in fantastic literature, displays a rather unique configuration, which renders this tension more vivid. In her 1996 novel *La Sorcière*, the fantastic is implicated in a critique of the banality, cruelty and superficiality of contemporary society. Supernatural themes such as sorcery and metamorphosis are intertwined with an evocation of the main character's dysfunctional family relations and monotonous existence in the contemporary Parisian suburbs. The fantastic emerges not only in the midst of the ordinary world, but within a reality that is itself disconcertingly dull and meaningless.

This section will explore the ways in which the author borrows from a repertoire of fantastic imagery in a unique fashion, so as to revive and estrange the reader's perception of contemporary life, and draw her attention to the 'extra-ordinary' nature of everyday phenomena and family relations within the home. NDiaye creates a fictional realm that we might qualify as *unheimlich*. It is one in which the contending codes of strange and familiar remain unresolved; one which is ordinary and domestic, yet in which the protagonist – and reader – cannot quite feel at home.[40]

In NDiaye's more recent novels, such as *Rosie Carpe* (2001) or *Mon cœur à l'étroit* (2007) and *Trois femmes puissantes* (2009), distortions of the codes of realism are relatively subtle, inducing a gentle estrangement of the reader's habitual expectations of the codes of collective reality. Strangeness is not so much event-related as written into the narrative language itself. Ordinary environments seem imbued with a sense of eeriness; characters appear to morph into others; social and natural laws are subtly transgressed.[41] However, in

---

[39] Claire Whitehead, *The Fantastic in France and Russia in the Nineteenth Century. In Pursuit of Hesitation* (London: Legenda, 2006), p. 13.

[40] As we will see, Marie NDiaye's writing shares some of the characteristics of Latin American magical realism. In her book on the genre, Wendy B. Faris states that its principal objective to represent an irreducible element which 'defamiliarises, underlines or critiques ordinary aspects of the real' in order to highlight the extra-ordinary nature of reality. See Wendy B. Faris, *Ordinary Enchantments: Magical Realism and the Remystification of Narrative* (Nashville: Vanderbilt University Press, 2004), p. 13.

[41] For example, as we will see later, in *Rosie Carpe* the protagonist's mother appears never to age and becomes pregnant at the age of retirement.

La Sorcière the fantastic assumes a more striking form. It manifests itself in more decidedly supernatural imagery and appears to co-exist with, rather than infuse, a nearly ethnographic portrait of contemporary France.

The novel relates the bland yet unusual suburban existence of Lucie, housewife and mother of twin daughters. Lucie's daily activities resemble those of any modern-day suburban parent: banking, dish-washing, defrosting dinners, mopping, coffee-making and looking after her daughters. Her world is dominated by domestic trivialities such as defrosting pizzas and banal neighbourly interactions, played out to the background hum of the television. However, although Lucie's run-of-the-mill lifestyle consists of the traditional tasks of motherhood in a typical French family, she is also a witch with prophetic visionary powers, inherited from her mother. This gift manifests itself externally through tears of blood which trickle down her cheeks during her visions. In the first chapter, Lucie initiates her 12-year-old twin daughters into the clairvoyant powers they too have inherited. To the witch's surprise, the girls' magical skills largely surpass her own. They eventually transform into crows and fly away. Abandoned by her husband, the pitiable Pierrot, vacation-package salesman of the Garden-Club, Lucie travels to Poitiers with her daughters in an attempt to retrieve him and to reunite her own separated parents.

The domestic everyday space that is problematized in *La Sorcière* differs from those of the other two novels studied in this chapter. While, in alignment with current tendencies in French fiction, the world of commonplace material objects does appear strangely amplified in NDiaye's text, it is the everyday space as a total experience that is rendered strange. While *La Moustache* and *En vie* focus primarily on the concrete phenomena of the everyday, NDiaye's 'everyday' is a combination of banal contexts, experiences and relationships within the home.

Sorcière de banlieue

Lucie's supernatural powers and status as a witch are represented ironically. The paradox of Lucie's clairvoyant gift is its banality, both because of the uninspiring content of the visions it allows her, and because of the capacity of the other characters and the fictional realm to integrate the existence of this power into everyday life. Clairvoyance is in fact nothing out of the ordinary,[42] since it only enables Lucie to foresee extremely inconsequential occurrences, such as foggy, deficient images of her husband, or trifling details surrounding the future circumstances she seeks to perceive: 'la couleur d'un habit, l'aspect du ciel, une tasse de café fumant délicatement tenue par la personne...'[43] Early in the novel, when Lucie's husband is late home from work and she would like to use magic to visualize his whereabouts, she is plagued instead with bland, undesired images of Steve, the odious boy next door. For the narrator (the story is related from Lucie's point of view) the existence of magic is just another element of everyday life, often interrupted or overridden by more prominent circumstances within the home and domestic respon-sibilities.[44] When Lucie is absorbed by one of her predictive visions, she suddenly remembers she forgot to clean the toilet, since Steve had recently visited and 'a pissé partout sur le siège' (S 27). When Lucie arrives in the bathroom, the urine has overflowed onto the floor tiles as well. In *La Sorcière* magic never suggests enchantment, but rather serves to reinforce the disenchanted nature of Lucie's suburban existence. At the end of the narrative, after being abandoned by her husband and children, Lucie puts her mediocre supernatural powers to work as a teacher at the 'Université Féminine de la Santé Spirituelle'. This institution offers guidance and magical training to young women gone astray, '(de) jeunes femmes fanées, flottantes, aux cheveux teints, blonds ou roussâtres' (S 160). She is ultimately imprisoned for charlatanism when the unreliability of her visions obliges her to invent them for her students.

---

[42] As Dominique Rabaté suggests: 'L'originalité de *La Sorcière* est ainsi dans le décalage qu'introduit un postulat merveilleux (il existe des sorcières) mais qui ne sert qu'à mieux éprouver la désolation de la vie'. Dominique Rabaté, 'L'Exaltation du quotidien', p. 234.

[43] Marie NDiaye, *La Sorcière* (Paris: Éditions de Minuit, 1997), p. 14. All other references will be given in the text, following the abbreviation S.

[44] The fact that Lucie is a visionary witch is taken for granted in *La Sorcière* and itself viewed as banal. When Lucie tells Steve's mother that she has seen her son in the future, Isabelle is more concerned with the lack of a tie, which indicates his eventual failure to be accepted at the École Polytechnique.

A meaningless world

Although Lucie's powers themselves are not outwardly disconcerting, the fictional world is nonetheless presented as a terrifying place. In the opening chapter, NDiaye paints a pessimistic picture of the middle class, suburban dimension of contemporary Paris. Relationships are dominated by alienation and superficiality, individuals by self-interest and avarice. We are first exposed to the financial complexes and extreme materialism of Lucie's husband Pierrot, who hesitates to invite his wealthy clients from the Garden-Club for an *apéritif,* fearing they might realize that 'malgré son costume gris perle et son écusson' he is only a modest sales representative, far from being as well-off as he has them believe (S 36). His feelings of social inferiority lead him to despise his substandard home and resent his wife. When Steve urinates on the floor in their home, Lucie strives to mop it up quickly, knowing that Pierrot would be angered to catch his wife performing such a lowly domestic task, no doubt entirely foreign to the well-off women of the Garden-Club. When Pierrot leaves Lucie at the end of the first chapter, he also flees with all the funds in their joint savings account. Given the references to the personal prestige and rewards packages Pierrot receives for his sales abilities at work, he is represented as the perfect self-made man, who has fully embraced consumer culture, delighting in the expensive taste he has managed to cultivate in his twin daughters, who, to his delight, have 'peu le sens de l'économie' (S 35), spending money on brand-name shoes, sophisticated toys and other trinkets.

Although there are numerous well-developed characters in the novel, these individuals are all somewhat disagreeable and naïve, lacking ambition and a sense of self, often behaving as automatons in a commercialized dystopia. Although nearly all of them remain self-absorbed and callous, details of their physical appearances and personalities continually fluctuate, always adapting to the newest trend. Isabelle, Lucie's next-door neighbour, is presented as an unpleasant, bossy woman who takes pleasure in spying on other inhabitants of the housing estate. In early descriptions of Isabelle, the author evokes her as crafty and unattractive, 'une petite femme boulotte et brutale, à l'œil étroit, stupide et malin' (S 82). The narrator's portraits stress, rather brutally, the anonymity of this character who appears to be the product of her uninspiring suburban environment. Overweight, plagued with acne scars, missing teeth, dressed in sports clothes, Isabelle is often encountered speaking sharply to her son or discussing the pursuit of her own self-interested projects. When Isabelle re-surfaces near the end of the novel, she informs Lucie that she has launched a new business: the Université Féminine de la Santé Spirituelle d'Isabelle O, where she provides self-help courses for abused women for 80000 francs per month. As a result of her lucrative enterprise, she appears to have undergone a strange transformation:

> Ses cheveux étaient coiffés avec soin, blondis et fixés en boucles courtes. Isabelle portait une jupe et une veste de lainage, couleur pêche. Je reconnus ses petits yeux curieux, sa bouche méfiante, néanmoins toute son allure semblait maintenant pleine de l'assurance bourgeoise, urbaine, qui lui avait fait défaut, ce qui me donna l'impression que ma dernière rencontre avec Isabelle remontait à de nombreuses années [...] Sa veste claire soyeuse, l'extrême finesse de son collant que je voyais enveloppant son genou robuste, l'élégante odeur de laque ou de gel qui flottait tout autour de sa tête parée, frisée, gonflée. (S 151-2)

From the description of her elegant clothing, in stark contrast to the 'combinaisons de sport' Isabelle often wore in the first part of the story, it seems that her cunning business scheme has emancipated her from her gloomy lower middle-class life, yet metamorphosed her into a frightening emblem of present-day *nouveau riche* prosperity and urbanism.

The strangeness of this transformation is highlighted when, uncannily, in a more striking incarnation of this theme of metamorphosis, Isabelle appears in the form of a bird. The first allusion to this event occurs when Lucie is on her way to the train station with her daughters and spots a large crow, which she realizes is Isabelle. Later at her mother's apartment she sees 'Isabelle' again, this time in the form of a large brown raven. It is interesting that when they occur in the text, many incidents of the fantastic appear to suggest or re-enact themes that have already attained full expression within the more realist framework of the narrative, as more convincing, yet highly cynical, analyses of modern life. The fantastic often appears to generate a reverberation of elements of the author's underlying commentary on the everyday, magnifying and estranging their significance.[45]

The unhomely

Within NDiaye's superficial, consumer-driven fictional world, the home is unable to reinstate value or meaning. The primary plot of the novel concerns Lucie's aimless meanderings through a bleak suburban landscape, as she negotiates a network of highly disagreeable family members and confronts a series of failed relationships. In *La Sorcière* the poignancy of the site of the family home is exploited by the author as a kind of counter-agenda to the family melodrama. Rather than emphasizing the family's capacity for love and sanctuary, or its ability to foster a sense of identity, NDiaye proposes a nightmarish tale of the inadequacies and cruelties that might equally underlie a representation of the family institution. Her depiction works against the grain of our attachment to thematic and mythological values of home and family, challenging both the way the latter shape our perception of the home, and the ways in which they are often inscribed in the literary text. The family is, most strikingly in her novels, an elusive site, which evades appropriation by moral and social codes.

At the heart of an industrial wasteland on the outskirts of Paris, Lucie's own home is a 'grosse maison froide, impayée' (S 155) and a site of platitude. The home is never portrayed as welcoming and hospitable, but is repulsive and alienating. Lucie is bothered by her husband's apparent disgust with their home, a place where he seems 'toujours vaguement en exil'. Every evening after returning home from work, 'sa morosité le reprenait, sa rancune diffuse et chagrinement entretenue' (S 34).

Lucie's home is only the first in a series of unpleasant houses which feature in the narrative. A particularly disagreeable portrait of Lucie's mother's home is related through Lucie's silent impressions of her visit there:

> Il m'avait toujours semblé que l'appartement était imprégné de l'odeur putride, tiède, que ce puits renfermait, et qu'au bout de quelques jours, les habits, la peau, exhalaient ce même relent indéfinissable et tenace. (S 84)

---

[45] Another strange metamorphosis is undergone by Lilli, Pierrot's sister, who becomes so fat that her parents must buy her a double bed (S 71).

Likewise, Lucie's stepmother's home, which she visits in search of her husband, is filled with an 'étouffante odeur de soupes quotidiennes et de réfrigérateur peu aéré' (S 119). The strange familial aromas of certain homes are a frequent atmospheric element in NDiaye's writing and participate in her tendency to reveal the unspoken, more un-pleasant corners of familiar, domestic settings. Her descriptions stress the claustrophobic, odorous, inhospitable nature of family spaces.

The unwelcoming evocation of family homes in the text is supplemented with disagreeable portraits of the home-dwellers themselves. The protagonist's own parents, also separated, figure fre-quently in the novel. After leaving Lucie's father, her mother has begun a new life with another man, Robert. This maternal figure appears somewhat disconcerting when she is encountered one morning, seated at the kitchen table:

> Elle tourna vers moi sa petite tête gracieuse, l'inclina légèrement, me sourit, comme autrefois, chez nous, lorsque je descendais le matin prendre mon petit déjeuner, dans la pièce déjà chaude et parfumée de ce que ma mère y avait préparé. Stupéfaite, il me sembla alors que ma mère était morte et que je n'avais devant moi que son apparition. Mais elle se leva, m'embrassa, et je reconnus dans son cou l'imperceptible odeur, rance, corrompue, qui était celle de son appartement de Paris et dont elle ne pouvait se défaire. (S 126-7)

The description begins by stressing the familiarity of the mother, whom the narrator perceives 'comme autrefois' before proceeding to describe her as a phantom-like, strange-smelling presence, so that the familiarity of the home suggests discomfort.[46] The mother's ambi-valent representation as both familiar and strange is perhaps reflected in the syntactical ambiguity of the adjective 'stupéfaite'. Since the writer opts to follow this word with the impersonal 'il' rather than with 'je' or 'elle' it is unclear, and perhaps intentionally, whether this adjective refers to the mother or the daughter. It may be that the mother's bewildered expression causes her to appear ghostly, or that the daughter's perception of this familiar family member provokes a reaction which would ordinarily accompany something unfamiliar or

---

[46] NDiaye's tendency to represent the mother as elusive and unsettling will be central to a discussion of her novel *Rosie Carpe* in the next chapter, which deals specifically with the theme of the family.

unexpected. As is almost always the case for NDiaye's characters, Lucie's central quest is to retrieve a sense of home and to reunite her dispersed family, yet the family, and especially the mother, is always absent or lacking in some way. This is reflected in Lucie's ponderings: 'Comme j'aimerais que ma mère entre dans la chambre, me dis-je avec ferveur, et qu'elle s'assoie sur mon lit quelques secondes' (S 126).

The family is constantly threatened by dislocation. In *La Sorcière* and nearly all of NDiaye's novels we find an unusual proliferation of fathers, mothers, brother, sisters, aunts, cousins, sons and daughters. Yet none of these individuals are capable of successfully performing their familial roles. Lucie is engaged in an incessant struggle to maintain the coherence of the family unit, a project which ultimately fails, since family members all appear to encounter great difficulty remaining in their proper places. Near the beginning of the novel, Lucie's already somewhat indifferent husband leaves her suddenly to return to his parents' home in Poitiers. Later, during the heroine's quest to locate him, her twin daughters also disappear.

Certain fantastic occurrences appear to suggest the presence of an irrational element within the family home, expressing this sense of family dislocation. In passages relating to Lucie's two daughters, the author first invites us to observe the girls' typically teenage apathy and nonchalance:

> Maud et Lise, mes filles, avaient de beaux yeux effilés mais remplis d'une énergie froide, d'une intelligence calculatrice, et, il me fallait le reconnaître, elles avaient le cœur sec, capable seulement de lamentations sentimentales, occasionnelles, vite endiguées, sur quelques misères entraperçues par inadvertance entre deux émissions. (S 64)

Lucie perceives her daughters as menacing and judgemental, and senses their hostility towards her. Uneasily shocked, bored and sassy, obsessed with fluffy fashion magazines and the television, Maud and Lise represent certain identifiable teenage tendencies or, at least, embody recognizable incarnations of these tendencies. During the course of the novel there are several allusions to the distance the author experiences between herself and her daughters, and to her difficulty in understanding and communicating with them: 'Il me semblait toujours que Maud et Lise vivaient en permanence dans un monde hypothétique et lointain, celui de leur gloire future, où les incidents du présent n'avaient pas leur place...'(S 60). Later, the girls' grandmother comments on their aloofness: 'Qu'est-ce qu'il t'arrive à tes filles? Pardonne-moi, elles me semblent lointaines, mauvaises. Qu'est-ce qu'il leur est donc arrivé ?' (S 116). Only M. Matin, a colleague of Lucie's husband, appears to be somewhat taken with the girls: 'Quelle jolie paire de perruches' (S 43).

These passing comments, which suggest the twins' increasingly distant attitudes in relation to their family, in fact foreshadow their literal metamorphosis into birds, which occurs later in the narrative. A description of adolescent remoteness exceeds the boundaries of realism when, one day on the train with their mother, the twins transform into crows – rather than budgies as hinted at by M. Matin – and fly away, leaving behind their lace-up boots, which growl and twist in front of the abandoned seats. After this initial incident, the twins' strange transformational tendencies are frequently acknowledged by the narrator: 'Je tâtai, de chaque côté, le bas de leur manche, saisis quelque chose que je lâchai aussitôt. C'était une aile, le bout d'une aile d'oiseau sombre' (S 136). At other times, descriptions of Maud and Lise borrow from a more striking and traditionally uncanny repertoire of fantastic imagery:

> Soudain, des manches de leur blouson, des cheveux de Maud et Lise, voletèrent quelques plumes légères d'un brun-noir, qui délicatement se posèrent sur le parquet poli. Mes filles riaient, enfantines, glorieuses. (S 101-2)

In this case, the fantastic theme of metamorphosis seems to echo a portrait of blasé adolescent attitudes and the distance and challenges in communication in the mother-daughter relationship, suggesting the twins' precocious desire to abandon their mother and 'leave the nest'. It is interesting that in each instance of metamorphosis where a character assumes the form of a bird, it is always an extremely commonplace, yet sinister bird, such as a crow or a raven. This is a world where magic exists, but its incarnations are no more remarkable than ordinary existence and therefore not entirely 'out of the ordinary'.

The integrity of the family structure is threatened by the fact that its members refuse to 'stay put', to acknowledge their relationships to other family members and to perform their expected roles within the family dynamic. Thanks to her visionary powers, Lucie

eventually re-locates her estranged husband, with a view to retrieving
the money he owes her. Pierrot has taken up residence in an apartment
block in the town of Bourges, with another woman and three children,
his new family. When Lucie mentions their daughters and reminds
him of his fatherly obligations to them, it appears he has renounced
his paternal role, feeling disgusted by his own children:

> La pâle et grasse figure de Pierrot se crispa de dégoût. Il fut sur le
> point de cracher, ravala sa salive, puis il s'essuya la bouche du
> revers de la main.
> – Ces saletés de petites sorcières! siffla-t-il en me lançant un coup
> d'œil haineux. (S 149)

The strange portrayal of fatherhood embodied by Pierrot in the
passage above is also visible near the beginning of the novel when we
are introduced to M. Matin, a former Garden-Club client of Pierrot's
who dines one evening with Lucie's family, having been rejected by
his own family. Feeling unappreciated by his own child and wife, M.
Matin plunges into a monologue concerning his own fatherly incapacity:

> Quand [ma femme] sort faire une course et je reste seul avec
> Nounou, je me sens vite tellement mal à l'aise, tellement gauche,
> observé et détesté, que je monte dans notre chambre pour respirer,
> car je ne respire plus, je suffoque quand je suis seul devant le
> petit. (S 53)

The conventional authoritarian father-son rapport is entirely reversed.[47] The child, Nounou, places his father in a strange state of
inferiority, anxiety and embarrassment, implying a reversal of the law
of the father. This representation of the vulnerability rather than the
authority of the father in relation to the son reflects a tendency in the
representation of the father within contemporary writing in the post-
Freudian period.[48] While the representation of this character suggests
that his fatherly unease is due to paranoia, it could also emanate from
his son, indicating the way that children now precociously absorb

---

[47] In the following chapter this point will be brought out more thoroughly in the
context of Savitzkaya's *Marin mon cœur*, a text which is founded on the reversal of
the more conventional father-son dynamic.

[48] See the next chapter where this idea is adressed more thoroughly.

unfavorable modern-day cultural representations of fatherhood.[49]

There is a sense that designators of kinship, although abundant in *La Sorcière*, are empty signifiers, since their incarnations within everyday life do not appear to live up to the expectations that might accompany these terms. When Lucie asks M. Matin 'Qui est Nounou?', rather than replying 'c'est mon fils' M. Matin responds: '...c'est cette petite bête qui me déteste' (S 49). M. Matin's description of his son as a 'petite bête' is an exaggerated response, but not an entirely implausible remark from a frustrated father. Later in the novel, this comment achieves a strange literal manifestation when Lucie discovers that her mother has used her magical forces against her own father literally to transform him into a 'petite bête', in this case a snail.

The presence of such fantastic incidents, the strange nature of which is not acknowledged by the characters, also generates absurd dialogue, causing the reader to perceive the collision of the word 'père' with the individual (or creature) that the term is supposed to designate in this context. Concerning the snail, Robert tells Lucie: 'Ta mère affirme que cette bestiole est ton père.' (S 173) Later, when a police officer finds the box containing the creature, the narrator tells us: 'Il lança mon père sur le bureau' (S 181). If the legitimacy of the signifier 'père' was not already questionable with respect to M. Matin's comments about Nounou and Pierrot's refusal to assume responsibility for his children, this particular incarnation of fatherhood overthrows any rational expectations the reader might have. Contrasted with the relatively plausible declarations of Pierrot and M. Matin concerning their own children, the representation of the father as a snail takes family indifference into a more far-fetched context, perhaps with the objective of rendering these dynamics more explicit. The fantastic presents a strange materialization of what the author is already telling us more subtly: that fathers do not always embody the characteristics of fatherhood we expect them to, that the home may be

---

[49] Another frequent feature of Marie NDiaye's novels, which is again present in *La Sorcière*, is that family members appear to have a quasi-fantastic sense of uncertainty when it comes to their progeny, parents, or siblings. M. Matin tells Lucie that Nounou is only a toddler, yet when she meets him, he is a young adolescent (S 51 and 55). A similar form of uncertainty is present in *Rosie Carpe*, when the protagonist mistakes her brother's friend for her brother when she's waiting for him at the airport, even though the former is a black man. See chapter 3 below.

a site of irrationality and cruelty. These strategies extract a monstrous quality from the more subtle forms of hostility present within everyday interactions and evoke a form of beastliness that lurks beneath the peaceful, functional image of family life.

The narrative technique at play here evokes the uncanniness of the omnipotence of thoughts. For Freud, the notion that things we say or think might be later produced in reality was a disturbing, unsurmounted archaic belief (U 247). In *La Sorcière*, passing comments or behaviours of the characters and the dysfunctional nature of home are capable of producing supplementary effects. What seem like relatively harmless moments of everyday life are pushed to an absurd limit, since the characters all have a strange ability to incarnate or produce the qualities of the world they inhabit. Yet the uncanny characters of NDiaye's fictional world are not the traditional ghastly figures of the conventional fantastic text. Unlike Hoffmann's Sandman or Shelley's monster, they are simply the ordinary individuals we encounter in day-to-day life.

The world Lucie inhabits is thus simultaneously insipid and paranormal. NDiaye often seems to be telling us that something is off-kilter in contemporary society. She portrays the modern world as a troubling place, where identities fluctuate, superficiality dominates and human relations are motivated by self-interest. In the midst of this, the subject is searching for home, for rootedness, for some kind of meaning to cling to. But something always prevents Lucie from feeling *chez elle*. Try as she might to reunite her family and reinstate the harmony and comfort of the family home, these domains constantly slip away, remaining intangible and incomprehensible.

Yet the reader cannot entirely sympathize with Lucie's condition, because there is something uncanny about Lucie herself. Although she invites the reader's identification and sense of familiarity due to her ordinariness, she has a disconcerting tendency passively to accept the outlandish nature of her environment. In *La Moustache*, the strangeness of the character's situation is the object of incessant reflexion; its interrogation by various characters determines the trajectory of the narrative. In *La Sorcière*, however, we find the formula of the presence of undeniably fantastic imagery with an unawareness of the strangeness of that imagery on the part of the characters. The passage which relates Lucie's reaction to her daughters' transformation exemplifies the banality of fantastic figures within the everyday. After dozing on the train to Paris, on the way to visit her parents with her twin girls, Lucie awakens to find her daughters have undergone a metamorphosis:

> Mes yeux se fermèrent, je somnolai quelques minutes. Lorsque je me réveillai, mes filles n'étaient plus là. Je parcourus le wagon, puis le train, et, soucieuse, je revenais à ma place quand deux gros oiseaux vinrent frôler la vitre du compartiment. Ils s'éloignèrent, disparurent à ma vue. Puis ils revinrent, dans un piqué joyeux, frotter leur aile au carreau, et je leur souris, soulagée. Ils me fixèrent d'un œil froid, malin – qui étais-je pour ces corneilles? Qui étais-je encore pour mes filles, certes tendres envers moi, mais déjà sorcières si accomplies qu'elles ne pouvaient certainement s'empêcher de ressentir, envers leur mère peu douée, une sorte d'indifférence condescendante? (S 111)

The knowledge of the fantastic event is absorbed with ease by the protagonist, whose attention is turned more to her own anxieties about her children growing up than to the transgression of the common real. In *La Sorcière* the fantastic never becomes an element of surprise or strangeness in itself, but is in fact often either cast aside, ignored or seamlessly blended into the commonplace interactions of characters. When Maud and Lise suddenly begin to sprout feathers in their grandfather's kitchen, for instance, no one is distressed and the conversation moves directly on to trivial familial exchanges between characters concerning Lucie's mother's new partner. Lucie's father hardly notices his grandchildren's transformation and appears more interested in discussing the reimbursement of the money Lucie has borrowed. In his methodological article 'The Psycho-Analysis of the Uncanny', Edmund Bergler suggests that there are twelve forms of uncanny experience. One of these is described as follows: 'A sense of the uncanny may be experienced when other people fail to display some typical affective reaction which we should "normally" expect to see in them'.[50] In *La Sorcière*, the mechanisms of the reader's identification with the characters are perturbed. All of the individuals in the novel appear to be extremely familiar, yet they appear to inhabit an extra-ordinary world.

The non-coincidence between the reader's expectations of the narrative realm and those of the protagonist prevent *La Sorcière* from

---

[50] Edmund Bergler, 'The Psycho-Analysis of the Uncany', p. 223.

behaving like a realist text, where identification with the character and a shared reality principle are expected. Yet the novel also challenges certain norms of the fantastic genre, reflecting the tendency of many contemporary French novels to elude characterization within either of these two genres. Fantastic tales by Romantic writers such as Hoffmann or Gautier are rich with adjectives of horror such as 'ghastly', 'wretched', 'monstrous', or 'uncanny', which qualify the characters' emotional responses to events which depart from the ordinary. In her study of the nineteenth-century French and Russian fantastic, Claire Whitehead argues that one of the generic conventions of the fantastic is that the characters display surprise or fear in reaction to irrational or supernatural occurrences.[51] In his *Introduction à la littérature fantastique,* Tzvetan Todorov also stresses the implicit function of the reader and likelihood of her identification with the bewilderment of the character: 'Le fantastique est fondé essentiellement sur une hésitation du lecteur – un lecteur qui s'identifie au personnage principal – quant à la nature d'un événement étrange'.[52] Without this affective solidarity between the reader and the character, the novel risks slipping into the genre of the marvelous or into allegory or poetry, where a more conventionally realist representation of the world is not expected.[53] Although Todorov's structural analysis imposes a rigidity on the fantastic which might appear contrived, he does point out certain tendencies within traditional fantastic writing which do not apply to many contemporary approaches. In the work of women writers such as Marie Darrieussecq or Linda Lê, for example, metamorphosis or imagery of the grotesque are integrated into the everyday lives of the characters, often appearing to reflect or at least to be intertwined with a revelation of disconcerting, or even monstrous elements of contemporary society.[54]

    In some ways NDiaye's approach thus resembles the mechanisms at work in Latin American and postcolonial Anglophone magi-

---

[51] Claire Whitehead, *The Fantastic in France and Russia in the Nineteenth Century, In Pursuit of Hesitation,* p. 125. As an exception to this rule she cites Gogol's short story 'The Nose', in which certain characters are only mildly shocked by the fact that Ivan Iakovlevich's nose is found in his loaf of bread. Ibid, p. 125-6.

[52] Tzvetan Todorov, *Introduction à la littérature fantastique,* p. 165.

[53] Ibid, p. 165

[54] Darrieussecq's first novel *Truismes,* for example, recounts the tale of a young masseuse who metamorphoses into a pig. See Marie Darrieussecq, *Truismes* (Paris: P.O.L, 1996).

cal realism. Critics of this genre often stress the fact that the super-natural events evoked by magical realists are stated in a matter-of-fact manner and never appear shocking to any of the characters.[55] However, another quality of magical realism is that it generally does not disconcert the reader.[56] Writers such as Garcia Marquez present a world in which the reader easily suspends her disbelief and accepts fantasy as reality. Likwise, in *La Sorcière*, fantastic events such as the metamorphosis of characters into birds or snails, or the visionary tableaux of the author's predictions, are everyday images, appearing no more or less strange than relationships, human behaviour and environments in today's world. It seems that fantasy for Marie NDiaye is neither a mode of escapism nor an expression of the enchantment of the everyday, but rather serves to generate an uncanny reflection of our own ordinary world.

To conclude, it might be suggested that in amplifying and re-configuring the fantastic tension between strangeness and familiarity, NDiaye's texts seem to lean towards a kind of 'uncanny realism' whereby fantasy expresses, often with humour, forms of absurdity and a sense of elusiveness that are extremely 'close to home': the discordance and communication gaps within day-to-day family relations, the fluctuating nature of contemporary identities, the groundlessness and superficiality of consumer society, the emptiness and banality of certain aspects of modern suburban life. This manifestation of the uncanny reflects many post-Freudian cons-tructions of the concept within cultural theory, discussed in the introduction to this book. While *La Sorcière* still displays the classic fantastical forms of metamorphosis and witchcraft, the author employs them in such a way as to suggest the strangeness of our familiar world.

However, it should be noted that while the fantastic often appears to serve as an uncanny echo for the author's statements concerning contemporary society, it is by no means reduced to a simple amplification or re-enactment of this theme. While this ob-servation brings out a certain quality or dimension of the fantastic in NDiaye's writing, it also risks imposing a sense of finality on the presence of the fantastic, which, in the novel, remains equivocal. In *La Sorcière* the codes of strangeness and familiarity are never resolved.

---

[55] See Amaryll Beatrice Chanady, *Magical Realism and the Fantastic: Resolved Versus Unresolved Antimony* (New York: Garland, 1985), p. 24.
[56] Ibid, p. 24.

The reader never has a sense of having come to terms with the strange forms that haunt NDiaye's narratives.

The novels of both NDiaye and Carrère appear to solicit a new form of realism in the space of an estrangement of the everyday. Both writers employ atmospheres of the fantastic to destabilize possible myths or illusions of the *chez soi*: the solidity of family relations, the certainty of the self, the normalcy of the home and the everyday. This tendency finds expression in a renewed commitment to transcribing the tumultuous inner experience of the individual, the mediocrity of the contemporary world, the absurdities and confusions of social relations and the forms and transgressions of family values and domestic space.

While this realism may be discursively and figuratively altered, and its subjects disjointed and unknowable, the realist vocation has in some sense been retrieved: to engage with the unease of the individual faced with the fragmentation of the social and political, to represent the subtle traumas and realities of the contemporary world. The uncanny contributes to a critique of contemporary society by encouraging the reader to perceive the strange banality and foreignness of ordinary components of modern life that we might take for granted. For NDiaye this takes the form of intrusions of fantastic imagery on her realist discourse, while for Carrère the fantastic is felt as an anxious atmosphere brought into proximity with the ordinary, one which subjects the signs of the familiar to a process of semantic estrangement.

In both *La Sorcière* and *La Moustache*, the atmosphere and imagery of the fantastic are employed ironically, even humorously, to express the absurdity and elusiveness of the everyday. The presence of the uncanny suggests a certain breakdown in meaning, and enhances the authors' representations of contemporary culture and values. They invite the reader to experience familiar, everyday life as foreign and to perceive the illusory nature of a stable, tranquil vision of the *chez soi*.

For both writers, the fantastic is also a means to announce the uncertainty of the authorial stance. As well as dismantling the home and the subject's modes of dwelling in the everyday, both writers reveal the excessiveness of the everyday, its invitation to alternative modes of literary appropriation. The most familiar objects and spaces take on lives of their own and refuse to cooperate symbolically or perform as background décor. Liberated from the mimetic ambitions of realism, these novels portray the everyday as a place of discontinuity and disorder, with which we nonetheless constantly attempt to re-familiarize ourselves.

The Home Comes to Life: Savitzkaya's *En vie*

In Eugène Savitzkaya's semi-autobiogaphical portrayal of everyday life within the home, the familiar once again asserts its refusal to be domesticated by the home-dweller and, by extension, its ability to lend itself to multiple representations. Unlike the first two texts examined in this chapter, which were decidedly novelistic, perhaps even realist, *En vie* (1995) blurs the distinction between poetry and prose. Although the work lacks a discernable plot and identifiable characters, reading more like a prose poem, the generic label placed beneath the title identifies it as a novel. In this text the uncanny becomes an eccentric language or narrative code which heightens our sense of the sublimity present in immediate, ordinary experience. As a domestic voyager, the narrator reinterprets the actions and décors of the household as a novel, nearly supernatural environment and pronounces the strangeness of this formerly familiar space. Diverse elements and moments of the home are dismantled and then lyrically reconstructed to generate an imaginative description of contemporary living.

Although Savitzkaya employs similar techniques of defamiliarization, his uncanny approach to writing differs from that observed in NDiaye and Carrère in that his narrative features a character who embraces the unhomely. In Savitzkaya's work, the uncanny may even be dissociated from negativity and anxiety and explored as a productive, playful or comical moment in the midst of day-to-day existence and reading. *En vie* provides a fascinating counter-example or *cas limite* to be contrasted with the depictions of the *chez soi* presented by Carrère and NDiaye, which are characterized by discomfort.

This discussion of *En vie* will begin by addressing the metaphoric interplay between the home and self in Savitzkaya's writing, with a view to situating the novel within the author's works. *En vie* marks an evolution in both the writer's style and his exploitation of the figure of home. This will be followed by an exposition of certain poetic strategies in the novel, through which the writer estranges banal domestic acts and objects. The analysis will then turn to the portrayal of home as a reflection of the self. Savitzkaya's defamiliarization of the *chez soi* is echoed in the distortion or exaggeration of familiar bodily imagery often associated with the home. As the home-dweller (and narrator) submits his domestic space to an estranging gaze, replacing his own subjective comfort with vulnerability, the description of the inhabitant and that of the home become intertwined. The home itself acquires certain qualities of subjectivity, such as body, voice and character.

Disfigured dwellings
In general, the representation of home is often intertwined with imagery of the body. In his psychoanalytic study of home, *L'Inconscient de la maison*, Alberto Eiguer describes the subject's need to conceive of the home through reference to corporeal figures. He develops the concept of 'habitat intérieur' to designate the subject's psychic projection of her own unified body onto her vision of home.[57] His term *asomatognosie* names the state of disorientation induced when the 'habitat intérieur' is lost. In certain patients, such a condition generates an internal perplexity which inhibits the subject from taking comfort in physical space and interferes with the geographical and intellectual mechanisms through which she acquires certainty about her physical environment.

Savitzkaya's writing reinforces the duality of the French *chez soi* as evoking both the home and the self, and exploits the imagery that underlies the literary and unconscious representation of both of these domains. It seems that, for Savitzkaya, and particularly in his younger period, writing is linked to such a state of homelessness, of *asomatognosie*. For him this is a state which may be achieved poetically and is both feared and desired. Savitzkaya's novels gesture towards a reality which is inaccessible from within the *chez soi* and display a yearning for union with a more primitive, pre-subjective

---

[57] Alberto Eiguer, *L'Inconscient de la maison*, p. 2

instance, one which constantly resists contemplation, but nonetheless drives the creative process.

The representation of states of utter homelessness dominates much of Savitzakaya's early work. His 1989 novel *Sang de chien* portrays the subject in a phase of interior physical confusion, which evokes a state of infancy or primary disorientation and dismemberment; body parts, images and thoughts attain the status of characters and participate in a disparate narrative, which enacts this inner turmoil. Place is constantly transformed back into space.[58]

Many critics have observed this quest in his writing for such a state of dislocation, which is both *heimlich* and *unheimlich*. For Henri Scepi: 'Tout l'art d'Eugène Savitzkaya tient, semble-t-il, à cet usage de la faille, trouée, inattendue et lumineuse où s'engouffre une perspective du sens, originelle et pourtant si familière, insoupçonnée et pourtant si coutumière'.[59] For Savitzkaya, writing endeavours to capture and figuratively extend moments where the *chez soi* is pulled towards dispersal, a condition that seems to imply a more authentic dwelling in the world.

Savitzkaya's characters are various incarnations of himself as writer and are thus constantly being beckoned away from home. The anxiety and non-unity of the writing subject is often mirrored in the topological and thematic representation of home, which consistently evades mythical or unconscious representations of the stable or comforting home. The distortion of the figure of home varies in degree from malodorous, dysfunctional, or disconcerting dwellings in *La Disparition de Maman* and *En vie*, to the entire devastation of home in the aftermath of cataclysm in *La Folie originelle*. The home is portrayed in its fragility, its potential for decomposition and crumbling, as a vulnerable, man-made entity, susceptible to invasion

---

[58] Marie-Claire Ropars-Wuilleumier distinguishes 'lieu' from 'espace'. A place differs from a space in that it is invested with subjectivity. A space is 'un rapport au lieu, et à ses lois d'orientation; mais ce rapport, qui est à construire, requiert tout à la fois l'inclusion d'un sujet humain, qui s'approprie cardinalement ses repères, et la mise en jeu d'une logique de l'observation, faisant de cette inclusion l'opérateur d'une expropriation du lieu lui-même'. See Marie-Claire Ropars-Wuilleumier, *Écrire l'espace* (Paris: Presses universitaires de Vincennes, 2002), p. 9-10. There is a sense that Savitzkaya's subjects have lost this sense of orientation and appear unable to transpose place into space.
[59] Henri Scepi, 'Eugène Savitzkaya: une poétique du continu', *Critique* 576 (May 1995), 399- 416 (p. 409).

or disintegration. At times, the home may also be a prison, as is seen in the 'maisons sans portes ni fenêtres' which lined the streets of the beach near his home as a child.[60] The home is often dark, claustrophobic and abandoned: 'Aucune maison n'était plus déserte. Aucune maison n'était moins traversée de vent et de lumière'.[61] Savitzkaya's writing is thus both an exploration and defamiliarization of the *imaginaire* of the home; associations and images of the home are interwoven with its very experience. The home constantly fluctuates between location, metaphor and emotion. It is a physical place from which the author writes, a memory or fantasy, and a subjective or authorial position.[62]

In these earlier texts, the *unheimlich* representation of home appears to reflect a threatened subject, and thus retains affiliations with the original anxiety of the Freudian concept. Many of Savitzkaya's more recent texts, however, continue to destabilize the home, but dilute this atmosphere of trauma and loss. In *En vie* and *Marin mon cœur,* for instance, the uncanny is exploited as an untroubled, more harmonious commingling of the strange and familiar. This shift in Savitzkaya's writing is accompanied by a movement towards a less dense, complex and poetic style, one which re-orients the reader within a more recognizable communal reality. In *En vie,* the defamiliarization undergone by the vicissitudes of day-to-day life takes on a less turbulent, gently humorous quality. This evolution in the writer's tone reframes his quest for uprootedness within a livable day-to-day framework, and generates a literary ethos of approaching and living in the ordinary world.

This observation evokes Kristeva's valuing of uncanniness as a potentially productive space, which might counterbalance the violence of abjection. The uncanny, for Kristeva, is a destabilization of experience, but one which preserves a place for language and signification. In *En vie*, Savitzkaya generates a distortion of home, but leaves the *chez soi* intact. By overcoming anxiety and the loss of the *chez soi*, Savitzkaya is able to see strangeness as positive and en-

---

[60] Eugène Savitzkaya, *La Disparition de maman* (Paris: Éditions de Minuit, 1982), p. 8.

[61] Eugène Savitzkaya, *Mentir* (Paris: Éditions de Minuit, 1977), p. 25.

[62] This is the vision of home that will be explored in the final chapter of this book in Savitzkaya's most recent novel, *Fou trop poli.* For Savitzkaya, the problematic of autobiography is that of defining a home, or origin, from which to write.

lightening rather than as a chaotic state in which the subject is disengaged from communication and common reality.

Domesticity reinvented

In *En vie*, by distorting and revalorizing the domestic site, the novelist directs the perception of otherness inwards, towards our own commonplace actions and environment, rendering exotic our habitual, unthinking modes of dwelling. Written in elegant and simple language and renouncing conventions of character and plot, the novel constitutes a lyrical geography of the home, doubled by a dreamlike depiction of the subject's bodily relation to individual elements of this domestic domain. As is the case with all of Savitzkaya's texts, traditional narration is essentially absent, since linearity would imply a compartmentalization of reality and the adoption of an economy of categorization, which are incompatible with the disarray and surrealism that prevail in his texts. Instead, Savitzkaya revisits the home through a poetic kaleidoscope of uncertainty. This perspective is achieved through narrative tactics that rely on the malleability of the strange/familiar dynamic: figurative and contextual techniques that confound strange and familiar, whereby everyday objects and activities appear overestimated or excessive; the slowing-down of our perception of ordinary domestic tasks through the amplification of detail; the exploitation of imagery of haunting and the fantastic to describe the commonplace; and the representation of the domestic space as a place of struggle and adventure.

The blurring of strange and familiar is first perceptible in the extraordinary representation of ordinary household entities. Everyday items of the home are placed in a state of connotative oscillation by being simultaneously identified by the narrator as banal and experienced as mysterious articles of fascination:

> En hiver, imbibé d'eau [un paillasson] gèle et devient la tablette (indéchiffrable). On le secoue lorsqu'il est saturé. Un paillasson n'est jamais éternel. Parfois, il semble immonde, peu à notre image. Il pue. Qui encore l'avait arrosé de vomissures? [63]

As it becomes the object of the writer's gaze, the doormat assumes a

---

[63] Eugène Savitzkaya, *En vie* (Paris: Éditions de Minuit, 1994), p. 13. All other references are given in the text, following the abbreviation EV.

freshly strange quality, whilst retaining its original associations.[64] Portrayed in its functionality and normality, it is a useful triviality, but it is accorded a perceptive attention. In many of the descriptions in the novel, household objects appear to the reader as both banal and sacred:

> La citerne d'eau de pluie est devant la maison, juste sous la terrasse. Elle émet des sons graves et lointains. C'est un vide qui se comble d'eau. Elle supporte, en plus du poids de l'eau, le poids des enfants, des visiteurs, de la table et des assiettes. On marche au-dessus du vide que les pas font résonner. Il est préférable de l'imaginer profonde et insondable comme un puits dont elle ne possède que le caractère souterrain. En se penchant dans l'ouverture, outre soi-même, on peut voir la muraille de la maison avec son toit en saillie et le ciel. C'est une sorte de richesse. (EV 111)

The poetic extraction of the tank from its ordinary role in the home is not performed by removing the object entirely from its contextual function, but instead by illuminating its habitual usage and milieu from an alternative or more concentrated angle. The attention drawn to its strange resonances, the sound of feet walking above it, elevates it from its position as a dismissable, functional component of the home to that of a peculiar musical instrument. The humble water tank assumes a distant and mournful significance, by being referred to as 'un vide'.

The process at work in some ways resembles that of the surrealist 'found objects' or readymades such as Duchamp's 'Fontaine', where banal objects acquire an absurd aesthetic value and are perceived differently by being displaced into an artistic context. Such artistic practices also invite us to reconsider ordinary entities, but the process at work is essentially one of estrangement. Savitzkaya's project is not simply a narrative equivalent to the readymade since the item is never detached from its original, familiar context. This context is simply expanded so that its significance appears to branch out into a world that exceeds the immediacy of the home and the everyday:

> Dans une maison, il est rare de ne pas pouvoir mettre la main sur

---

[64] This technique perhaps follows more closely the logic of the uncanny effect produced by repeating a familiar word over and over until it resonates nonsensically, a phenomenon alluded to by Nicolas Royle on the first page of his book, *The Uncanny.*

une aiguille [...] Il y a toujours une aiguille piquée dans un rectangle de carton noir ou blanc, ou dans le corps d'une bobine, repérable à la queue de fil lumineux, comme d'une comète. (EV 39-40)

The familiar needle is placed within an excessive descriptive framework. Strangeness is portrayed as an extension of the everyday; a common experience or quality already present in the ordinary use-value or role of the object within the home is magnified or lyrically empowered to such a point that it moves beyond the familiar. As they become objects of focused, literary depictions, screws, nails, mops, brooms, slippers and dish towels also develop as natural wonders of the home, significant in themselves, rather than by-passed as simple instruments of convenience.

Similar processes of textual exaltation are found in the representation of activities in the home. The writer reconstructs familiar, daily life as a series of magical or foreign events, which branch off into strange literary microcosms. One of these processes involves the amplification of instances of home that are taken for granted, through the representation of what would normally be unquestioned physical or intellectual affinities between the subject and her environment. By extracting a poetic quality from the dynamics of the subject's interaction with his domestic milieu, the novelist encourages the reader to reconsider the unthinking ways in which the body engages with the outside world:

Les mêmes mains accomplissent toutes les tâches. Elles scient et transportent le bois, allument le feu dans le poêle et profitent de la chaleur de la pièce, elles manipulent les papiers. Je suis à la fois à la roue et au moulin. Les mêmes mains servent à tout et font communiquer les parties du monde, la terre avec le ventre, la bouche avec l'anus, l'assiette avec la cuvette des latrines et l'alphabet avec le cœur du bois. (EV 13-14)

The literary evocation of the diverse elements associated through unconscious movements of the hands, illuminates certain unseen relationships which do not ordinarily infiltrate our immediate reality, such as that of 'la bouche avec l'anus'. This sketch of the criss-crossing of the daily pathways of objects and the body reveals a surprising narrative space, since these movements are, in a sense, so familiar that they seem to be exempt from articulation.

Another technique of defamiliarization involves slowing down our perception of habitual tasks around the home through meticulous transcriptions of their processes. This is first simply the effect of textually acknowledging, and thus deepening, extremely banal domestic chores, by bringing them into the literary text. A large part of the novel consists of series of short chapters or fragments dedicated to individual household chores. The author's exuberant poetic gaze magnifies the banal, challenging the distinction between detail and event. Peeling apples, for instance, becomes a surreal ballet, which occupies the greater part of two pages in the novel. The writer concentrates scrupulous attention on the material qualities of the knife, the sensation of piercing the apple skin, and finally, the majestic unraveling of 'une sorte de phylactère qui indique la superficie totale du fruit' (EV 59). The banality of routine practice and method is augmented, transformed into something new, without departing from familiar experience: 'enlever d'abord la plus fine membrane possible et ensuite, avec la pointe du couteau, se débarrasser de la chair meurtrie et faire sauter les logettes à pepins' (EV 60).

We also observe a technique of estrangement which is the opposite of the magnification process evoked above. At times the writer achieves a similar effect by assuming a very distanced perspective on the activity. For example, he describes the bustle and activity of clearing up after dinner as a strange orchestra of sound effects: 'cliquetis, chocs, chutements [...] qui profitent autant à ceux qui se reposent qu'à ceux qui s'activent' (EV 25).

Such descriptive strategies might perhaps be viewed as a literary enactment of the renewal of the everyday advocated in Michel de Certeau's *L'Invention du quotidien*.[65] For de Certeau, while the everyday might be viewed as a docile, non-innovative domain which is submitted to, rather than lived, the heterogeneity and the singularity of everyday individual acts within this space harbour a plethora of mysteries and poetic potential. As summarized by Bruce Bégout:

> Derrière la soumission apparente de l'homme ordinaire à la rationalité instrumentale et formelle qui s'exprime dans le champ

---

[65] Michel de Certeau, *L'Invention du quotidien,* 3 Vols, Vol. 1, *'Arts de faire'*, coll. 'Folio essais' (Paris: Folio, 1994), p. 146. De Certeau's theories of the *quotidien* are not limited to domestic everyday spaces, but extend to other realms of subjective experience such as the urban environment or the workplace.

économique, technologique et politique, se cache une subversion muette, dispersée et particulière, minimale et marginale, mais réelle.[66]

In Savitzkaya's novel, this 'subversion muette' is found in the distinctiveness of the individual's existence within his home as he engages uniquely with the space around him, constructing, demolishing, reforming, modifying. The home is not a passive space, but may be viewed as one of constant creativity and invention: 'Il n'y a pas qu'une seule manière de ranger, mais des milliers, toutes nécessaires pour structurer et baliser l'existence de la maison [...]'(EV 42). Thus, daily chores, such as the washing up, generate a moment for reflection and rediscovery:

> On plonge les verres dans l'eau savonneuse et ils s'y dissolvent pour réapparaître dans la lumière, humbles et précieuses ampoules qui pourront à nouveau contenir le lait sirupeux, le vin fragile et l'eau sœur. (EV 24)

The literary amplification of these ordinary tasks is most often a celebration of their gloriousness: 'Existe-t-il un plaisir plus grand que de nettoyer les vitres d'une véranda inondée par le soleil du soir'? (EV 23) However, at times the author employs a vocabulary of struggle to evoke instead the frustration or sense of obstacle which might characterize the events which occur in the home: 'Il faut lutter contre l'aspirateur [...]' (EV 27).

The writer often revives the banal by employing imagery and language of the fantastic. This imagery is rarely unsettling and does not appear to express hostility. It may simply be a way of ascribing a certain power to the familiar. Cooking soup becomes the act of creating a monstrous concoction: 'Dans la marmite cuit chaque jour le monstre aux cent mille têtes et aux deux milles bras qui use de cent mille façons de se dérober à la cuisson' (EV 50). Old clothes contain 'des trous autour desquels le tissu n'est plus qu'un fantôme' (EV 35). Dust which must constantly be removed from various household surfaces is 'un grand dragon éternel' (EV 93). These fantastic descriptions reveal a surprising quality in simple objects, revitalising

---

[66] Bruce Bégout, 'La Découverte du quotidien', p. 569.

their monotonous roles within an ordered reality, by modifying their purpose.

This constant reinvention of home leads the writer to develop an alternative discourse to express its marvels. Familiar household acts are described in an eccentric vocabulary. This new domestic language tends to distort common occurrences in the home by renaming or re-describing them to draw attention to an aspect of their role in the home which is often overlooked, or just slightly absurd. At times, the narrator appears to have forgotten the ordinary word to designate a particular act, forcing him to offer an alternative explanation of the activity, the same way a non-native speaker of a given language might attempt to evoke an unknown term for a simple phenomenon. Thus '*cuisiner*' becomes 'préparer et cuire ce que quatre bouches vont manger' (EV 45). '*Casseroles*' are 'les ustensiles dans lesquels la cuisson s'est faite'. *Repasser* is 'fai[re] disparaître les plis des vêtements' (EV 34). The family members are referred to as simply 'mangeurs'. Often a new description of a given act involves its glorification or exaggeration, rather than a simplification: '*Épousseter*', for example, becomes 'la lutte contre les poussières' (EV 26).

To accompany this unusual vocabulary, the writer develops a new conceptual domestic logic and invents alternative regulations and values to govern the home. He relates, for example, his experience of cooking vegetables, a task he performs in order to 'les détourne[r] du pourrissement' (EV 65). The act of dressing is performed 'pour cacher mes épaules, pour cacher mes genoux' (EV 74). Cleaning also possesses its own new set of objectives: 'Puisque ni les fourmis, ni les souris, ni les oiseaux ne sont admis dans la maison, il faudra balayer les miettes [...]' (EV 28). The floor is mopped because: 'Il ne faut pas que les visiteurs s'effrayent au premier pas dans la demeure' (EV 30). We must sweep regularly 'pour effacer les traces de notre passage' (EV 26). Washing up is not performed in order to clean the dishes, but 'les rendre transparents' (EV 24). Cooking is given a purpose other than that of simply nourishing the family: 'J'ai cuit le riz, des asperges et du poulet afin de les attendrir, d'en extraire le parfum et d'en rendre la saveur plus humaine' (EV 26). Domestic experience is re-located into gaps in conceptuality, into the extra-ontological, the extra-functional. For Savitzkaya, such fleeting moments of rupture become an entire way of perceiving, a re-categorization of experience whereby the singular becomes the only possible universality.

As in Carrère's *La Moustache*, Savitzkaya's descriptive strategies expose an alternative story of the familiar, which runs at an oblique angle to the image of the everyday as a constant, uneventful space. Once again, the novelist achieves this effect through an unhoming of the inhabitant. The narrator revisits the banal scenery of the home through the uncertain gaze of a subject who has lost the *chez soi*. While in *La Moustache* the main character was placed in a state of paranoia, in Savitzkaya's text the narrator willingly adopts a more humble position within the home. In the examples above, this is often performed by assuming a perspective of fascination which attributes to the banal a spell-binding power, constantly unsettling a controlling or passive appreciation of the home. The narrator perceives everything as if for the very first time.

However, another technique employed by the author in order to reveal the unseen or unacknowledged elements of the domestic sphere is a strategy of figurative reversal, which is applied to the representation of the narrator's home. The most intimate corners and concealed moments of the home are brought to the forefront in such a way as to figuratively turn the house inside out. The writer exteriorizes the vulnerable, non-functional or private aspects of the house and directs an othering attention at what is buried under our ordinary perception of its immediate reality: the hairs found in the hairbrush in the bathroom, the crumbs under the table, the dust that invades from the outside: 'aucune surface n'y échappe' (EV 92).

The veiled disorder of the home comes across through the voicing of household obstacles, catastrophes and infestations such as odours, mould, dust, floods, drafts, leaks and insects which invade the home, unable to be repressed by the inhabitant, despite his efforts to exclude them. Often it seems that the narrator has accepted the fragility of his home:

> Dans cette maison, il n'y a que la clenche qui brille, la clenche de la porte d'entrée. On ne peut plus fermer les robinets. Les portes s'ouvrent au moindre courant d'air. Le jet d'eau de la plupart des fenêtres est pourri par les pluies. L'eau s'infiltre par les fissures des pierres de taille. (EV 7)

The writer's description depicts the inhabitant in a state of striving to define and maintain the borders of the home; home is revealed in a constant state of quest and struggle.

The crumbling chez soi

The narrator in *En vie* alludes to a female character, perhaps his wife, who appears to exercise a form of mastery over the domestic environment: 'Ranger les jouets des enfants, les objets éparpillés par la tourmente et les vêtements, confère à celle qui connaît la place de chaque chose une stature quasi divine' (EV 41). He, however, has come to terms with both the unthematizable and untamable nature of the home. The Savitzkayan home-dweller knows that he is rarely in such a position of certainty, but more often, in one of vulnerability. He is frequently found on his knees, searching for lost objects, cleaning, polishing or striving to protect his home from outside invasion. He lives in fear that at any given moment, he may be exposed in one of his more defenseless states: 'que personne ne me surprenne un torchon à la main et des caoutchoucs aux pieds!' (EV 30). The inhabitant has renounced all illusion of being 'master in his own house' in order to adopt a more humble position within its configuration. He loses some of his subjective authority and recasts himself as a simple element that is absorbed into the home's continuum, as one strange phenomenon among others:

> Je balaie la sciure que je sème. Je ratisse les feuilles des arbres que j'ai plantés et celles des arbres que j'ai laissé croître. Je ramasse les fientes des pigeons que je tolère. Je lave les vitres que ma buée ternit. Je secoue le paillasson que je crotte. Je nettoie l'assiette que je salis. Je vide le cendrier que je remplis. Je lave la sueur que j'émets. Je débarrasse la cuvette que j'encombre [...] (EV 22-23)

The description seeks to express an impossible moment, where the unthinking movements of the everyday become self-aware and thus necessarily strange. The narrator locates himself in the midst of the multiple, infinite, cyclical tasks of home. The use of 'je' in such phrases, which evoke nearly unconscious acts, is somewhat ironic, since the instinctive actions of home described above do not ordinarily have a declared subject. By figuring as the subject of both the main and subordinate clauses, the 'je' is portrayed in its domestic, almost trancelike busyness, perpetually engaged in the mindless rituals of organization and inhabitance.

The body of home

Alberto Eiguer, for whom the stability of self is linked to the stability of home, affirms that '[l]a maison est le reflet de ce que nous sommes'.[67] Savitzkaya also views the home as a mirror of the self: 'ce dépotoir que nous avons créé à notre mesure' (EV 47). In *En vie*, the home's representation constantly recalls the comparison between the home and the human body. The writer emphasizes its physical composition as a mass of vital organs, entrances and exits and dwells on its internal workings, tubes, openings and crevasses. The home is 'un agencement de portes, de fenêtres et de murs, un grand système d'alvéoles' (EV 42).

Savitzkaya's text reveals the strangeness and sensitive limits of this familiar metaphor of the home as body, by amplifying this corporeal portrayal. Like the inhabitant, the home is full of creative energy. It moves from a foundational place, a stable background, to a strange force which expresses personality and resistance; the home is a living thing, which grows, develops, mutates, and the inert, inorganic objects which fill it begin to move and speak. In *En vie*, the bodily metaphor that relates self and home is thus defamiliarized as the writer reveals its less reassuring side. If home takes on too much personality it becomes *unheimlich*, uninhabitable. Strange noises emitted by the home, its ingestion of uninvited, foreign elements, for example, can detract from its comfort.

The writer stresses the more disconcerting, repressed or unspoken bodily elements of home. Like a body, the home is mortal. It metamorphoses and ages as an entity composed of matter 'en désagrégation permanente' (EV 71). Like a body, it must expel its waste: 'Il faut sans cesse se débarrasser de ce qui a germé, de ce qui a fané, de ce qui a moisi, de ce qui s'est gâté dans l'ombre des garde-manger et des frigidaires' (EV 60). It contains numerous strange smells: 'L'odeur de vomi de certains torchons de cuisine est tout simplement époustouflante...' (EV 63). The home is a strange monster that stirs, groans and devours objects. In descriptions such as that of the water tank, featured earlier in this section, the writer draws our attention to the grumbling innards of the home by exposing and giving voice to its various hidden internal organs. The home thrives on money, which it requires to remedy its various ills: 'Le manque

---

[67] Alberto Eiguer, *L'Inconscient de la maison*, p. 14.

d'argent, dans cette maison, est ponctuel comme la migraine, la douleur viscérale, l'acidité de l'estomac ou la crise de nerfs' (EV 44). Often the home's disintegration is reflected in bodily imagery and the representation of the narrator himself as a physical being: 'Peu à peu, au fil de la journée, s'affirme le caractère disparate de mon corps. Des morceaux menacent de tomber. Des pans entiers se détachent' (EV 16).

This bodily or living representation of the home is further reinforced by the reanimation of certain household objects. For Henri Scepi, Savitzkayan objects 'échappent à la clôture du regard géométrique comme à l'emprise de la réduction conceptuelle'.[68] This is particularly pronounced in *En vie*, where they uncannily come to life, almost becoming characters in the narrative. Aside from the techniques of poetic recontextualization evoked earlier in this analysis with regard to the doormat, water tank and needle, the novelist employs certain writing strategies which poetically attribute a living status to the material world.

Piles of dirt and crumbs swept up by the inhabitant take on a life of their own, since the narrator believes that with these remains it might be feasible to 'recomposer un quelconque homoncule apte à gesticuler' (EV 26). Through ironing, clothes assume a living form: 'le travail consiste à effacer les traces et les figures. Il s'agit de faire surgir du fouillis la silhouette humaine, dans sa grâce et sa fragilité. La silhouette grotesque' (EV 34).

This revival of the object is sometimes observable on the level of language, in the personification of non-living matter, through the attribution of human-related verbs to inanimate items. The dust in the home is represented as capable of purposefully locating or reaching for specific items. The narrator speaks of the need to place things 'hors de portée de la poussière' (EV 42). When the floor is cleaned, 'il proteste en répandant une forte odeur de bois mouillé'; laundry is capable of movement: 'le tas de linge jamais ne diminue. On dirait que, vivant, il fermente et lève' (EV 35). Objects often appear to engage in dialogue with one another: 'Contre l'extrême agressivité de l'aiguille a été conçu le précieux dé à coudre qui est comme une bague obtuse' (EV 38). As in *La Moustache*, household items become ungraspable, attaining force over the home-dweller, rather than

---

[68] Henri Scepi, 'Eugène Savitzkaya: une poétique du continu', p. 406.

behaving as objects of possession. The author nearly creates the impression of a poltergeist within the home, a spirit or ghost that manifests itself by moving and influencing inanimate objects, so that it appears as though they have a life of their own. This animated description of inert household objects, which is not necessarily disconcerting, suggests a subtler version of the uncanny effect of the blurring of boundaries between the living and the non-living. In his original study of the uncanny, Jentsch tells us that 'the effect of the uncanny can easily be achieved when one undertakes to reinterpret some kind of lifeless thing as a part of an organic creature, especially in anthropomorphic terms, in a poetic or fantastic way'.[69]

In *En vie*, the home is both a metaphor for the self and a place in which the self dwells. The home and subject are constantly reconfigured in various domestic encounters. The narrator is unsure of his place within the home, although desirably so, and constantly reinterpreting the *chez soi,* adopting a position of self-estrangement and vulnerability. This vulnerable stance assumed by the inhabitant of the home is often brought out in expressions of his awareness of how the other, a potential visitor, might view his home:

> Il se pourrait que tu voies bien d'autres choses encore qui appar-
> tiennent à la maison, et que tu sentes l'odeur de cette maison où je
> vis. Il n'y a pas lieu de t'offusquer. Ce que tu ne dois pas voir a
> été soigneusement rangé. Mais il se pourrait quand même que
> certains détails te choquent. (EV 46)

Acknowledging the possible strangeness of his home as perceived by the other is also a gesture of hospitality on the part of the narrator. Despite the *unheimlich* nature of the space the author has described, there is no need to take offense, as these particularities are to be enjoyed and even shared. The narrator's constantly open and evolving perception of his home leads him to extend an invitation to the reader, to expand her own concept of home by acknowledging the absurdities and wonders of domestic existence.

Savitzkaya's approach is reminiscent of Cixous's *poéthique,* which, we might recall, is founded on the abandonment of the *chez soi* in order to attain what she describes as a writerly position, chara-

---

[69] Ernst Jentsch, 'On the Psychology of the Uncanny', trans. by Roy Sellers, *Angelaki* 2, 7-16 (p. 13).

cterized by 'l'œil nu'.[70] For Cixous this quest is tied up with claims of a more authentic transcription of reality. While the question of realism does not seem to be primary for Savitzkaya, Cixous's choice of vocabulary is interesting in relation to *En vie*, since the reader often has the impression that the author has 'stripped away' the conventionally acknowledged subjective filters through which the *quotidien* presents itself to the subject. The Savitzkayan subject appears to be engaging with his domestic environment without the *chez soi*. Objects and phenomena remain familiar, yet they assume a foreign quality by being re-inscribed in a textual space which is, to a certain degree, released from the domesticating tendencies of the perceiving subject.

Like the previous novels examined in this chapter, Savitzkaya's poeticized representation of the home accords a certain foreignness to the unthinking space of routine, so as to renew our experience of the everyday world. The home is reconfigured as a space hospitable to a certain unfamiliarity or unhomeliness.[71] His approach differs from the others explored in this chapter. Although his text displays several of the elements of uncanniness present in the *La Moustache* and *La Sorcière* – the blurring of the boundaries of strange and familiar, the destabilization of home, intellectual uncertainty – Savitzkaya dissolves much of the anxiety that accompanies these dynamics. Instead of predominantly mobilizing atmospheres or tropes of the fantastic, he creates a framework of amazement and adopts a stance of hospitality, which affects his representations of the home, the self and the writing process itself. Although such an approach may at first seem removed from the feelings of unease which are most often the starting point for reflection on the uncanny, Savitzkaya's text might gesture towards some of its forms as advocated in Kristeva and Cixous's analyses, which were, ideally, divorced from repression.

---

[70] See page 66 above.

[71] As the author says in an interview: 'il me faut peu de choses pour me sentir dépaysé. Je ne m'ennuie jamais. La moindre activité me procure du plaisir'. Antoine de Gaudemar, 'Interview avec Eugène Savitzkaya', *Libération* (April 1992), http ://www.lesÉditionsdeminuit.fr/extraits/2003/interviewsavitzkaya.pdf (accessed 9 December 2007).

All three narratives discussed in this chapter present us with *unheimlich* homes. In *La Sorcière*, we find dismal suburban houses and a dismembered family. Lucie's everyday life is a constant struggle to maintain the coherence of the family unit. Family relations are portrayed as irrational and often hostile. In *La Moustache*, the home is transformed from a site of material and emotional comfort into a zone of hostility and uncertainty. The protagonist is constantly seeking to re-establish the harmony of the everyday as a way of securing his identity. The home appears to be inextricably linked to the self. In *En vie*, the home appears to take on a life of its own. Endowed with its own identity and body, it appears to speak back to the home-dweller, suggesting that he is not as *chez lui* as he might think. Each writer offers the reader a conceptual repertoire to relive, in diverse ways, the domestic space of the everyday under an uncanny light. The subject's relationship to the familiar is not one of continuity and harmony, but primarily one of doubt, conflict and re-evaluation. All three novelists thus challenge the image of everyday life in the home as a secure, comfortable space and show that it is equally capable of presenting an obstacle to subjective stability.

Each narrative displays a refusal to resolve or expel the uncanny, and instead insists on strangeness as fostering a dynamic for every vision of the ordinary. The uncanny is often constructed as a quality of the ordinary itself, rather than an external form or trope. For NDiaye and Carrère this implies the development of a contemporary form of 'uncanny realism', while for Savitzkaya the unhomely leads him to locate a form of 'uncanny lyricism' through which he recreates domesticity and figures his own unhomeliness as a writer. This approach perhaps reflects some of the commentary presented in the previous chapter of this book, which suggests that the uncanny might promote a renewal of the self-same. It may perhaps provide a way of achieving a different perspective on ordinary life and familiar surroundings. Of course, what comes across well in the work of all three writers, is that this is already the role of literature.

In his article 'Le Romanesque du quotidien', Michael Sheringham concludes that although the everyday is indeed 'romanesque', the novel is not traditionally a 'bon conducteur de quotidienneté'.[72]

---

[72] Michael Sheringham, 'Le Romanesque du quotidien', in *Le Romanesque*, ed. by Michel Murat and Gilles Declercq (Paris: Presses Sorbonne Nouvelle, 2004), pp. 255-66, p. 258.

While the novel is capable of detailing, classifying the everyday in its *simplex* form, its concern for immanence and structure renders it incapable of providing a genuine reflection on the everyday in its *complex* form, that is, as lived experience. However, near the end of his article, Sheringham suggests that paradoxically it is often 'des expériences romanesques où l'artifice du roman est souligné, ainsi que son manque de coïncidence avec le réel, qui témoignent d'une volonté de dire le quotidien'.[73] This statement indicates that, for Sheringham, the everyday might achieve a rich representation when portrayed as being in rebellion against the narrative order that the author seeks to impose on it. Sheringham's statements might be particularly relevant with regards to the everyday as represented in or theorized by the *Nouveau Roman*, in such texts as Sarraute's *Planétarium* or Robbe-Grillet's *Trois Visions Refléchies*. The contemporary novel may owe its fascination with the everyday to this heritage. However, the assertion in the *Nouveau Roman* of the elusiveness of the everyday is connected to the greater agenda of portraying the indeterminacy of the literary text itself, a goal which is certainly less prominent in the writing of the authors studied here.

Yet in all three texts examined in this chapter, the everyday is, in a certain sense, represented as being beyond the grasp of the novel. For Carrère and Savitzkaya especially, its representation is carried out through a dethroning or unhoming of the narrating voice. While they seek authentically to transcribe the everyday, they are each obliged to assume a stance of reticence, since this domain evades the narrative orders which seek to possess it. In all three texts, a moment of representational breakdown, or a forcefulness attributed to the familiar, reveals the incapacity of certain collective or narrative structures to account for it. The notion of an uncanny authorial position will be developed in the final chapter of this book, where the concept comes to found a possible ethics of non-fiction.

By bringing the disconcertedness and estrangement of the uncanny into proximity with the landscapes of home and day-to-day life, all three authors elaborate a similar configuration of the representation of strangeness in the literary text. As was suggested in the previous chapter, within their work, the strange often appears to emanate from the familiar itself, giving the impression that the known

---

[73] Ibid, p. 259.

world has transformed, throwing the subject's way of dwelling in everyday life into question.

The uncanny is also a concept which may be seen to illuminate these authors' particular approaches to the 'return' to the banal in contemporary French writing. As was suggested in the introduction to this chapter, many of today's writers inscribe within their narratives an attention to the space of the everyday. For NDiaye, Carrère and Savitzkaya, the absurdity or enchantment of this domain is an object of particular interest and an important source of narrative inspiration.

De-familiarization[1]

In his book *L'Inconscient de la maison,* Alberto Eiguer alludes to the positive emotional resonances called to mind by the notion of kinship: 'La filiation évoque un sentiment unique sinon exceptionnel d'intimité, de confiance et de compréhension réciproques'.[2] However, in the post-Freudian era we are also highly conscious of the *unheimlich* nature of family relations. Since the discoveries of psychoanalysis, there is a sense that underneath apparently normal family interaction and relationships lies a secret story of irresolvable tensions. With the popularization of concepts such as the Œdipus complex within culture and literature, the family is now commonly viewed as both a pathway and an obstacle to the development of the subject.[3] Although it is supposedly the institution which nourishes the child's identity and facilitates her passage into the symbolic domain and the social community, the family also feeds the conscious and unconscious dynamics of repression, desire and hostility through which individuality is constituted. This dual perception of the home, as both wholesome and detrimental with respect to subjectivity, is reflected in Alain de Mijollai's description of the family in his book *Préhistoires de famille*:

> Dans notre société occidentale, même si des évolutions récentes
> ont un peu brouillé ce schéma, cet entourage, inclus dans le tissu
> d'une nation et d'une culture, possède un nom et une structure.
> C'est la 'famille', ou telle organisation artificielle qui, avec plus

---

[1] The hyphenation serves to distinguish this term from the notion of 'defamiliarization' as theorized by the Russian formalists, and also to accentuate the root 'familiar' and its connection to the word 'family', which is the theme of the present chapter.

[2] Alberto Eiguer, *L'Inconscient de la maison,* p. 117.

[3] For example, Steven Bruhm suggests that what distinguishes contemporary Gothic texts from the traditional Gothic is that they demonstrate an explicit awareness of Freudian rhetoric and the role of the unconscious, especially in terms of the representation of family dynamics. He suggests that in today's writing, 'Freudian machinery is more than a tool for discussing narrative; it is in large part the subject matter of the narrative itself'. See Steven Bruhm, 'The Contemporary Gothic: Why We Need it', in *The Cambridge Companion to Gothic Fiction,* ed. by Jerrold E. Hogle (Cambridge: Cambridge University Press, 2002), pp. 259-76, p. 262.

ou moins de succès, prétend en adopter les caractéristiques. Toute reconnaissance, toute identification provient d'elle, d'un ou de tous ses membres, dans une suite de rapports qui oscillent sans cesse entre symbiose – c'est la racine même de l'identification, le rapport primitif à l'objet – et intrusion, forçage de ce 'facteur X' qui finalement spécifierait l'identité.[4]

De Mijollai's comments also evoke the increasing diversity displayed in the composition of today's family. Contributing to the concomitant strangeness and familiarity that now characterize visions of the family is the fact that its traditional Freudian structure is undergoing a transformation. In her book *La Famille en désordre,* Élisabeth Roudinesco addresses the current dissolution of the traditional Western nuclear family. The threat of the 'famille mutilée' is today a source of great uncertainty, which challenges dominant meaning and cultural institutions that depend on family-based ideologies to anchor their discourses.[5] Yet Roudinesco points out that, although it is currently evolving, the family is thriving and easily fulfilling its reproductive and societal functions. Furthermore, family-related social statuses and identities have never been more desired: '[La famille] est aimée, rêvée et désirée par les hommes, les femmes, et les enfants de tous âges, de toutes orientations sexuelles et de toutes conditions'.[6] It seems that, despite the family strangeness revealed by psychoanalysis and the constantly broadening definition of the family in society, we also remain attached, at the level of the collective imagination, to the ideas

---

[4] Alain de Mijolla, *Préhistoires de famille* (Paris: Presses Universitaires de France, 2004), p. 110.

[5] Recently much consideration of the family and home has been directed towards upsetting the stability of these terms as transcendental signifiers operating in favour of a particular ideological framework. For Michael J. Shapiro, political structures and cultural institutions depend on what he calls the 'neoconservative family imaginary'. Rather than an institution in and of itself, the nuclear family is, for Shapiro, a symbolic discursive structure, a myth of the collective imagination and a regulatory ideal. It has little connection to actual incarnations of the family, which are currently becoming more disparate. Shapiro considers that dominant ideology misrepresents the family by privileging its image as a naturally stable, heterosexual, nuclear unit. See Michael J. Shapiro, *For Moral Ambiguity, National Culture and the Politics of the Family* (Minneapolis, London: University of Minnesota Press, 2001), p. 2.

[6] Élisabeth Roudinesco, *La Famille en désordre,* p. 243. Roudinesco raises the point that even groups such as homosexuals who would have rejected the family institution in the past, considering it to be oppressive, are now seeking recognition within in it through structures such as the 'PACS' in France. Ibid, p. 7.

of home and family relations as positive sources of comfort through which to define the self.

Certain critics have suggested that a great part of the vitality of the contemporary French novel lies in its drawing inspiration from the family and exploring its complexities and repercussions for identity. For Christian Michel, within the contemporary French novel the theme of the family emerges from a background or contextual role to become an object of investigation in and of itself: 'La famille semble entrée, elle aussi, dans l'ère du soupçon'.[7] Michel further describes the family as represented in current fiction as a 'lieu instable qui menace de s'effondrer sur lui-même'.[8] The *récit de filiation,* associated with writers such as Marie Nimier, François Vigouroux or Pierre Bergounioux, constitutes a vibrant incarnation of the novel, and has roots in autobiographical fiction by Serge Doubrovsky, Annie Ernaux and Nathalie Sarraute. Often semi-autobiographical, these texts reflect an attempt on the part of the writer to come to terms with his or her origins and situate him or herself with respect to a parental figure or ancestor. The story of the other is a detour which leads back to the self. As Dominique Viart suggests, these texts often emphasize the uncertainties and shortcomings of the family, even though they arise from a willingness to approach or comprehend a relative: 'Le récit de filiation s'écrit à partir du manque: parents absents, figures mal assurées, transmissions imparfaites, valeurs caduques' (LFP 91). The complexities and difficulties of family relations come to the forefront not purely as an interrogation of the vicissitudes and traumas of home, but as a revelation of the confusion that characterizes an individual's attempt to comprehend the most familiar figures and the challenges inherent in representing them. As Viart proposes:

> Ces textes montrent bien à quel point le sujet contemporain se sent redevable d'un héritage dont il n'a pas véritablement pris la mesure et qu'il s'obstine à évaluer, à comprendre, voire à récuser. Le besoin de comprendre se lie ainsi à une interrogation de l'origine et de la *filiation.* Absence sans recours ou présence excessive, les figures paternelles et maternelles se dérobent au récit et impriment à la langue même une défiguration telle que l'écriture s'en trouve perturbée, et perturbante. Le sujet contem-

---

[7] Christian Michel, '"Le Réel dort aussi": un panorama du jeune roman français', p. 44.

[8] Ibid, p. 45.

porain s'appréhende comme celui à qui son passé fait défaut,
constat qui invalide la conscience sûre de soi et favorise les
égarements identitaires. (LFP 88)

The encounter with a familiar person exercises an estranging, unsettling effect on the self, in this case the writing subject, and this effect
is inscribed in the form or language of the representation itself.

Although they may not be *récits de filiation* in the strict sense,
the three novels examined in this chapter all reveal the presence of a
destabilizing impact on the self and on the writer's mode of representation, which results from the quest of a narrator or character to
come to terms with her origins or with a particular family member. In
Rosie Carpe, La Classe de neige and *Marin mon cœur,* close relatives
are a great source of uncertainty rather than reassurance. Approaching
or attempting to understand a sibling, parent or child reveals this
person's elusiveness, or even hostility, problematizing the individual's
relation to the outside world, rather than reinforcing identity and
generating feelings of comfort. NDiaye, Carrère and Savitzkaya all
portray ties of kinship as a context for interrogating the self, but also
as a source of ambiguity that may damage or disturb one's sense of
being *chez soi*, leading to self-estrangement.

This chapter will be an exploration of the ways in which
stories of most familiar people become stories of the strange. In
interpreting relations of kinship and subjectivity within the contemporary home, all three authors draw upon motifs of the uncanny. They
appeal to the themes of intellectual uncertainty, alterity, unhomeliness
or fragmentation in order to represent the turbulence and peculiarities
of child-parent relations in the contemporary world. In alignment with
Viart's observations concerning the *récit de filiation*, the interaction
with a familiar figure appears to exercise a deforming effect on each
writer's representational approach. Narrative expression and ordinary
environments as they appear in the novel are perturbed as a result of
family uncertainty. While in *Rosie Carpe* and *La Classe de neige* a
certain degree of monstrosity is attached to the parent, these
approaches are, once again, counterbalanced by Savitzkaya's narrative
tactics. In *Marin mon cœur,* a reinterpretation of the family dynamic
and the acknowledgement of the otherness of a familiar person are a
source of enchantment, poetry and innovation, rather than anxiety.

'*Où est ma famille?*': NDiaye's *Rosie Carpe*

In an interview granted to the literary magazine *Lire*, NDiaye compares the aesthetic of her novel *Rosie Carpe* (2001) to the strange yet familiar experience of standing extremely close to a painting. At a certain point, the coherent image is no longer visible and instead the spectator perceives a collection of 'petits points [...] Le dessin d'ensemble disparaît et la chose qu'on voit devient curieuse, bizarre, incompréhensible'.[9] This metaphor proposed by the author suggests that she considers her writing to be a transfiguration of our intuitive glance onto contemporary society and inter-subjective relations. In *Rosie Carpe*, the strangeness of certain characters or situations and the deformations of common reality reveal our contemporary world in the form of an arbitrary, chaotic collection of 'petits points,' absurd occurrences, signs and objects, which have renounced their former transparency. However, this metaphor might also provide a vivid image through which to conceive of the author's representation of family relations. In the visual domain, the reference to the 'petits points' denotes an uncanny moment of spectatorship, where the viewer's proximity to the image has an effect of estrangement in relation to a previously familiar form. The beholder gains awareness of the painting in its strange, resistant materiality and its refusal to form a coherent image. Likewise, in *Rosie Carpe,* the author's close-up interrogation of family life, is 'too close for comfort'. Despite the writer's intense concentration on family dynamics and the plethora of familial signifiers that form the content of this narrative, the homely, identity-affirming associations we might have with the notions of kinship are continuously revealed to be mythical. Through the ambivalence and simultaneity of codes of strange and familiar and an emphasis on the shortcomings and hostility of family relations, the family emerges as a fundamentally *unheimlich* phenomenon. Ties of kinship, supposedly the closest relations one can have, are portrayed as those most capable of unsettling or even annihilating the self. For Rosie Carpe, who desires nothing more than a sense of origin and to know her place within the family unit, a loss of meaning and a sense of fear ensue from every movement towards home.

---

[9] Catherine Argand, 'Entretien avec Marie NDiaye', *Lire* 294 (April 1, 2001), p. 35.

A monstrous family

Rosie Carpe recounts the life story and family quest of a young woman, banished from her family home following her scholarly failures in Paris. Rosie endures a series of traumatic experiences, miserable jobs in the suburbs, unwanted pregnancies and periods of severe alcoholism, before traveling to Guadeloupe with her son, Titi, in an attempt to retrieve and reunite her lost family. The action unfolds primarily in Guadeloupe, although the character's youth and young adult life in France are later reconstituted for the reader in a lengthy flash-back. Although the fantastic does not intervene as directly in *Rosie Carpe* as it does in *La Sorcière*, a macabre, surreal atmosphere dominates the text and renders the narrative events opaque and dreamlike. Following *La Sorcière,* this subtly fantastic mood is often the result of the author's tendency to accentuate the nightmarish elements of ordinary reality. The island of Guadeloupe is depicted as a debased tropical inferno, full of consumer-driven, leathery-skinned holiday-makers, 'de vieillards hâlés, musclés, candidement vêtus de slips miniscules, de soutiens-gorge panthère'.[10] The sun and the heat are suffocating, rather than welcoming, as they only intensify the odours 'de décomposition, de pourriture déjà faite' (RC 204) and provoke nausea and anxiety.

Rosie Carpe represents well the author's tendency to reintroduce and re-appropriate more traditional novelistic features such as plot, linear temporality, character development and symbolism. In his review of the novel in *Le Monde,* Pierre Lepape observes this return to the novelistic in *Rosie Carpe*:

> Voilà en tout cas un roman à qui l'on ne pourra faire le reproche de ne pas être romanesque. Il s'en passe des choses dans *Rosie Carpe*! Il y a des intrigues multiples, des personnages qui vivent des aventures, des rebondissements, des surprises, de la couleur, des décors, des atmosphères, des sentiments et même des meurtres.[11]

The theme of the family constitutes one such revived feature. *Rosie Carpe* displays and manipulates elements of realism, family melodrama and even mythology and biblical narrative to produce

---

[10] Marie NDiaye, *Rosie Carpe* (Paris: Éditions de Minuit, 2001), p. 178. All other references are given in the text, following the abbreviation RC.

[11] Pierre Lepape, 'Meurtre au paradis', *Le Monde des livres* (March 9, 2001), p. 2.

alarming contemporary incarnations of parent-child and sibling relations. The action is situated almost entirely within the family context, to the degree that all other elements of character and plot are relegated to the background so as to bring this family scene into the spotlight. We learn very little, for instance, about Rosie's studies in Paris or her day-to-day experiences outside the family dynamic. It is entirely with respect to their familial roles that the writer depicts the realities of Rosie and others. Yet this close focus on family-related emotions, scenarios and identities follows a distressing and para-doxical logic in the novel. Although the family dominates the plot and obsesses the characters, it appears in the story primarily as an absence. The yearning for family and home is evident in the frequent ponderings made in passing by various characters, who can never quite seem to unify or retrieve their families: 'Où sont mes enfants?' or 'Où est ma famille?' are fragments of this form of nostalgic dialogue that recurs throughout the novel.[12] The comfort of the family is experienced solely as the object of a quest on the part of these individuals.

As we observed in connection with *La Sorcière* in the previous chapter, in NDiaye's fictional world, the family appears fundamentally flawed, dysfunctional and threatened by dismem-berment. As we shall see, the author appears to propose a distortion, or renewal of codes of representation for the family by depicting betrayal, abandonment, incest and enmity as banal occurrences, pre-sent within the everyday reality of home. Every family in *Rosie Carpe* is dispersed or displays some transgression of family norms. Marriages are often cross-generational, defying traditional family hierarchies, or bordering on the incestuous. For example, Rosie's mother and father separate and begin relationships with a father and daughter respectively. At the end of the novel, the daughter, Lisbeth, leaves Rosie's father to marry Titi, this man's grandchild. This incessant reconstruction of the various ties between members of the 'family unit' causes it to appear as an impossible ideal, rather than a norm.

---

[12] See, for example, page 318 of the novel.

Family failures

Family members in *Rosie Carpe* are rarely capable of performing
gestures of kinship or fulfilling the duties expected of them by others.
During the course of the novel, Rosie experiences a series of family-
related disappointments. The first of these occurs in the opening
chapter when her brother, Lazare, fails to arrive at the airport in Point-
à-Pître to collect Rosie and Titi:

> Mais pas de Lazare, rien que de la confusion et de l'embarras,
> ensuite une sorte de colère mauvaise lorsqu'elle se rappela qu'elle
> était venue précisément pour en finir avec ces sentiments-là, de
> gêne et de honte, et c'était son frère Lazare qui les lui faisait
> éprouver de nouveau, alors qu'elle débarquait à peine et ne vou-
> lait, sur cette terre nouvelle, rien connaître de ce qu'elle quittait,
> en fait de tracas et de pesanteur. Voilà que son frère Lazare lui
> recollait le nez dedans, avant même de s'être montré, et voilà
> qu'elle était, encore et de nouveau, mortifiée. (RC 9-10)

Rosie's interior monologues, which figure abundantly, often display
this obsessive and ironic repetition of family members' names and
their supposed functions. The more Rosie reiterates Lazare's status as
brother, the more prominent is his absence and his failure to fulfill his
'brotherly' obligations. Although Rosie never gives up hope of reuniting with Lazare after their banishment from the family home, he is
a constant source of letdown. When he finally visits her in Paris in a
distraught and penniless state, she is overjoyed and rushes out to
spend her month's earnings, buying him food and new clothes.
However, this 'sisterly' gesture, perhaps a sign of Rosie's attachment
to the idea of recreating a family life with her brother, is not met with
gratitude. When she returns home from the supermarket, Lazare has
disappeared and broken into her boss's house, where he has made
himself at home. As Max tells Rosie: 'Il est chez moi, Rosie. Chez
moi et ma femme, à la maison. Il est même dans notre chambre, notre
lit […] Ton frère dort dans mon lit et ma femme est à moitié morte de
peur et elle s'est enfermée dans la cuisine' (RC 106). Later, Rosie is
saddened to learn that Lazare has left town, without even bidding his
sister good-bye.

In addition to their inability to fulfill the basic expectations of
others, most family members appear incapable of love, generosity,
sacrifice or affection. NDiaye represents the family not as a source of
sanctuary or warmth, but a site of passive violence. It seems that no

compassionate or mutually comprehensive inter-subjective relation is possible among family members. The cruelty of the family and absence of physical or emotional contact is often revealed in passing fragments of dialogue. Rosie's brother reports near the end of the novel: 'Ma sœur, je ne l'aurais touchée pour rien au monde' (RC 312). When Rosie is an older woman in the final chapter, living with her son, Titi tells Lagrand: 'Personne ne s'approche de Maman. C'est la règle. Je ne veux pas que les gosses la touchent et je ne veux pas qu'elle mange à notre table' (RC 328).

These affective deficiencies are especially pronounced in the parent-child relationship. Rosie and Lazare's parents abandon their children after they become wealthy through the stock market and move to Guadeloupe. Rosie's mother refuses to acknowledge her maternal responsibility towards her children, as she tells Lazare's friend Lagrand: 'Mes deux grands enfants ne me manquent pas […] Je me suis détachée d'eux […] J'ai eu une vie dont ils faisaient partie, puis j'ai une autre vie, toute neuve, qui ne leur appartient pas' (RC 207). Lazare later becomes a neglectful father himself and hardly acknowledges the existence of his daughter, Jade, or even that of the child's fifteen-year-old mother. Rather than encouraging the child's development and his or her integration into society, the family forestalls it, having lost its supposed capacity to transmit positive values or traits. This is expressed in Rosie's frequent reflections concerning her parents: 'Brive et les parents Carpe leur avait si peu appris, si peu légué, hormis la gêne, la docilité, et une sorte de béance maussade et défiante devant les imprévus de l'existence' (RC 59). Despite and perhaps also because of the intense concentration on family identity and roles in the novel and the prevalence of familial designators, none of the characters come close to fulfilling adequately their roles as fathers, mothers, brothers and sisters.

Disconcerting mothers

The fearsome quality attached to certain family members, and the failure of these characters to live up to received roles or familial prototypes, are most pronounced in descriptions of the mothers in the narrative. The impossibility of motherhood appears to be the fundamental problematic of NDiaye's fictional world. The image of the maternal might generally be perceived as evoking the ultimate site of home. However, this image is incarnated very differently in *Rosie*

Carpe, where mother figures tend to reinforce and emblematize the characters' more general troubles of origin.

Completely counter to the image of the self-sacrificing, eternally generous, life-sustaining mother, the mothers in *Rosie Carpe* are anxiety-provoking and a source of great damage to the child.[13] Rosie's own mother is not only neglectful, but also one of the most disconcerting figures in the novel. Without being manifestly demonic or ghostly, Madame Carpe subtly defies natural law by appearing never to age and by becoming pregnant with another child at retirement age. She often surfaces in the midst of a yellow hue, with her 'effroyable ventre jaune' (RC 205), surrounded by an unpleasant vegetal odour. She also has a fluctuating identity and changes her name when she moves to Guadeloupe, to correspond with her new life-style as the owner of an apartment complex in a holiday resort. As she tells Lagrand: 'Il n'y a plus de Danielle Carpe, monsieur Lagrand. Il n'y a plus que Diane, gérante de la Perle des Iles, future jeune maman de nouveau' (RC 197).

Rosie also embodies this impossibility of the maternal. After her banishment from the family home, she takes on a miserable hotel job in the suburbs. Seduced by Max, the obnoxious hotel manager, she conceives her son, Titi, under the gaze of a camera during the production of a pornographic film. As a result of the circumstances of the child's conception and perhaps of her own mother's nonchalance towards her, Rosie repeats these maternal failures herself and is unable to care for her sickly, unloved son. On the second page of the novel we witness Rosie's lack of compassion towards the child and the feelings of embarrassment he evokes in her, rather than maternal tenderness:

> Qu'allait penser Lazare, se demanda-t-elle, lorsqu'il arriverait enfin et découvrirait cet enfant maigre et pâle, aux jambes si blanches, si osseuses, sous le large short colonial [...] Son frère Lazare verrait un petit monsieur de six ans démodé et fragile [...]

---

[13] Barbara Johnson suggests that the concept of motherhood in our culture connotes the very opposite of violence: 'a recourse against it and a refuge from it'. However, such an image of the maternal is a collective myth, which conflicts with reality in a world in which there is child abuse. She says that this reduction of the concept of motherhood to self-sacrifice is itself violent: 'The very exclusion of violence is itself violent'. Barbara Johnson, *Mother Tongues* (Cambridge, Massachussetts and London: Harvard University Press, 2003), pp. 77-8.

(RC 10)

There are frequent descriptions of the child's unsightly physical characteristics, which lead Lazare and Lagrand to refer to him as 'Barbapapa': his unusually large head, his constant heat-induced nose-bleeds, his overly prominent veins, signs of 'son sang pauvre' (RC 33). Titi's unusual appearance seems to incarnate his mother's lack of love towards him and invites a similar rejection on the part of other characters.

Two particular occasions on which Titi has near-death experiences poignantly reveal Rosie's lack of maternal instinct and secret desire for Titi to cease to exist. The first episode occurs when Titi is still an infant and Rosie suddenly discovers she is no longer able to breast-feed the child, having inexplicably run out of milk. She leaves him in his crib to cry until finally Max, Titi's father, discovers him and rushes him to the hospital, where he is diagnosed with severe dehydration. Later Titi becomes ill after eating guavas contaminated by rat urine. Although Rosie appears to acknowledge his condition, she is trapped in a strange state of impotence and cannot bring herself to take him to the hospital. This time, Lagrand intervenes and rushes the child to emergency, while Rosie entertains the notion that Titi has passed away: 'Pas question que je revoie Titi, de toute ma vie [...] Il n'y a plus de Titi, dorénavant, pour Rosie Carpe' (RC 285). Titi's death appears to be the condition necessary for Rosie to found her own life. She views it as a kind of sacrifice, and imagines Titi as 'son misérable agneau qu'elle avait laissé aux Grands-Fonds pour qu'il y subisse le sort qui est celui des agneaux' (RC 292).

Rosie has three maternal opportunities in the novel and each time she manifests her incapacity to prolong or promote life. After Titi's birth she discovers she is pregnant again, following relations she has had with a neighbour, and she has an abortion. Her third pregnancy is an enigma, since she cannot recall having been with any man. Given the frequent allusions in the novel to Rosie's former name, Rosie-Marie, and the abundant biblical references and other saints' names, such as Lazare, the obscurity surrounding the pregnancy suggests an ironic incarnation of Immaculate Conception. Near the end of the novel, this last child is lost when Rosie has a miscarriage.

Another disconcerting maternal figure in the novel is
Lagrand's mother. We learn of Lagrand's hostile feelings towards this
person, who abandoned him at a young age, and the complexes this
experience has instilled in him. His own solitary childhood perhaps
explains his sympathy towards Titi and his repeated urges to rescue
him from Rosie's neglect. Near the end of the novel, Lagrand visits
his mother at the psychiatric hospital, where she is being detained, in
the hope that she will recognize him as her son. When she sees
Lagrand, she laughs and, although she affirms that she is indeed his
mother, she refuses to acknowledge the uniqueness of their relationship and imagines that all the patients in the psychiatric unit are her
sons as well: 'Tous les fils m'appartiennent' (RC 277). The theme of
motherhood, like that of the family more generally, is ironically
incorporated into the story. This woman is everyone's mother and yet
not a mother to her real son.[14] We are confronted with multiple
mothers, but there are no confidence-inspiring maternal behaviours.

As in *La Sorcière*, part of the aesthetic discomfort the reader
experiences in *Rosie Carpe* results from the author's technique of
writing against the attachment the reader might have to notions of the
family as a stable, nurturing environment and portraying it instead as a
source of malignance and disillusionment.[15] NDiaye's alarming por-

---

[14] In this case, NDiaye's representation of motherhood is not so much a complete
subversion of the self-sacrificing mother myth as one which eludes common
prototypes of motherhood, by oscillating between too much and not enough. E. Ann
Kaplan examines the prevalence of melodramatic portrayals of the mother figure in
popular culture and television from a Lacanian perspective. She suggests that the
institutional, familial and religious codes that surround us are deeply embedded in the
patriarchal unconscious and thus tend to construct the mother in ways which confirm
existing images of motherhood. She deems a text to be 'complicit' if it represents the
mother from the perspective of the patriarchal fantasy, that is, in accordance with
myths of the mother figure as either saintly and self-sacrificing or phallic and evil. In
opposition to this melodramatically inscribed mother, who obeys this polarized logic,
Kaplan presents a series of texts and films which she considers to be 'resisting' texts,
defying mythic paradigms. She is interested in finding innovative subjective positions
for the mother so that motherhood as a concept is not essentialized. However, while
Kaplan's proposed framework offers an interesting description of possible representations of motherhood, in my view this theory is not entirely applicable to
NDiaye's work. See E. Ann Kaplan, *Motherhood and Representation: The Mother in
Popular Culture and Media* (London and New York: Routledge, 1992), p. 125.
[15] Of course it could be argued that today's readers are no longer attached to such
family ideals. Since modernism, and writers such as André Gide, the family has been
represented in literature as failing to adhere to the values, myths and emotional

trait of the contemporary family exaggerates its cruelties and insufficiencies, yet presents those distortions as the norm by dispersing these qualities throughout an entire family saga. She thus infuses ordinary family dynamics with a subtle monstrosity. Like the 'petits points' in the author's aesthetic metaphor, the plentiful fathers, mothers, brothers and sisters in the novel all assume a certain opacity. They refuse to adhere to the reader's most basic expectations of moral and human decency among family members or comply with structural norms of the family. The family is simultaneously abundant and absent, excessive and lacking. The more profuse and banal these terms become, the more frighteningly deficient the individuals in the novel appear. Yet this portrayal of the family as hopelessly deficient is not simply a pessimistic affirmation of declining family values or broken family myths. In her article on the representation of the family in contemporary French women's writing, Shirley Ann Jordan proposes that the 'conspicuous superfluity'[16] of family-oriented themes and terminology in NDiaye's works serves to promote the reader's inclination to reflect on ties of kinship and familial roles, asking questions such as: 'What does it mean to stand in a particular role relationship to another family member – to be a 'sister', 'mother', 'father', 'aunt', etc? What are the programmes of action, the tacit contracts which are understood to adhere to these roles within the moral framework of the family?'[17]

This dualism of overload and shortage that founds the representation of the family is also apparent on the level of symbolism. There are numerous signs and images in the novel, but they appear to be deprived of their usual evocative value. This is seen in the religious theme that runs throughout the narrative. The reader observes frequent biblical references, such as the theme of Immaculate Conception and the names of Saints or other religious figures.[18] Churches and hymns

---

resonances we might associate with it. However, the dialogue between family ideals and particular family incarnations is very striking in NDiaye's writing, especially since her characters appear so attached to, and indeed obsessed by, the mythical, Bachelardian images of home as a nurturing, re-assuring place.

[16] Shirley Ann Jordan, 'Figuring Out the Family: Family as Everyday Practice in French Women's Writing', in *Affaires de famille. The Family in Contemporary French Culture and Theory* (Amsterdam, New York: Rodopi, 2007), pp. 39-58, p. 57.

[17] Ibid, p. 57.

[18] Lazare has a friend named Abel for example.

often figure in the background décor.[19] However, due to the heartlessness of the family and the excessiveness and vulgarity of the
Caribbean holiday environment that constitutes the backdrop for the
novel, there is also a sense that nothing is sacred and that no faith or
goodwill of any kind exists.

This irony is also present in the employment of certain literary
symbols. The family, as a missing place of origin and comfort which
might provide a locus for meaning and the construction of selfhood, is
perhaps symbolized by the magnolia tree from the Carpe family's first
home in Brive-la-Gaillarde. While this tree has great significance for
Rosie's brother, who regularly alludes to it and remembers it in detail,
Rosie cannot recall that such a tree existed:

> Lazare, plus tard, dirait à Rosie qu'il avait le regret profond, dou-
> loureux, de l'énorme magnolia de Brive, qui chaque printemps
> ouvrait dans leur jardin ses fleurs blanches, épaisses, aux durs
> pétales empesés et duveteux, il lui dirait encore que le bonheur à
> Brive avait pour lui les couleurs de ce magnolia inodore et un peu
> raide sur leur bout de pelouse maigre. Rosie, elle, ne se
> souviendrait d'aucun magnolia, de nulle splendour douteuse. (RC
> 53)

Portrayed as a missing token of familial happiness and harmony, and
as an object of disagreement between Rosie and her brother, the
magnolia tree is a central, yet absent emblem in this novel. While a
description of an ancient and magnificent tree might have evoked
ideas of rootednes, lineage and family solidarity, this magnolia symbolizes both the impossibility of communication among members of
the Carpe family and its failure to incarnate mythical family values.
The tree's 'durs pétales', 'splendour douteuse' and the adjectives
'inodore' and 'raide' evoke a waxy, artificial tree, rather than an
organic 'tree of life'. The tree's fictional status is thus accentuated,
suggesting the irony of nostalgic or melodramatic family values in the
context of the Carpe family. NDiaye's tendency simultaneously to
subscribe to and to reject more traditional narrative practices, such as
symbolism, has been frequently discussed within recent criticism.
Pierre Lepape says of her approach: 'Le roman contient toujours une
critique du roman comme sens commun littéraire; du roman comme

---

[19] See, for example, pages 28-9 of the novel. Upon her arrival in Guadeloupe, Rosie
waits in the truck with Lagrand for Lazare's new family to finish their church service.

narration qui va de soi'.[20] NDiaye herself acknowledges this quality of her work: 'Je n'ai pas une stratégie de déception du lecteur, mais mon esprit me conduit naturellement vers des scènes ou des expériences qui déjouent les attentes que le roman classique aurait fait naître.'[21] Maud Fourton suggests that Marie NDiaye 'raconte la désuétude de la tradition romanesque, la met en récit'.[22]

Misrecognition and selfhood

The literary scenario in which a family member oscillates between the strange and the familiar is present across eras and genres and is often at the heart of a reflection on the self. A standard feature of Greek tragedy, for example, is the 'recognition scene' or *anagnorisis,* a moment when a character moves from ignorance, or nonrecognition, to acknowledgment of the other, often of kin.[23] Such scenes often involve a family member who has formerly appeared to another one with a different identity and is later 'recognized' by that individual for who they really are. An example of such an occurrence would be the experience of Clytamnestra in Aeschylus' *The Oresteia.* Her son, Orestes, poses as a stranger to her, bringing her news of his own death. She only recognizes Orestes when he later resurfaces to murder her. Frequently, the recognition that occurs is ruinous for the character, or accompanied by a tragic realization, as in the classic example of Œdipus, who discovers that the woman he takes to be his wife is his mother. However, in *The Poetics,* Aristotle linked such scenes to both *katharsis* and self-discovery.[24] In his catastrophic realization, Œdipus recognizes his true identity in relation to his family and the accuracy of the prophecy made about him.

---

[20] See Pierre Lepape, 'En panne de famille', *L'Atelier du roman 35* (September, 2003), 42-7 (p. 43).

[21] Alain Nicolas, 'Le Cœur dans le labyrinthe,' *Humanité* (1 February 2007), http://www.humanite.fr/2007-02-01_Cultures_Le-coeur-dans-le-labyrinthe (accessed 5 February 2007).

[22] Maud Fourton, 'Marie NDiaye, *Rosie Carpe*: du tant bien que mal au malgré tout', in *Christian Oster et cie, retour du romanesque,* ed. by Aline Mura-Brunel (Rodopi: Amsterdam, NewYork, 2006), pp. 49-63, p. 55.

[23] For an interesting psychoanalytic study of the recognition scene, see Bennett Simon, *Tragic Drama and the Family: Psychoanalytic Studies from Aeschylus to Beckett* (New Haven and London: Yale University Press, 1988), p. 52.

[24] Aristotle, *Poetics,* trans. by Kenneth A. Telford (Chicago: Henry Regnery Company, 1967; first published in 1961), pp. 26-27.

In her book *Roman des origines et origines du roman*, Marthe Robert advances the view that all novelistic writing contains resonances of Freud's 'family romance'.[25] The 'family romance' refers to the fiction that every child invents in order to overcome the disappointment experienced when the idyllic image of the parents, which supports the child's primary narcissism, begins to crumble. Within Freud's theory, one very early element of the plot of this fiction concerns the child's pre-Œdipal image of the parents. When her overestimated representation of these figures begins to be challenged by the realities of the external world, she unconsciously transforms them into strangers and on some level disowns them, doubting her origins. The child often develops a fantasy in which these parents are replaced by 'better' ones.[26] For Robert, the novel is deeply embedded in this great family disillusionment, which constitutes a decisive stage in the development of the self: 'qu'il soit populaire ou savant, ancien ou nouveau, classique ou moderne, il n'a de loi que par le scénario familial dont il prolonge les désirs inconscients'.[27]

The tragic recognition scene and the pre-Œdipal chapter of Freud's family romance develop according to opposing forms of logic. The first example features a person thought to be a stranger, who is revealed to be kin, whereas the second recounts the estrangement of a familiar relative. In both instances the equivocal quality that a loved one is found to possess brings about an unsettling of the self, but one which is connected to its discovery or development. The doubly strange and familiar quality of ties of kinship incarnated in these scenarios also underlies the experience of the heroine of *Rosie Carpe*. For Rosie, any reunion with a family member reveals his or her duplicitous nature. However, rather than providing a pathway for self-discovery, the experience of coming face-to-face with a family member only further unsettles Rosie's already troubled sense of who she is. As Sara Bonomo observes, the parental figure in NDiaye's novels provides a mirror for the inadequacy and disorientation of the

[25] See Marthe Robert, *Roman des origines et origines du roman* (Paris: Gallimard, 1981; first published in 1976).

[26] See Sigmund Freud, 'Family Romances', in *The Standard Edition of the Complete Psychological Works of Sigmund Freud*, Vol. IX (1906-1908), *Jensen's 'Gradiva' and other works*, trans. by James Strachey (London: The Hogarth Press and the Institute of Psychoanalysis, 1959), pp. 237-41.

[27] Marthe Robert, *Roman des origines et origines du roman*, p. 63.

self:

> C'est par rapport au parent que le personnage mesure sa propre
> inadaptation, sa propre insuffisance; c'est en le regardant et en se
> reflétant en lui qu'il évalue à quel point il est mal dans sa peau, à
> quel point il est perdu.[28]

The discussion of *Rosie Carpe* elaborated in the first part of this section primarily concerns the author's tendency to defamiliarize the familiar site of home, by distorting certain emotional, moral and novelistic codes of the family. The remaining portion of this study of the novel will be dedicated to an exploration of the repercussions of this familial strangeness for subjectivity, as manifested in certain peculiar encounters that Rosie has with her relatives. While the protagonist constantly turns to home in order to retrieve a sense of stability and origin, the greater her proximity to her family, the more foreign and impenetrable its members appear and the more they trouble her ability to feel at ease in the world around her.

The reader constantly perceives the tension between Rosie's apparently misguided illusions of the family as a nourishing institution, and so the solution to her anxieties, and its materialization in the fictional world as damaging and disparate. Since her rejection from her family home, Rosie's inner existence has been dominated by strange memories and grotesque images which appear to be symptommatic of her severance from home and from the community. She is portrayed as an unfortunate character, exaggeratedly flaccid and submissive, and suffering from an 'éternelle tentation d'hébétude' (RC 20). She often seems to be trapped in a curious stupor, staring blankly at other people, rather than acting or communicating. From the opening chapter, she is constantly ill at ease, perspiring and at odds with her environment: 'Sa peau la démangeait à la taille, là où le pantalon humide l'enserrait. De grosses gouttes salées perlaient à son menton, au bout de son nez qu'elle avait un peu long et fin […] Elle lui semblait flotter maintenant dans une poche d'eau aigre, irritante' (RC 27).

She is plagued by nostalgic, uncertain impressions of her childhood, 'une longue période constante, brumeuse, d'un jaune pâle

---

[28] Sara Bonomo, 'La Mise en œuvre de la peur dans le roman d'aujourd'hui: *Rosie Carpe* de Marie NDiaye', p. 219.

et uni, dans sa mémoire' (RC 90). Her disconcerting memories of her parents, from years ago in Brive-la-Gaillarde, are also surrounded in her mind by this strange yellow glow: 'Elle vit en esprit leur visage sévère nimbé de jaune, leur tête privée de tronc, pâle, froide, posée légèrement au cœur d'une gloire jaune éclatante' (RC 90). This colour also appears to cloak her self-perception: 'J'étais Jaune autrefois, disait-elle encore, lointaine, l'œil vide, ne se comprenant plus très bien et indifférente, vide' (RC 52).[29] Many of NDiaye's critics have contemplated the significance of the colour yellow in *Rosie Carpe*. As Maud Fourton points out: 'le jaune se signale d'abord comme une couleur ambivalente – à la fois la plus divine et la plus terrestre selon Kandinsky – simultanément symbole de l'or des dieux et du soufre de Lucifer'.[30] In this light, yellow would seem a suitable colour to express the vagueness of Rosie's general rapport with the outside world and, especially, of her family memories and sense of identity.[31]

Throughout the novel Rosie appears to suffer from a form of ontological uncertainty. Cut off from her family, she perceives herself as an invisible, phantom presence on the margins of the community, deprived of any real existence:

> Il semblait à Rosie que les regards la traversaient de part en part et que, si elle se trouvait devant un mur, c'est le mur qu'on voyait au-delà d'elle et non pas Rosie, grande silhouette emmitouflée et frissonnante, les cheveux tirés en arrière, les yeux pâlis de froid, le sourire incolore et qui semblait flotter juste devant ses lèvres indécises. (RC 82)

Rosie's detachment from her own smile is a sign of her symbolic alienation, her estranged sense of self and her distance from the language and logic of the community. This exclusion is a constant obstacle for Rosie. Feelings of unreality and self-doubt are integrated into her general sense of being.

---

[29] Rosie also refers to herself as 'Rose-Jaune'.

[30] See Maud Fourton, 'Marie NDiaye, *Rosie Carpe*: du tant bien que mal au malgré tout', p. 58.

[31] The colour yellow also prevails in every description of Rosie's mother in the novel. In this case the ambivalence evoked by the colour might qualify Rosie's uncertain relation to this woman which will be described in more detail further on. Despite Madame Carpe's threatening manifestations in the novel, Rosie appears to remain attached to her as a source of comfort and identity.

Rosie often turns to the idea of family as the only means of resolving this confusion. Her lacking sense of origin, which constantly troubles her identity quest, is often evident in Rosie's inner thoughts. This self-interrogation is a perpetual, uncertain background to her daily activities. She yearns to retrieve a sense of identification with her proper name, and more importantly, with the surname that connects her to her family:

> Une jeune femme longeait les haies bien entretenues d'une petite rue paisible et discrètement cossue d'Antony. Rosie était cette toute jeune femme, nommée Rosie Carpe, qui marchait le long des haies de fusains en laissant courir sa main sur les grillages, les treillis. Elle savait qu'elle était Rosie Carpe et que c'était bien elle, à la fois Rosie et Rosie Carpe[32], qui marchait en ce moment d'un pas tranquille longeant les haies bien taillées de ce quartier résidentiel, silencieux, d'Antony. (RC 127)

The character's repetition of her own name suggests the absence of a stable relationship between the person and the name. The circularity of the syntax, in which Rosie finds herself in both the subject and predicate, reflects a confused moment of self-perception where the subject appears to be chasing unity and correspondence with its own ideal image and proper name. This circularity reflects Rosie's multiple failed attempts to come to terms with her familial origins. Her re-iteration of the surname Carpe suggests her ambiguous relationship to her family.

However, at moments when Rosie turns directly to the family as a means to reinstate a lacking sense of origin, her uncertainty is almost always intensified, since familiar characters reveal their foreignness and refuse to provide the certainty she seeks. Often this is related through a sense of duplicity in Rosie's emotional reaction to a family member. This is the case in the description of Rosie's much anticipated reunion with Lazare in Paris after a year of separation:

> C'était son frère Lazare. Il puait insupportablement. Elle se rapprocha de lui, l'entoura de son bras. Lazare était revenu, se disait-elle. C'était un fait que rien ne pouvait modifier ni altérer, pas même la honte qu'elle aurait de lui inévitablement, plus tard,

---

[32] Rosie's repetition of her name is both a desire to belong to the Carpe family and the expression of her distance from it since she was originally know as 'Rose-Marie' by her parents and became 'Rosie' only after leaving the family home.

> quand la joie serait retombée et qu'elle ne pourrait plus feindre
> qu'il était sans importance d'avoir retrouvé un frère Lazare qui
> sentait la pisse et qui ne s'était pas lavé ni changé depuis un an.
> Elle savait, tout en étreignant, qu'elle aurait honte de lui. Mais
> elle savait qu'il resterait Lazare au cœur même de la honte qu'elle
> ne pourrait manquer d'éprouver, son frère Lazare qui était revenu.
> (RC 101-2)

Rosie's encounter with Lazare reverses the logic of the tragic recognition scene. Rather than staging an encounter in which an outsider turns out to be a familiar relative in disguise, NDiaye often describes scenes in which a family member whom Rosie desires to 'recognize' and who she hopes will help her recognize herself, reveals a foreign or disconcerting aspect and prohibits the feelings of comfort she seeks. Rosie's meeting with Lazare hovers between repulsion and tenderness, shame and acceptance, affection and rejection. She is desperate to establish a familial bond and wishes to dwell in the joy of retrieving her long lost brother. However, she also experiences feelings of disgust. Despite her insistence on Lazare's disagreeable appearance, the last line of the passage suggests that more important than Lazare's shortcomings is the tie of kinship they share. Rosie insists on achieving this identification, even if it must take place 'au cœur même de la honte'.

Another encounter between the two siblings is in fact a 'misrecognition' scene, in which Rosie mistakenly recognizes another character as her brother. When Lazare is late to collect her and Titi in the airport upon their arrival in Guadeloupe, his friend Lagrand, whom Rosie has never met, arrives instead. As if in a dream, Rosie believes this man is indeed Lazare, even though Lagrand is a black man. She appears to have the capacity to accept the fact that Lazare has simply transformed:

> Et qui était Lazare, qu'était-il devenu, Lazare, frère aîné? Il y
> avait maintenant cinq ans qu'ils ne s'étaient vus, depuis le jour où
> il avait choisi de s'exiler vers cette terre inconnue d'eux, dans
> l'espoir d'y prospérer. Mais, à présent, comment être certaine que
> celui-là n'était pas Lazare, avec sa peau sombre, ses cheveux ras à
> la ligne bien nette sur le front et les tempes? (RC 12)

Again Lazare appears to Rosie in an unexpected form and Rosie's prevailing desire to retrieve her brother seems to allow her to accept his failure to incarnate her expectations of him.

It is interesting to note that NDiaye often relates Rosie's thoughts using free indirect discourse, which generates some uncertainty as to the question of who is speaking. In the above passages, the author's exploitation of this type of discourse brings to the forefront the spontaneous, confused inner emotional reality of the character, giving the reader the impression of being in unusual proximity to Rosie's thoughts. The level of intimacy the reader achieves with the character's inner world generates the strange effect that this world has not yet been filtered through the narrative voice. This technique accentuates the uncanniness of the omniscient narrator as a disembodied figure who is everywhere at once, able to read the thoughts of all the characters.

The uncertainty that dominates Rosie's inner thoughts seems to proliferate, rather than dissipate, at moments where she must approach or interact with another family member. Although she constantly yearns to rediscover feelings of familiarity and her proper place within the family's configuration as a means to regain her sense of self, the closer she gets to its individual members, the stranger it appears and the more it further perturbs her already precarious ontological state. Despite her desire to reunite with Lazare in Guadeloupe, from the moment Rosie arrives at the airport in Pointe-à-Pitre with the promise of retrieving him, her physical state evokes fear and unease. The reader is aware of Rosie's inability to feel at home in her surroundings, even in her own body: 'Les poings serrés, elle se concentrait de toutes ses forces sur la nécessité de faire refluer la nausée' (RC 12). There are frequent references to her fear-induced discomfort, and these feelings are associated with Rosie's imminent encounter with home. Her physical and emotional stress is amplified when Lagrand is driving Rosie and Titi to Lazare's house: 'Le Toyota filait tout au long des cannes plaintives. L'anxiété revint d'un coup s'abattre sur Rosie, trempée de sueur. Elle percevait sa respiration bruyante et se sentait importune, sale, surabondante' (RC 20). As Bonomo observes, a striking feature of NDiaye's novels is 'l'équation que l'on y trouve entre l' "autre" en tant que déclencheur de peurs, et les membres de la "famille"'.[33] As well as suggesting Rosie's sense of fear and discomfort in relation to her family, this description of her

---

[33] Sara Bonomo, 'La Mise en œuvre de la peur dans le roman d'aujourd'hui: *Rosie Carpe* de Marie NDiaye', p. 218.

physical state echoes the Sartrian feeling of being 'de trop', as experienced by the protagonist of *La Nausée*. Rather than providing Rosie with a sense of 'fitting in' or finding her place, the encounter with family produces feelings of excessiveness and dispensability.

It is in the encounter with the parent, and in this case the mother, that we perceive the degree to which Rosie's family quest is tied up with an identity search that fails to produce answers. In a scene that immediately follows the free indirect discourse description of Rosie's identity struggle while walking along the street in Antony (cited above), she has an interaction with her mother in which this person's strange and familiar qualities coalesce to further dismantle Rosie's sense of self. On her morning stroll, Rosie discovers that the Carpe parents have a house in the very same suburban Paris neighbourhood where Rosie lives. She suddenly perceives her mother in the garden of this house after years of separation. As in the encounter with Lazare at the airport, Mme Carpe first embodies familiarity, but then elusiveness:

> C'était Mme Carpe, mais si différente de ce qu'elle avait été qu'elle aurait pu ne pas être Mme Carpe et qu'elle, Rosie, aurait pu alors se contenter d'un petit signe de tête accompagné d'un sourire d'excuse pour son indiscrétion, puis se détourner et poursuivre sa route. Mais les yeux sévères et petits, hardis, sûrs d'eux, étaient ceux de sa mère, les yeux, qui avaient la brillance et l'éclat inexpressif d'un verre bleuté, de la Carpe dont elle était issue, elle, Rosie qui tout à l'heure encore, dans le bien-être de sa marche, ne faisait qu'un avec Rosie Carpe. (RC 129)

This reunion with the mother is revealed to be unsettling rather than anchoring. The mother fluctuates between signifying origin, as 'la Carpe dont elle était issue', and foreignness, since she has changed so much that Rosie hesitates to identify her as her mother. This oscillation of the mother between strange and familiar qualities further problematizes Rosie's sense of self, since she now experiences herself as split, dislocated between Rosie and Rosie Carpe. Following the previous representation of mothers in the novel as capable of destroying their progeny, Mme Carpe's resistance to Rosie's instinct to recognize her, challenges the daughter's well-being and sense of identity, threatening the destruction of any sense of being *chez elle*.

Each attempt on the part of the protagonist to pin down her relationship to her family members and to obtain a sense of being rooted is destined to fail, since these familiar characters always reveal their strangeness. However, for NDiaye, despite this elusiveness inherent to the proximate other,[34] the family is also the primary measure of selfhood. A collision is generated between the desire and expectations of the protagonist, still very much attached to the notion of home as a site of comfort, and the manifestation of the family, which constantly sabotages these heartening associations. *Rosie Carpe* displays a constant disharmony between the character's attachment to the family as a place of reassurance, grounding and familiarity, and the incarnation of the family in the novel as violent, identity-destroying and inherently strange.

With *Rosie Carpe*, NDiaye achieves a similar aesthetic of discomfort to that produced in *La Sorcière*, only without appealing so directly to fantastic imagery. In *Rosie Carpe*, the reader experiences metamorphosis, the mutilated family and the beastliness of certain parents, but these themes are often transposed into a subjective inner reality which allows the atmosphere of the uncanny to emanate from Rosie's thoughts and impressions, often related through NDiaye's use of free indirect discourse, rather than from the level of narrative content. Rosie herself appears to dwell in an uncanny position with respect to the ordinary world. Once again, as in *La Sorcière*, these distortions or exaggerations of the less positive moments of family life, and the author's appeal to the motifs of the uncanny and codes of alterity to express the subject's relation to the family, are perhaps methods of figuring certain forms of strangeness that the author sees as present within contemporary society and inter-subjective relations.

The Family Secret: Carrère's *La Classe de neige*

Freud's etymological investigation uncovered the precariousness of the German *heimlich*, a term which first meant 'belonging to home' and then evolved to incorporate what is disclosed from the eyes of strangers, and thus 'hidden, secret'. Freud equated this second definition with that of the term *unheimlich,* which was 'foreign, gloomy, ghastly, uncomfortable': '[thus] *heimlich* is a word the meaning of

---

[34] 'L'autre proche' is Paul Ricœur's term for characterizing relatives. See Paul Ricœur, *La Mémoire, l'histoire, l'oubli* (Paris: Éditions du Seuil, 2000), pp. 161-63.

which develops in the direction of ambivalence, until it finally coincides with its opposite, *unheimlich*' (U 226). His decision to reduce the notion of secrecy to foreignness may have been somewhat hasty, since these two meanings are not synonymous. However, this simplification provided Freud with a semantic basis for his theory of the uncanny, which was centred on the castration complex, a phenomenon that is both *heimlich* and *unheimlich*, familiar, yet repressed in the adult psyche and thus experienced as foreign when called to mind by certain images.

Recent psychoanalytic readings of Freud's essay, however, have returned to the theme of secrecy, which was downplayed in Freud's account by being reduced to foreignness. Nicolas Rand and Maria Torok re-read Hoffmann's tale and attribute its uncanniness to the return of the family secret, rather than to the return of the repressed. In their interpretation, the theme of the eyes and the impairing of vision in the story are related not to the fear of castration, but to information that is hidden from Nathaniel concerning his family and the secret activities of his father and the lawyer, Coppelius. The frightening figure of the Sandman, whom the child equates in his fantasies with his father's acquaintance, and the ocular imagery in the narrative, represent 'the hero's thwarted attempt to see, to inquire, to discover'.[35] In a sense, Rand and Torok's analysis repeats Freud's mistake of attempting to isolate and reduce the uncanny by providing a one-dimensional interpretation of Hoffmann's tale.[36] In trying to challenge Freud's repression-based theory, they isolate the family secret as the primary source of uncanniness in the text and distinguish this idea from that of repression, perhaps overlooking the parallels that may exist between the two. After all, the family secret may well be 'repressed' and these two concepts are not necessarily clearly distinguishable.

However, Rand and Torok's exploration of the theme of secrecy as constitutive of uncanny experience reveals a point of over-

---

[35] Nicolas Rand and Maria Torok, 'The Sandman Looks at 'The Uncanny', in *Speculations after Freud, Psychoanalysis, Philosophy and Culture*, ed. by Sonu Shamdasani and Michael Münchow (London and New York: Routledge, 1994), pp. 185-203, p. 188.
[36] In their account, even the doll Olympia is reduced to an emblem for the family secret, as simply 'the embodiment of the dust thrown in Nathanael's eyes'. Ibid, p. 197.

lap for various interpretations of the uncanny. As in 'The Sandman', part of the strangeness of Emmanuel Carrère's novel *La Classe de neige* (1995) is due to its complex layering of different uncanny themes, including that of secrecy. In bringing the ideas of the secret and of intellectual uncertainty into proximity with the figure of the authoritative father, Carrère's novel reveals the uncanniness of the child's life-world and childhood experience, and the difficulty of separating one uncanny theme from another.

In *La Classe de neige*, the uncanny often appears to be an expression of incomprehensibility or a feeling induced by the prohibition of knowledge, and is a means for the author to figure the experience of the child, excluded from the 'rational' world of adults. Themes of bodily dismemberment and metamorphosis, which are dispersed throughout the story and occupy the main character's inner thoughts, appear to be products of young Nicolas's overactive imagination, and an amplification of everything that perplexes the child, everything he undergoes without being able to grasp it. As we shall see, the uncanny is both an expression of terror and a way for Nicolas to survive his immediate reality and keep fear at bay.

An uncertain world

Like *Rosie Carpe*, Emmanuel Carrère's *La Classe de neige* is a subtle horror story of the family. Discomfort, anxiety, abandonment and foreignness constantly undermine the qualities that might define more idealistic portraits of family life. Again, this novel features an anxiety-ridden anti-hero who suffers from problems of integration and is plagued by uncertainty as a result of strangeness within the home. At the same time, Nicolas is in search of home and seeks something from it that will contribute to his sense of self. However, NDiaye and Carrère express the strangeness of these uncanny families differently. NDiaye's approach involves the distortion of family roles and an exaggeration of the cruelty or heartlessness of family relations and particularly of the mother. Carrère's text exploits the themes of secrecy and suspense, which he attaches primarily to the absent and disconcerting father figure.

Although the author does not introduce explicitly fantastic events, he succeeds in attaching an unthematizable, anxious quality to the character's familiar environment. Seen through the eyes of Nicolas, an ill-at-ease 10-year-old, the ordinary world undergoes the distortion of a sensitive, childlike gaze. The young boy's childhood nightmares and uncertainties are multiplied when he leaves his family to participate in a school ski trip. Unable to integrate properly into the school community, he is plagued by youthful anxieties, such as his fears of bed-wetting and class bullying. These seemingly minor concerns assume the same proportions as his fear of his own death, or that of his loved ones, which also resurface in the form of fantasies throughout the narrative: 'Il mourrait de froid pendant la nuit. On retrouverait son corps au matin, bleu, durci par une fine pellicule de gel, presque cassant [...] Il faudrait prévenir ses parents. Toute l'école assisterait à son enterrement'.[37] A sense of danger hangs over Nicolas, a danger that cannot be located precisely, but that is felt from the very beginning of *La Classe de neige*. The questions of the precise origin and authenticity of this danger that threatens Nicolas are destined to plague the reader throughout the novel.

At times, it may appear to be an uncontrollable external danger. In the first chapter we learn of the tragic school bus accident in the community which has caused concern among the parents at Nicolas's school, who know that their own children are soon leaving for a school ski trip. There is also the story of the monstrous crime, recently committed in a nearby village, which the children learn about during the trip. The police are investigating the abduction and murder of a little boy, René, who is approximately Nicolas's age. The knowledge of this event weighs anxiously on the minds of Nicolas and his classmates.

At times, this danger may be an internalized exaggeration of Nicolas's day-to-day experience. He is fascinated by everything gruesome, and horrific thoughts prevail in his inner existence. He is constantly ready to extend the vividness of his fantasies to his external surroundings and seems to expect the worst from reality. When passing the scene of a minor car accident with his father, for example, he imagines 'les corps sanglants qu'on emportait sur les civières dans le tournoiement des gyrophares' (CN 11).

The sense of danger that pursues the protagonist is also incarnated by the many 'monsters' that surround Nicolas, all the more frightening because they are often very close to him, a parent or a

---

[37] Emmanuel Carrère, *La Classe de neige* (Paris: Folio, 1995), p. 75. All other references are given in the text, following the abbreviation CN.

peer. There is Hodkann, the bully of the class: 'Depuis le début de l'année, il avait une peur terrible que Hodkann le remarque, lui demande quelque chose, et à plusieurs reprises avait fait des cauchemars dans lesquels il le choisissait pour souffre-douleur' (CN 20). There are also the monsters in the horror stories found in the deliciously terrifying book, *Histoires épouvantables*, which Nicolas sometimes steals from his parents' bedroom.

Family dangers
Amongst the various sources from which this danger appears to emanate is Nicolas's own family. It may be tempting to blame Nicolas's fears on his sheltered childhood and overprotective mother and father. He is trapped in a parental grasp which appears to impede his development and his ability to make friends and feel part of his social milieu. He is not permitted, for example, to have his lunch at the school cafeteria, 'où survenaient souvent des bagarres' (CN 21). These protective impulses on the part of his parents, who take him home during the break each day, result in his alienation from his peer group:

> Pendant son absence on s'était envoyé des petits suisses à la figure, on avait été puni par les surveillants, on avait conclu des alliances et chaque fois, quand sa mère le ramenait, c'était comme s'il avait été nouveau et devait reprendre à zéro les relations nouées le matin. (CN 21)

The social consequences of this parental suffocation are further exposed in the second chapter when, out of concern for his safety, Nicolas's parents refuse to let him travel with the rest of the students on the school ski trip. Their insistence on transporting him to and from the destination, against the advice of the school psychologist and mistress, results in his feeling excluded from the group. This is apparent when the school mistress brings him to greet the other students: 'En franchissant le seuil derrière elle, il ressentait les pénibles impressions du nouveau à qui rien n'est familier, dont on va certainement se moquer' (CN 17). When Nicolas's father mistakenly drives away with his back pack, he experiences further humiliation, since he must borrow pyjamas from another pupil and is without ski equipment, and cannot participate in any of the winter activities with the other children. The inconvenience of the missing bag also means

Nicolas does not have the protective mattress cover necessitated by his bed-wetting problem, already a source of anxiety, so he must force himself to stay awake at night to avoid an accident. These difficulties of integration only worsen when Nicolas becomes ill with a fever, and must sleep in the office of the chalet, instead of in the dormitory with his fellow classmates. Perhaps it is partly this sense of fear instilled in him by his parents, along with his consequently marginal existence, that confer a tone of strangeness on his ordinary world.

A strange father
Aside from the exaggerated protectiveness of Nicolas's parents, which poses a challenge to Nicolas's ability to constitute his subjectivity in the social world, the child's uncertainty often appears to be linked to an unknown family secret. Nicolas is unable to see clearly into murky affairs within this family home, particularly in relation to his father. There is a feeling of something *unheimlich* in Nicolas's home, something which, to go back to Freud's essay, 'ought to have remained secret and hidden but has come to light' (U 224). The theme of secrecy is announced in the opening chapter when we learn that, for Christmas, Nicolas's father has given him a small trunk, 'pour [s]es petits secrets' (CN 10). The trunk has a lock that requires a code that only Nicolas knows. However, the most important secret in the novel is not his own, but concerns his father. This secret is constantly sensed by Nicolas, and throughout the novel we observe the boy's uneasiness when the question of his father arises. This is apparent, for example, when the schoolmistress attempts to contact his home to acquire a phone number or itinerary for his father, who is in possession of Nicolas's bag: 'Cet appel le mettait mal à l'aise. Ils en recevaient très peu, à la maison, et les rares fois où le téléphone sonnait, surtout en l'absence de son père, sa mère s'en approchait avec une angoisse visible' (CN 42). We also learn that, a few years previously, Nicolas's family suddenly left his childhood village for reasons that were unknown to him (CN 120). The father and the family home in *La Classe de neige* are endowed with an aura of mystery.

Nicolas's father is in fact missing throughout most of the novel and his character is conveyed primarily through Nicolas's childhood memories, which are dominated by disconcertedness. He recalls an inattentive, absent father, 'tout le temps sur les routes' (CN

27). He describes him as an elusive figure who would sleep for long periods of time and occasionally, upon passing Nicolas playing in the hallway, stop and stare at him 'avec inquiétude' (CN 35):

> Au crépuscule, leur père sortait de la chambre en pyjama, pas rasé, le visage maussade et bouffi de sommeil, les poches gonflées par les mouchoirs en boule et les emballages crevés de médicaments. (CN 35)

Nicolas has uncomfortable recollections of his father's affectionate mumblings at his bedside, and remembers how, at other moments, he behaved like a complete stranger:

> Il posait des questions bizarres, demandant par exemple à Nicolas en quelle classe il était. Nicolas répondait docilement et il hochait la tête, disait que ça devenait sérieux et qu'il fallait bien travailler pour ne pas redoubler. Il semblait avoir oublié que Nicolas avait déjà redoublé une fois, l'année où ils avaient déménagé. (CN 36)

The opening line of the novel prepares the reader for the possibility that this character's absence or disappearance may be the central problematic of the novel: 'Plus tard, longtemps, jusqu'à maintenant, Nicolas essaya de se rappeler les dernières paroles que lui avait adressées son père' (CN 9). However it is not until the end of the story that the reader is enlightened concerning the strange behaviour that Nicolas remembers. The ambiguous circumstances conveyed in the final chapters of the novel suggest that this man may have some connection with the brutal murder of René, the boy who recently went missing in the area. However, just like Nicolas, we are kept in the dark concerning the details and veracity of this crime; the adult reader is not permitted to transcend the child's point of view.

The father occupies an ambivalent role in Nicolas's mind. Just as he continuously oscillates between strange and familiar, he is also both too absent and too present, a source of humiliation and pride, of admiration and rejection. This dynamic of dualism is perhaps partially explained by the particular phase Nicolas is experiencing in his individual development. The novel takes place at a time of change and conflict in the evolution of this boy's identity, a time when the family is both desired and oppressive. Although Nicolas remains attached to his parents, a fact which is evident in his reluctance to leave home for the school trip, he is also beginning to experience their omnipresence

as claustrophobic and is forging new relationships, seeking to
distinguish himself from his family. In the first chapter of the novel,
when he is dropped off for the school ski trip, we learn of Nicolas's
discomfort with respect to his father:

> Il lui dit au revoir à la porte du chalet, répéta des conseils de
> prudence, mais Nicolas était tellement gêné de sa présence, il
> avait tellement hâte de le voir repartir qu'il n'avait pas écouté. Il
> lui en voulait d'être là, d'attirer des regards qu'il devinait
> moqueurs et s'était dérobé, en baissant la tête, au baiser d'adieu.
> (CN 9)

However, Nicolas is at other times extremely proud of this man. He
later reveals his admiration for his father's profession as a medical
sales representative when his classmate, Hodkann, inquires about his
job.

We also learn that Nicolas both desires and fears his father's
death. He admits to being jealous of Hodkann, whose own father's
death is an asset to his social status in the class, 'la source de son
prestige', and with whom the schoolmistress is overly lenient (CN
102). However, he is also saddened and afraid to think that his own
father may have been killed in a road accident, which would explain
his failure to return to the ski chalet with Nicolas's bag: 'Peut-être la
voiture avait-elle glissé sur une plaque de verglas, embouti un arbre, et
son père agonisait, la poitrine défoncée par le volant' (CN 44). Such
fantasies are often accompanied by a certain degree of guilt, as he
fears that thinking such thoughts may render the event of his father's
death more likely: 'Ce serait atroce. Il serait non seulement orphelin,
mais coupable, terriblement coupable. Ce serait comme d'avoir tué
son père' (CN 61).

Foreign experiences

Nicolas's partial detachment from his father is facilitated when he
finds a new role model in Patrick, the ski instructor who befriends him
at the beginning of the trip and gives him a Mexican bracelet in the
first chapter. Patrick represents the beginning of Nicolas's liberation
from his parents. When Patrick takes him shopping for ski clothes,
Nicolas enjoys being permitted to do things he could never do at
home, such as sitting in the front of the car and listening to loud guitar
music: 'il aurait voulu que sa vie entière soit ainsi. Voyager toujours à

l'avant des voitures en écoutant ce genre de musique, et plus tard ressembler à Patrick: aussi bon conducteur, aussi à l'aise, aussi souverainement libre de ses mouvements' (CN 51).

The emotional richness of this period in Nicolas's development is exhibited in a dream he has one night in the dormitory. He relives a day he spent at a theme park with his father, but Patrick replaces this man and takes him on the caterpillar ride that his father had prohibited. This dream has blissful, erotic overtones for Nicolas, who wishes he could perpetuate this exhilarating experience and the physical proximity to the ski instructor it permits: 'le ventre de Patrick contre son dos, ses cuisses autour des siennes, son souffle dans son cou, et le vacarme, et le creux, et le ciel' (CN 66). It is through this dream that we learn that fantasy and fiction are often ways for Nicolas of coping with the traumas and absurdities of growing up and with secrets, both those he wishes to hide from others and those he desires to know. When he awakens to find 'une colle humide entre son corps et le drap', he fears his stomach has opened and that blood is pouring from his body. He feels terribly alone and, for the first time, has his own secret: 'Il sentait, dans l'obscurité, son visage se crisper, ses yeux s'écarquiller d'effroi à l'idée qu'il lui arrivait quelque chose d'affreux qui n'était jamais arrivé qu'à lui, quelque chose de surnaturel' (CN 68). In a sense, the anxiety of this experience is also related to the absent father, since Nicolas's confusion and fear imply that his father has never discussed the onset of puberty and its symptoms with him or prepared him for the changes that would occur.

For Nicolas, imagery of the uncanny is often a way of expressing the incomprehensible nature of childhood experience. When faced with the unknown, Nicolas turns to imagery he recalls from literature as a means to come to terms with alterity. Confronted with the foreignness of his own body, he recalls a terrible tale he read in *Histoires épouvantables* in which a man swallowed a magic elixir, which caused his body to 'se décomposer, se liquéfier, se transformer en un magma noirâtre et visqueux' (CN 68). But this gruesome fantasy, which reinforces his fear, evolves into a warmer, more comforting image when he recalls a passage from the story of *The Little Mermaid* where the Mermaid's tail is transformed into legs so that she might win the heart of the prince: 'A tâtons, elle glissait les mains le long de son corps et là, sous le nombril, où depuis sa naissance commençaient ses écailles, la peau, la si douce peau continuait' (CN 74). Imagination and fiction thus intensify Nicolas's trepidation, but also alleviate it, by postponing or circumventing his real experiences and making him feel less alone.

The fragmented body

Nicolas's fantasies nearly always involve bodily imagery. One of his favourite stories, also from the stolen book of horrific tales, is that of a son chopped into pieces and delivered to his parents by his killers. In the first chapter of the novel, we learn of his general fascination with anatomy and that he collects Shell petrol coupons in the hopes of accumulating enough of them to win a plastic figure whose body opens to reveal its internal organs. We know that Nicolas routinely sneaks into his parents' bedroom to read the medical book they keep on a shelf above their bed. His fantasy world, an extension of this interest in the body, is centred on the theme of the fragmented, mutilated or mutating body.

For Freud, dismembered limbs and images of severed heads or hands were highly uncanny and constituted various incarnations of the castration complex (U 244). He thought the proximity of the paternal theme to that of the mutilation of the eyes in Hoffmann's tale evoked the myth of Œdipus, who was blinded after killing his father. For Lacan, the 'imago' of the fragmented body, which includes visions of castration, harks back to a traumatic moment in the construction of subjectivity, which precedes the construction of the ego.[38] However, it seems that what renders Nicolas fearful is not so much a type of castration, as it is a sense of impotency that results from being excluded from the adult world and from his peer group and lacking the

---

[38] In *Vocabulaire de la psychanalyse*, Laplanche and Pontalis define the term 'imago' as: 'Prototype inconscient de personnages qui oriente électivement la façon dont le sujet appréhende autrui; il est élaboré à partir des premières relations intersubjectives réelles et fantasmatiques avec l'entourage familial'. See J. Laplanche and J.B. Pontalis, *Vocabulaire de la psychanalyse*, ed. by Daniel Lagache (Paris: Quadridge/PUF, 1967), p. 196. For Lacan, during the mirror phase, the child perceives its body on the specular register as whole, but experiences it as fragmented. The ego is formed through identification with the complete specular self. Even after the construction of the ego, the subject continually oscillates between these images of wholeness and fragmentation, between the unified image and the real body in pieces. This sense of fragmentation may be expressed in images of mutilation, castration, the bursting open of the body and dismemberment. See Jacques Lacan 'Le Stade du miroir comme formateur de la fonction du "Je"' and 'L'Agressivité en psychanalyse', in *Écrits* (Paris: Éditions du Seuil, 1966), pp. 101-24, p. 104.

knowledge that they possess and refuse to impart. For Nicolas, fantasies of fragmented bodies seem to be both a coping strategy for, and the expression of, the incomprehensible, or of what Nicolas is not allowed to know. Versions of this fragmented body fantasy occur at various moments throughout the novel when Nicolas is curious or uncertain about something. When he fantasizes about Hodkann's father's death, for example, he imagines him 'mort de façon terrible, démembré ou jeté dans un puits' (CN 39). Although Nicolas visualizes a bodily attack, this experience of fragmentation is nearly always linked to his inability to comprehend. In her analysis of the uncanny, Cixous suggests that intellectual uncertainty, the hypothesis that Freud rejected, and the experience of being deprived of one's ability to reason, or to make sense of one's environment, are themselves forms of intellectual 'castration':

> Bizarrement, Freud lui-même semble ne penser la castration qu'en termes de castration 'proprement' dite, portant sur une partie du *corps*, que ce soit le pénis ou un substitut du pénis, à l'exclusion d'une 'castration' intellectuelle. Or, si Coppélius menace les 'yeux' de l'enfant, ce qu'il menace en même temps, c'est tout de même sa raison, ce sont les yeux de l'esprit. C'est en crevant la raison et non ses yeux que Coppélius [...] fait plonger ou plonge Nathaniel dans les ténèbres, dans la mort (PP 102-3).

While the parallel Cixous establishes between the castration complex and the ambiguity of intellectual uncertainty might seem a bit of a jump, her evocation of the sense of threat or confusion experienced by an unknowing subject reflects Nicolas's plight. The theme of bodily fragmentation is perhaps emblematic of the disjointedness and uncertainty of the world as it might appear to Nicolas. As a child, and especially one who is plagued with family secrets, Nicolas only has access to fragments of adult reality. On several occasions we sense his frustration at being deprived of the 'whole story'. One example is the police investigation concerning René, the missing child. Due to his illness, Nicolas must wait in the lodge café while the other children take their ski lessons. When two police officers enter to question the café owner about the missing boy, Nicolas observes from the corner with curiosity. Eager to be let in on the secret of René's disappearance, he attempts to get involved and asks to view the photograph of René, claiming he might have seen the boy. Later, the children are waiting in the bus at the ski hill. Through the foggy windows, they

perceive a group of distraught people outside the café. Their suspicion
that René has been found murdered is confirmed by their teacher, but
they are told to remain on the bus and, deprived of the details of the
case, are left to their own racing imaginations and questions concerning the circumstances of such an incident: 'Est-ce que les parents
de René étaient là, dans ce groupe rassemblé sur la place et dont les
séparait maintenant le mur de buée opaque? Est-ce qu'ils étaient tous
encore là? [...] Est-ce qu'il y aurait une fin à ce silence, à cette horreur
qui les enveloppait tous et avec laquelle lui, à l'insu de tous, avait
partie liée' (CN 107)?

     Other fragmented experiences of the world as lived by Nicolas
involve moments where he knows that he is the subject of dialogue
between teachers, but either cannot hear the conversation properly, or
hears only one side. Near the end of the novel, the mistress receives a
mysterious phone call, following which it is decided that Nicolas must
immediately be sent home to his mother. From the bits and pieces he
gathers, Nicolas concludes that something horrible has happened,
something related to his father, but he is banished from the room
while his fate is discussed by the teachers. The next morning, he
awakens to overhear fragments of a conversation between Patrick and
the mistress who are discussing these same mysterious troubles that
have emerged in his home: 'N'importe comment [...] les gosses vont
le savoir très vite. Et puis si les gens du village apprennent qu'il est
ici, dans l'état où ils sont, on ne sait pas de quoi ils sont capables' (CN
138). Another fragment of information is acquired by Nicolas when he
and Patrick stop at a petrol station for breakfast on the way to
Nicolas's house. Although Patrick attempts to hide the morning newspaper from him at the station, he glimpses the word 'monstre' in the
headline and the photograph on the front page, which we suppose
contains information about his father (CN 142).

     It is in the figure of the father, and in Nicolas's inability to
penetrate the enigma surrounding him, that the theme of secrecy and
the image of the fragmented body, as an expression of uncertainty,
illuminate one another. As a travelling sales representative who sells
prosthetic limbs, Nicolas's father incarnates and perhaps explains
some of the child's anxieties and obsessions with detached body parts
and bodily imagery. The disconcerting associations a child might have
with such a profession are evident in Hodkann's reaction when
Nicolas explains his father's occupation: 'si j'étais ton père, je me

servirais de toi pour faire les démonstrations. Je te couperais les bras et les jambes, j'adapterais les prothèses et je te montrerais comme ça à mes clients' (CN 29). We also know that Nicolas has never been allowed to see these prosthetic limbs. When Hodkann promises not to harass Nicolas during the ski trip in exchange for a glimpse of the equipment in his father's car, Nicolas is tormented by the risk involved in breaking into his father's secret boxes: 'Nicolas voyait Hodkann penché sur le coffre ouvert, forçant les mallettes, éprouvant sur le gras de son pouce le tranchant d'un bistouri, faisant jouer les articulations d'une jambe en plastique, si fasciné qu'il en oubliait le danger' (CN 37-8). The danger threatening Nicolas this time is his authoritative father, who would be angered to discover the two boys investigating the boot of his car.

The father's connection to this theme of the body is also evident in Nicolas's fear of kidnapping and organ trafficking, the fate he believes to have befallen René. Even more frightening for Nicolas than the *Histoires épouvantables* are those which, allegedly true, are recounted to him by his father. The most vivid of these in his mind, and the source of many of his nightmares, is one that was told to him at the fairground. On one occasion his father refused to leave Nicolas's younger brother with a stranger so that he and Nicolas could go on a ride that required the presence of an adult. Nicolas remembers that when he contested his father's reluctance to leave his brother and accompany him, he told him the story of a small boy who was abducted by strangers from a crowded area, and whose kidney was subsequently surgically removed by organ traffickers. These traffickers were presented as terrifying men 'qui rôdent autour des parcs d'attractions, ou près de la sortie des écoles' (CN 34). As the origin of these fears of mutilation and abduction, the father seems to be the pivotal point of Nicolas's uncertainties. Every new or foreign event is experienced by Nicolas as a version of the original family secret, which concerns this very strange and familiar person. He is a 'castrating' father, if only in the sense that his mysteriousness and overprotective character are inhibiting to Nicolas, and a challenge to his subjective development and certainty about the world.

Buried alive

The affinities between these images of physical mutilation and the fragmentation of knowledge are brought out in another story that haunts Nicolas, again conveyed to him by his father. This one concerns a boy who was admitted to hospital for a routine operation and, due to an error on the part of the anaesthetist, woke up entirely paralyzed, deprived of his sensory capacities, unable to see, speak, or hear. Nicolas vividly recreates this scenario in his mind and it provides him with a means to envision the plight of René, the kidnapped child, who, he imagines, was transported to the site of his murder in the boot of a car:

> Dans un monde tout proche, mais à jamais coupé du sien, ses parents, les médecins, décomposés d'horreur, scrutaient son visage cireux sans savoir si quelqu'un, derrière les yeux mi-clos, ressentait et pouvait comprendre quelque chose. D'abord, il avait dû penser qu'on lui avait bandé les yeux, peut-être plâtré le corps, qu'il était dans une chambre obscure et silencieuse, mais que forcément quelqu'un allait venir, allumer la lumière, le délivrer. Il devait faire confiance à ses parents pour le tirer de là. Mais le temps passait, sans mesure possible, des minutes ou des heures ou des jours dans le noir et le silence. L'enfant hurlait et n'entendait même pas son propre cri. Au sein de cette panique lente, inexprimable, son cerveau travaillait, cherchait l'explication. Enterré vivant? (CN 111)

Even before the final question, this passage evokes the terror of the classically uncanny image of being buried alive, which Freud referenced in his essay (U 244). Freud associated the uncanniness of this strange and familiar thought with the feared and yet desired maternal womb. In this context however, the image serves as a metaphor for the terrifying experience of the child René, and is perhaps also a product of Nicolas's own lack of insight into the family secret. This image of the boy who awakens from his coma, deprived of sensory information, reflects Nicolas's plight throughout the narrative, lacking the details that might help him understand the many mysteries that everyday life brings, especially those surrounding his father. While images of fragmentation, bodily destruction and live burial appear imaginary, what is real for Nicolas in his ordinary existence seems to be this impossibility of insight and knowledge.

From his own experience of being deprived of information, Nicolas also appears to understand the power of the secret, and he exploits this power to win over Hodkann, the toughest, most respected student in the class.[39] From the beginning of the novel, Nicolas expresses his desire to befriend Hodkann. He often fantasizes about situations where Hodkann might confess his true insecurities to Nicolas, by entrusting him with one of his own secrets, such as his emotions surrounding the death of his own father:

> Il imaginait leurs chuchotements, la proximité du grand corps chaud de Hodkann, et se plaisait à penser que sous cette puissance tyrannique qu'il déployait il y avait aussi du chagrin, une fragilité que Hodkann lui confesserait [...] Hodkann, si railleur, avouait à Nicolas qu'il avait peur, qu'il était lui aussi un petit garçon perdu. (CN 39)

In order to forge a relationship with Hodkann, Nicolas invents a secret, in the form of information about René's murder. He solicits Hodkann's attention one evening in the chalet and constructs a plot, based on the story of the organ traffickers told to him by his father at the fairground. He claims that his younger brother was also a victim of such a crime and that his own father is currently seeking revenge on the individuals responsible. By possessing this secret and promising to impart it to Hodkann in order to capture his interest, Nicolas reverses the power relations at work in their relationship and places Hodkann in his own usual unknowing position: 'Nicolas le sentait captivé, jouissait du rôle nouveau qu'il tenait' (CN 99). Nicolas learns that while being left in the dark about something one is desperate to know puts one in a position of inferiority, possessing a secret and proposing to divulge it to another person can earn him the respect and the interest of others.

This dynamic reflects an aspect of the relationship created between reader and author by narrative suspense, which, in *La Classe de neige*, rests upon the secrets the author keeps from the reader. Part of the uncanniness of the novel results from the reader's inability to emerge from this position of being deprived of knowledge, from not

---

[39] Eric Bordas makes this point in his reading of *La Classe de neige*: 'C'est l'exaltation du pouvoir du secret qui anime Nicolas, en exerçant un contrôle sur ce qu'il sait (ou croit savoir) et que l'autre ne sait pas (ou ignore savoir)'. See Eric Bordas, 'Le Secret du petit Nicolas' in *Modernités* 14, 'Dire le secret', ed. by Dominique Rabaté (Bordeaux: Presses Universitaires de Bordeaux, 2000), pp.171-82, pp. 178-9.

being able to gain a firm footing from which to interpret the narrative events.[40] This position resembles that of Nicolas throughout the story, and that of Hodkann in the scene commented on above. Because the reader of *La Classe de neige* experiences the world through the eyes of the child, she too shares an experience of enigma with respect to the family mystery and the fragmented experience of reality that Nicolas constantly encounters. She asks herself questions that resemble those which are at the origin of Nicolas's constant uncertainty: 'What is the relationship between the fantasy world of this young boy and the fictional events of the novel'? 'What does the father have to do with this imagery of bodily mutilation and monstrosity'? There is a feeling that the author is always hiding the most important realities. As Freud and the many other interpreters of Hoffmann's tale also discovered, reading is in a sense the act of attempting to decode secrets, which often have no solutions. For Cixous, this desire to eliminate the secret of the uncanny by defining it was Freud's mistake in his approach to literary interpretation. For her, the impossibility of assigning a fixed meaning to a text is necessarily an incarnation of the uncanny: 'C'est que ce qui est manifesté reste inapprochable, reste interdit, n'est pas récupérable par le familier. Il y a une part de l'*unheimlich* qui résiste toujours l'approche du *heimlich*' (PP 52).

For Nicolas the uncanny is both a position of defenselessness or lack and a productive force, which serves many purposes. It is a means to approach or sublimate what he cannot understand about growing up, about his own secrets and about the mysteries of his family and those of the outside world. Not yet initiated into the world of adults or privy to the codes of this realm, Nicolas is obliged to invent and fill in the gaps. With the aid of his gruesome fictions, stolen from his parents' bedroom, and the stories recounted to him by his father, he imagines the secrets of adults.

---

[40] Noël Carroll links the notion of suspense to a sense of doom: 'Specifically, suspense in fiction generally results when the possible outcomes of the situation set down by the story are such that the outcome that is morally correct, in terms of the values inherent in the fiction, is the less likely outcome (or, at least, only as likely as the evil outcome)'. See Noël Carroll, *The Philosophy of Horror, or Paradoxes of the Heart* (New York and London: Routledge, 1990), p.138. For Todorov the uncanny and suspense appear to be intertwined. We might recall his formalist description of the uncanny as a period of hesitation experienced by the reader when faced with an implausible event. (See pages 41-2 above).

The uncanniness of the family secret is also at the heart of an authentic experience of growing up. It is through wrestling with the family secret and transposing his anxieties into various imaginative forms that Nicolas learns and constitutes his subjectivity. For François Vigouroux, the family secret is an 'endroit de souffrance'[41] at the core of human experience: 'Le secret, c'est par lui que l'homme se crée. C'est en cherchant à l'élucider, consciemment et inconsciemment, que nous créons notre vie et prenons sens. C'est dans cette interrogation, entre obscur et lumineux, entre dissimulation et révélation, que nous prenons naissance.'[42] In the final chapter, Patrick leaves Nicolas at the doorstep of his family home and it is at this moment, while he waits for the door to open, that Nicolas knows he has grown up and must face the responsibilities of the 'real' world, where the true terror begins: 'La moquette, à l'intérieur de l'appartement, étouffait les pas, mais Nicolas savait que la porte allait s'ouvrir, qu'à cet instant sa vie commencerait et que dans cette vie, pour lui, il n'y aurait pas de pardon' (CN 148).

In a sense the ending of *La Classe de neige* resembles that of *La Moustache,* where the main character destroys himself, thus putting an end to his uncertainty. It is in fact the fluidity of the margin between the worlds of fantasy and reality, strange and familiar, that keeps Nicolas safe. As long as he can continue to fantasize, he can postpone the true monstrosity that emerges from his own home at the end of the novel. However, Nicolas fears, as does the reader, that these two worlds will one day coalesce. Ultimately, the reality proves worse than the fiction and the home is a greater source of unfamiliarity and danger than the other potential threats suggested by Nicolas's parents or found within his own anxiety-ridden thoughts. Rather than being the source of his fear, the uncanny space of fantasy is paradoxically presented as a temporary dwelling place, or refuge, in which Nicolas is spared from the violence of the real.

In *La Classe de neige*, the uncanny displays echoes of Freud's castration hypothesis, but also of Rand and Torok's theory of secrecy, an idea raised by Freud, but perhaps 'repressed' in the interest of promoting the coherence of his psychoanalytic theory. Possibly, the notion of secrecy was too close to Jentsch's definition of the uncanny

---

[41] François Vigouroux, *Le Secret de famille* (Paris: Hachette Littératures, 1993), p. 126.
[42] Ibid, p. 8.

as 'intellectual uncertainty', which Freud was attempting to undermine. Or perhaps, the notion of family secrets in Hoffmann's story was a little too close to home for Freud himself. In their article 'The Secrets of Nature and the Nature of Secrets', members of the Freudian Study Group unearth some of the family secrets that plagued Freud's own upbringing. They hypothesize that Freud sublimated his ambivalent, traumatic relationship with his own mother, whom he loved but connected with 'deadly powers',[43] into his dedication to the pursuit of the 'secrets of nature', his vision of the science of psychoanalysis.

The Un-homed Father in Savitzkaya's *Marin mon cœur*

For Freud, the anxiety of the uncanny was associated with the figure of the father. He linked the ocular motif in Hoffmann's tale to the plight of Œdipus and claimed that the fear of losing one's eyes was a mitigated form of the castration complex. In passing, however, he also cited the image of being buried alive as an uncanny thought, since it harks back to the strange and familiar idea of existence in the maternal womb. It has been suggested both by readers of his essay and by his biographers that what Freud feared most was the feminine and the absence of the paternal function.[44] After all, the figure of the authoritative father was the pivotal point of Freud's psychoanalytic theory of the uncanny and, more generally, of his description of the human psyche. On a personal level, Freud's own anxiety surrounding unresolved ambiguities in his relationship with his own mother may have led him to privilege the role of the father in his own analysis and in the hypotheses he formulated.[45] Taking into account both the maternal and paternal aspects of the uncanny, as asserted or manifested in Freud's essay, it appears that he viewed the uncanny as a momentary return to a pre-symbolic or primitive state in which the individual

---

[43] James W. Barron et al., 'Sigmund Freud: The Secrets of Nature and the Nature of Secrets', *International Review of Psychoanalysis*, Vol. 18 (1991), pp. 144-63, p. 150.

[44] We might recall that Cixous's reading of Freud's essay was based on Freud's repression of the difference of the feminine, which was for her his true fear. The comments about the uncanny female body scattered throughout the essay often seem to support this interpretation.

[45] See James W. Barron et al., 'Sigmund Freud: The Secrets of Nature and the Nature of Secrets'.

dwells prior to the construction of his adult subjectivity, one that, according to Freud, is abandoned when the authoritative father calls him forth into the social and linguistic community.

However, it is often suggested that contemporary society is dominated by a form of anxiety that results not from excessive paternal authority, but from the waning of the paternal function, in both a literal and metaphorical sense, within culture, ideology and government. As Jean-Claude Stoloff tells us: 'Aujourd'hui nous est prédit le déclin irréversible du père en tant que figure imaginaire incarnant une domination masculine condamnée par l'Histoire'.[46] Michel Biron observes that unease about the disappearance of the father figure and of paternal discourses is visible within institutions, politics and in the questioning of identity and family within contemporary writing: 'Qui suis-je si je me sens fils de personne, si je n'ai pas de père à tuer'?[47] Laurent Demoulin evokes the 'désarroi intérieur' of postmodern writers who 'semblent pâtir de cette remise en cause du père et de la loi, de la mère et de la langue. Ils sont perdus et la psychose n'est pas loin'.[48]

Élisabeth Roudinesco speaks of the current dissolution of traditional family structures, which is provoking a 'terreur d'une fin du père' resulting in the 'toute-puissance des mères'.[49] However, for Roudinesco, the fall of the father is not to be mourned, but is rather an incentive to re-define the dynamics of the family. She examines the figures of Hamlet and Œdipus, who strongly influenced twentieth-century psychoanalytic thought. Hamlet may be viewed as a key character in our contemporary world, as the descendant of a mutilated patriarch. Roudinesco holds that the role of the father requires reinterpretation within the discipline of psychoanalysis, which is now faced with the task of finding meaning for the family beyond the notions of patricide and incest. The current evolution of the family dynamic and the paternal function paves the way for a less repressive, less authoritarian image of paternity:

---

[46] Jean-Claude Stoloff, *La Fonction Paternelle* (Paris: In Press Éditions, 2007), p. 193.

[47] Michel Biron, 'Fils de personne', *Voix et images*, Vol. 81, pp. 566-571, p. 566.

[48] Laurent Demoulin, 'Eugène Savitzkaya à la croisée des chemins', p. 54.

[49] Élisabeth Roudinesco, *La Famille en désordre*, p. 11.

À la famille autoritaire de jadis, à celle, triomphale ou
mélancolique, de naguère, succéda la famille mutilée d'aujour-
d'hui, faite de blessures intimes, de violences silencieuses, de
souvenirs refoulés. Ayant perdu son auréole de vertu, le père, qui
la dominait, donna alors une image inversée de lui-même, laissant
apparaître un moi décentré, autobiographique, individualisé dont
la psychanalyse tentera d'assumer, tout au long du XXe siècle, la
grande brisure.[50]

It is such a de-centred, uncertain father who emerges in
Savitzkaya's novel *Marin mon cœur* (1992) and, in so doing, brings
forth a more primordial, fluid space where meaning is not yet fixed.
However, this collapse of paternal logic is visibly divorced from
unease. In this semi-autobiographical text, written for his son, the
author elaborates an innovative portrayal of paternity which evades
the anxiety of either the absent father or the overly present
authoritative father. The author writes against paternal myths by
representing a world in which the infant or child determines meaning.
In a movement away from the representation of the anxiety-producing
father from *La Classe de neige*, *Marin mon cœur* describes the
uncanny experience undergone *by* a paternal figure. Rather than
portraying the father as he who facilitates or commands the child's
passage into the social and symbolic universe, the author values the
un-homing capacity of the child, who causes him to re-think familiar
scenarios and landscapes otherwise, through an innovative, child-like
gaze. As the narrator observes the existence and development of his
son and contemplates the more primitive, pre-linguistic realm he inhabits, his own everyday environment and his role within it undergo a
distortion. Once again, for Savitzkaya the strangeness that emerges
from the midst of the familiar is desired and willingly prolonged. The
uncanny is a means to extricate an element of tenderness, sensitivity
and subtle humour from the father-son relationship, rather than to
evoke discomfort or peril.

Before turning to this text, it is useful to consider the
evolution of the figure of the father in Savitzkaya's writing. In his first
novel, *Mentir,* the paternal role is articulated according to a more
traditionally Œdipal logic. In this work the author employs a sparse,
child-like language to string together a series of descriptive portraits
of his mother. The narrative subject, who remains indistinct and

---

[50] Ibid, p. 24.

unidentified, appears to be consumed or haunted by the mother. His anxieties about how to represent her generate the unsettling flux of the text. The mother as subjectivity is in effect absent, and the story develops from the gaze of the son as a spectator who obsessively observes the mother, an object he can never fully reach. The impossible desire for union with the maternal seems to be sublimated into a representational, textual impossibility. This impossibility is suggested to some extent by the statements the author makes about having seen the mother, which are subsequently doubted or contradicted by the same narrating voice: 'J'ai vu ma mère'[51], 'Ai-je vu ma mère?' (ME 25), 'J'ai peut-être vu ma mère […]' (ME 27), 'Rien à voir' (ME 31). The prohibition of maternal desire is implied by passages that suggest a quest for something that cannot be granted: 'Ces fleurs ne sont pas pour moi, dit-elle, ces pivoines, ces marguerites, ces fleurs blanches ou pourpres, ce cerisier […] ne seront jamais plus dans mes bras, entre mes doigts ou dans mes cheveux comme des morceaux de couleur […]' (ME 7). The description of the flowers, depicted here as desired and later as 'énormes et repoussantes' (ME 14), appears to mimic the ambiguity of the maternal as simultaneously sought and repressed. The narrative presents a duality whereby writing is simultaneously what brings the narrator into proximity with the object of his desire and what suggests the distance between him and his mother, forestalling their union and preventing him from successfully telling the story of his mother and his childhood.

Although the father is essentially absent in *Mentir*, the narrator's description of the mother is frequently disrupted by violent visions of a thirsty black panther, 'une bête un peu floue' (ME 57) that the narrator envisions attacking a young woman or a child, or skulking in its cage:

> Comment buvait la panthère, tirant la langue, l'énorme langue écarlate, léchant les bords de son écuelle. Panthère luisante. Et comment flambait sa robe, son épaisse fourrure noire bien lustrée. Un animal peigné soigneusement selon les différents sens de ses poils. Comment tournait la panthère assoiffée. Comment le liquide éclaboussait les barreaux de sa cage. (ME 74)

---

[51] Eugène Savitzkaya, *Mentir* (Paris: Éditions de Minuit, 1977), p. 23. All other references are given in the text, following the abbreviation ME.

The panther often occupies the mother's frame of vision or attention and appears to intrude on the story as an incomprehensible obstacle to her possession by the narrator. This threatening figure of the panther has been interpreted as a paternal symbol that forbids the subject's incestuous desire for the mother and intrudes on his attempts to appropriate the mother through writing.[52] However, this interpretation is questionable when one considers Savitzkaya's choice of creature; the panther is a feminine word in French and the feline part of a very feminine *imaginaire*. The author's description of the panther, full of words such as 'robe', 'fourrure', and 'soigneusement' might be seen to confirm this association in the present context.

In *Marin mon cœur,* the father-son relationship transcends the negativity and anxiety that some critics have observed in *Mentir*. Savitzkaya creates a form of paternity and a foundation for meaning that are exempt from the law of the father. In a sense, this is attained through the narrator's refusal of his traditional paternal role. The qualities ordinarily associated with fatherhood, such as didacticism, authority or legislation, are replaced by observation, withdrawal and humbleness. The novel takes the form of a series of succinct chapters which recount, in a simple, gentle and often poetic language, disparate episodes from the story of a father who observes the coming to subjectivity of his child. A strange peculiarity of this represented world is the absence, not of the father, as in *Mentir*, but of female characters. Although there is a single reference to Marin's 'petite sœur' and, on another occasion, one to his mother, the entire narrative is centred on the father-son relationship. With his father at his side, Marin is learning his place in the microcosm of the home and acquiring the linguistic and intellectual skills necessary to move in his environment and participate in the community. However, the more the reader progresses in her reading, the more she realizes that the traditional parent-child dynamic is often reversed, so that it is in fact Marin who teaches the parent about the more plural, fantasy-driven world of the child.

The author employs an eccentric terminology of 'géant' and 'nain', derived from a father-son make-believe game, to describe the interaction between himself and his son, only very rarely making use

---

[52] See Adeze Igboemeke, 'Le Père silencieux: la métaphore paternelle chez Eugène Savitzkaya', *Neophilologus*, Vol. 85, No. 4 (October 2001), 519-27.

of the terms 'père' and 'fils': 'Aujourd'hui (pour la quantième fois?), j'ai joué avec Marin au géant et au nain'.[53] This fairytale vocabulary lends a playful quality to the language, placing the gestures and interaction of father and child within a distanced, dream-like theatre. The narrator whole-heartedly embraces this role of giant and employs this terminology retrospectively to look back on the vicissitudes of Marin's infancy through this fantastical lens: 'Après avoir baigné le nain, le géant l'a habillé avec ses vêtements de ville et lui a fait prendre l'air de la ville, qui, ce jour-là, avait un odeur de coing. Le géant a nourri le nain à la petite cuillière' (MMC 38).

The narrator is thus a friendly giant, loving and gentle towards the dwarf. He reminds us more of the benign, child-befriending figure in Roald Dahl's *The BFG* than of the malicious ogres we might recall from such tales as 'Jack and the Beanstalk'. This figure of the mollified giant well suits the softened paternal portrait that Savitzkaya presents in the novel. As the author explains during an interview with *Libération*: 'L'enfant a tous les droits. La plupart du temps, c'est lui le géant et moi le nain. Il n'a aucun préjugé et distribue les rôles à sa convenance'.[54] Since in the novel the father is in fact nearly always the giant, it seems that when the writer suggests the flexibility of these roles, he means that it is often Marin who is the more domineering of the two, as we shall see further on. But in addition, this imagery of giant and dwarf, which suggests the alterity with which these figures often view one another (one being excessively large and the other excessively small), assists the narrator in conceiving of the relationship between these two family members as one which must embody strangeness as well as familiarity. His willingness to adopt an innovative language to portray the father and son within the home, suggests his openness to, and celebration of, the elusive quality that may emerge from the most familiar places and people.

Perceiving the other

The story opens with Marin's birth, an experience which introduces the author's dual perception of the child as simultaneously foreign and extremely familiar: 'Il n'avait pas encore expiré, il était pâle et bleu comme après un effort surhumain, une grande frayeur ou un chagrin

---

[53] Eugène Savitzkaya, *Marin mon cœur* (Paris: Les Éditions de Minuit, 1992), p. 37. All other references are given in the text, following the abbreviation MMC.

[54] Antoine de Gaudemar, 'Interview avec Eugène Savitzkaya'.

[...] il avait l'étrangeté de l'axolotl en dépit de sa forme indéniablement familière' (MMC 13). The use of the term 'axolotl', defined in the *Petit Robert* as 'Larve d'amblystome qui peut se reproduire à l'état larvaire', is an example of Savitzkaya's fascination with obscure or very specific biological and botanical terminology, which runs through his work. He often uses such terms as if they were the most common words, a tendency which itself perhaps emphasizes the blurring of the strange and familiar which he asserts in this passage and many others. This simultaneity of the strange and the familiar is an underlying tension in Savitzkaya's representation of the family and appears to be the quality of general experience that his writing seeks to name. Even the cries of the cats in the garden are 'pas suffisamment familiers ni tout à fait étrangers' (MMC 40).

This duality is the founding idea of the novel. In Marin the writer recognizes a part of himself and often expresses his emotional and physical proximity to this person, and the comfort he acquires through encountering him in the home or witnessing his familiar noises and gestures: 'C'est alors que le nain toussa et le bruit de cette toux parvint aux oreilles du géant comme le son familier par excellence, une preuve étincelante de leur profonde parenté' (MMC 36). However, he also locates in Marin the infinite difference of the other and affirms the incomprehensibility of the world he inhabits: 'Une partie du nain lui devenait aussi proche que sa propre chair mais l'autre partie lui demeurait totalement étrangère' (MMC 62). The narrator constantly draws the child nearer through observation and affection, while distancing him conceptually by representing him in a way that maintains his otherness in its integrity. The poetic language, which often veers towards fantasy, calls the toddler back into the realm of the familiar through description and metaphor,[55] while maintaining the child's resistance to his father's interpretation:

> Au géant, Marin apparaît en songe sous la forme d'un animal aux longs cheveux flottants s'approchant radieux d'un œil-de-bœuf. Un courant agite la longue chevelure et le visage change continuellement de couleur et d'aspect, influencé par le passage incessant d'énormes nuages. Il est clair que le nain a échappé à l'emprise du géant. Mais à la question de savoir dans quel élément il s'ébat il n'y a pas de réponse. (MMC 64-5)

---

[55] Marin is evoked as 'dauphin riant' (p. 80) and 'haricot vert' (p. 79).

This surrealist imagery of bewildered internal visions is the means by which the author finds a place in his text to articulate thoughts of wonder and perplexity towards his son and to inscribe this wonder, intact, within the story. Despite his familiarity, Marin is never pinned down or defined, but is constantly transforming: 'Il est à la fois le nain, le merle, la fourmi, la souris, l'ours et le géant' (MMC 66).

A pre-symbolic universe
This duality of strange and familiar also informs the writer's representation of the outside world, which he desires to re-live from a renewed angle. Because Marin's experience of reality is wholly unknowable, the narrator can only imagine the newness and richness that he sees within the ordinary. Savitzkaya seeks to establish a sympathetic literary standpoint to match that of the toddler who sees the rational adult world through an infant's lens of uncertainty and surprise, perceiving everything for the very first time. This is achieved by placing a child-like filter over a series of selected moments of life in the home, which often also constitute Marin's first discovery of those phenomena:

> Le premier riz se prend à l'âge où un bon nombre de dents sont là pour aider la langue à faire le tri et le compte des grains à avaler. Le premier riz rendit Marin de si bonne humeur qu'il fit le compte à l'envers, expédiant les grains hors de sa bouche un par un, deux par deux, trois par trois [...] (MMC 28)

The author interprets Marin's reactions to various new experiences. Here, he combines his own observations of his son's behaviour with a description of the possible joys, sensations or complications that Marin might discover with a new food. He suggests possible descriptions of his son's experiences in a tone of questioning and wonder, without claiming to fully apprehend or see what Marin encounters, without reducing the strangeness of Marin's environment to his own cognitive or intellectual codes. In this way, the author creates a language which allows for the intertwining of the father's observations of his son and the son's possible observations of the outside world:

> À la première bouchée de chair de poisson, il fit la grimace et son sourcil droit se leva. Ne lui déposait-on pas sur la langue un morceau de lui-même, une saveur par trop familière ou si légère

> qu'il ne parvenait pas à la distinguer du goût de sa bouche?
> (MMC 25)

The narrator is fascinated by the child's exclusion from the clearly
defined borders and categories that define the world of adults, which
permits him to play and manipulate objects without subscribing to the
norms of separation and logic that dominate in communal reality. His
description of Marin's experience is nourished by an emphasis on
Marin's pre-linguistic condition in order to envision the familiar not
only as never previously experienced by the little boy but also, as
much as possible, from a perspective uninformed by symbolic, social
or practical preconceptions. In play, Marin defies certain orders and
thus enjoys an innovative experience of worldly phenomena:

> Il transporte le sable de la rivière sur le plancher de sa chambre et
> les coussins de sa chambre au bord de la rivière. Il mélange les
> lieux et se les concilie. Et vit deux fois. Dans un même gobelet, il
> dépose des châtaignes, de l'eau de mer, de l'herbe et sa propre
> buée. (MMC 56)

The author privileges the illogicality of the child's play. Marin crosses
boundaries of inside and outside and manipulates entities in a singular
fashion, one which to the adult mind appears nonsensical.

An interrogative tone often serves as a way of conveying the
ungraspable nature of Marin's experience and locates a strange unexpected and yet charming quality in trite moments. In the following
passage, the child-like, inquisitive tone of the writing represents the
pure curiosity of Marin when confronted with something as ordinary
as a case of children's head-lice:

> Sur le cuir chevelu de Marin, parmi ses cheveux, des plaies
> suppurent. Il les touche et les gratte.   Qu'est-ce que c'est?
> Nouvelles oreilles en train de pousser? Jeunes bouches s'ouvrant à
> la lumière? Nouvelles dents ou cornes comme on en voit chez les
> bouquetins pour de nouveaux affrontements tête contre tête avec
> le bélier géant? (MMC 81-2)

Through this questioning approach, the author imagines some of the
comparisons and conclusions the ordinary world may provoke in the
mind of the child and the minor discoveries or crises experienced each
day by Marin as he grows and develops.

The pre-symbolic experience of the everyday that the author

seeks to bring out is also reflected in his representations of the child's body. The father imagines Marin's perception of his physical self in fragments while submerged in his bathwater 'dans laquelle flottent ses cheveux, ses bras et ses jambes' (MMC 21). This fantasy informs his conception of the child. He does not view him as a unified being, but as bits and pieces of a person not yet inscribed in an order that demands the integrity and mastery of his body parts:

> C'est alors que, ouvrant enfin le poing, il esquissa le signe qui devait le rendre solidaire des principaux éléments du monde. L'index était dirigé vers la lumière. Le majeur et l'annulaire formaient les ciseaux capables de découper l'air lui-même. Le petit doigt, auriculaire ou aurifère pointé, négligemment en apparence, vers les secousses du plancher, indiquait son origine. Le pouce légèrement replié prouvait que la main était encore intacte. L'index comme sémaphore. Le médius et l'annulaire comme lames taillant la lumière. L'auriculaire en goutte de sang ou de mercure et le pouce en vigilant ergot. (MMC 14-15)

What for the narrator are distinctly labelled body parts, may be experienced as miscellaneous digits for Marin. The metaphors of chopping and direction established by the narrator to describe the child's bodily movements generate a fantastical or eccentric meaning for these gestures, but one which is not necessarily intended by Marin since the child's physical self is not yet symbolically codified.

Many of the narrator's observations of Marin portray the child's lack of language as simply another way of seeing things, rather than as an inferior phase of human development. He makes efforts to adopt and comprehend the early linguistic attempts of his son, and allots them meaning in his novel as possible descriptions of the outside world: 'De la plupart des êtres, il connaît davantage le langage que le nom. Ainsi le cheval est celui qui piaffe, le rat celui qui zigzague, le cochon celui qui renifle sa morve et grogne [...]' (MMC 33). Marin does possess language, but it is one all of his own:

> Au cours de la sieste de l'après-midi, le sommeil a échappé au nain, qui a appelé le géant. Il l'a appelé d'une voix très basse où seules les consonnes étaient perceptibles. Voulait-il, tout en rappelant son existence et sa dépendance vis-à-vis de lui, que le géant ne vienne pas trop vite ou simplement vérifiait-il le bon fonctionnement de son instrument vocal? Un stratagème inique permit au géant d'entendre ce qu'il voulut bien considérer comme

un appel impératif et il obtempéra illico et put surprendre sur le
visage emmitouflé du nain le fameux sourire de Chinois. (MMC
54)

In Marin's crying for his father, the reader instantly recognizes the
portrayal of a customary scenario, which characterizes the father-son
rapport, but this instance is articulated in an inquisitive tone. The
inscrutability of Marin's expression, referred to as a 'sourire de
Chinois', accentuates the impenetrability of his world. However, the
father dedicates a significant amount of thought to interpreting and
contemplating his son's language, rather than considering it to be
simply nonsensical.

In certain psychoanalytic accounts, such as that of Jacques
Lacan, the paternal function bestows upon the child stability of
meaning through the possibility of language. When the child acquires
the Name-of-the-Father and recognizes the symbolic order, he
becomes a subject.[56] In the context of Marin and his father, however,
this schema is reversed as the author stresses the child's language as a
form of pre-verbal authenticity. Meaning does not begin with the
subject's acquisition of language, but is fuller and richer before this
step has taken place. This father does not attempt to close the irrational world of the child by promoting his movement into the
symbolic domain, but rather seeks to enter this world himself. This is
seen in the fact that Marin's story ends, rather than begins, with the
acquisition of language. In the last few pages of the novel, the world
begins to take shape as a series of linguistically construed phenomena
as opposed to a collection of chaotic incidents. However, the language
learned by Marin is itself estranged, belonging to the other:

Marin parcourt la maison dont il dresse l'inventaire. Mais ce n'est
pas lui qui parle. Porte, dit quelqu'un dans sa bouche. Armoire, dit
quelqu'un dans sa bouche. Poubelle, dit le même personnage dont
la voix sort par la bouche de Marin. Chaise, dit le petit bonhomme
assis sur sa langue. (MMC 89)

Here, ordinary speech and vocabulary are rendered foreign, spoken by
another, and the child's adoption of language is portrayed as a form of
alienation. With the image of the little man sitting on Marin's tongue,

---

[56] Jacques Lacan, 'La Signification du phallus', in *Écrits II* (Paris: Éditions du Seuil,
1966), pp. 685-95.

Savitzkaya stresses the absurdity of language itself and presents communal language as perhaps inferior to Marin's own personal forms of expression. Not only are the world and language of the dwarf more magical, but they are also represented as being, in some sense, more authentic. Marin appears to possess a form of insight that the giant cannot access. The author is fascinated by Marin's more emotional, primordial space; indeed his descriptions suggest that it is richer than the adult world: 'Lorsqu'il pleure, son chagrin semble probant et inextinguible. Il n'y a que les chats qui pleurent aussi longtemps et aussi fort' (MMC 19). This highly emotive life-world that the child inhabits is represented as a simpler place, untainted by external demands and complexities: 'Marin connaît la grande et la petite tristesse. La première ne peut se résoudre. La deuxième ne se résout que par le bain de larmes. Le bain de larmes vivifie, lave les entrailles et promet une grande clarté' (MMC 61).

Marin mon cœur, like many other Savitzkayan texts, reflects the writer's fascination with the primitive. The technique of imagining a child-like space before language is acquired is one of many employed throughout Savitzkaya's oeuvre with a view to retrieving a certain original, organic reality that precedes the laws and structures of the common real. While in some of his earlier texts he tends to abandon familiar scenarios and landscapes entirely in favour of fantasy and a more psychological, visionary form of representation, in his more recent novels, he appears increasingly interested in depicting ordinary life infused with glimpses of this primitiveness. Laurent Demoulin sees *Marin mon cœur* as a turning point in Savitzkaya's writing:

> La réalité y reprend ses droits. Mais pas pour autant le réalisme, car ce qui est décrit ici, pour être connu de tous, n'en suscite pas moins un regard neuf et déroutant. Nous sommes passés d'un roman qui racontait l'inouï comme si c'était normal à un autre qui décrit le banal avec des mots inouïs.[57]

Due to his lack of boundaries and his perpetual state of unhomeliness, which leads to innovation, the child is venerated as an insightful figure who can encourage others to perceive differently. The child is a

---

[57] Laurent Demoulin, 'Eugène Savitzkaya à la croisée des chemins', *Écritures contemporaines 2* (1999), 41-56 (p. 47).

character within the ordinary world who possesses the ability to de-familiarize.

Nain et géant

As Carrère did in *La Classe de neige,* so, in *Marin mon cœur,* Savitzkaya reinvents the world through the eyes of the child. However, Marin's marginality and distance from the symbolically and morally codified adult world do not place him in a position of trepidation or vulnerability. While for Nicolas the incoherence of secrecy was an obstacle to his comfort and certainty, the frag-mentation of Marin's world and his lack of access to social norms and knowledge make him the object of reverence on the part of the narrator and father. As Savitzkaya explains in an interview, 'Marin m'a permis d'être comme lui. C'est un privilège, une chance. Ça m'a en quelque sorte réoxygéné'.[58] The child is represented as a kind of visionary who has an insightful perception of reality, and the father-son relation is re-written in the light of this gift.

In his relationship to the dwarf, the giant must recognize his inferior position and the power of the dwarf, which is 'proprement illimité' (MMC 37). Although the nature of this realm is such that these two individuals are obliged to 'cohabiter et s'entendre' (MMC 58), it is paradoxically by virtue of his marginality, or lack, that the dwarf possesses a certain authority over the giant, who must look after his well-being: 'Si le nain est tributaire du géant, le géant est responsable du nain' (MMC 39). Often, the author's representation of this relationship does not require the invention of new parent-child scenarios, but simply involves drawing the reader's attention to moments which already exist within the home and presenting them as evidence of an alternative reality, one shown to defy the image of the authoritative parent. It is not the father who dictates what the child should or should not do, but the child who imposes his own desires: 'un nain ne mange que ce qu'il veut et il lui est permis de retirer de sa bouche les morceaux non-désirés' (MMC 38). Rather than ordering the home or instructing the child, the father is often represented in a subservient role, conforming to Marin's wishes, picking up the objects that the child throws on the floor and fulfilling the roles determined for him by the dwarf in play: 'Le nain est le chamelier et le géant le

---

[58] Antoine de Gaudemar, 'Interview avec Eugène Savitzkaya'.

chameau' (MMC 43). The last fragment of the novel expresses the omnipotence of the dwarf, who commands the giant: 'Fermez la porte et ouste! ordonne le nain assis sur son pot dans le cabinet au géant qui en prend toute la place' (MMC 91). We recognize a celebration of the narcissistic phase of infantile development as a subversion of and response to the more traditional representation of fatherhood as imposing or restrictive: 'Dans la maison du géant, le nain possède maintenant sa maison. Il y invite le géant qui pour entrer doit se plier aux lois de la réduction. On n'entre pas impunément dans cette demeure où Marin est le maître absolu' (MMC 51). Marin and not the father is the master of the house.

At times the writer employs a nearly spiritual or biblical language to represent Marin as a kind of venerated god. The narrator's description of worldly phenomena is inspired by his recognition of Marin's supremacy and mystical qualities: 'Ne sera vivant que ce qui aura été oint. Ne germeront que les graines qui auront séjourné sous sa langue. Ne bourgeonneront que les rameaux qu'il aura sucés. Ne mûriront que les fruits qu'il aura émaillés de son suc' (MMC 26).

The author's privileging of Marin's vision of things is also evident in the representation of play between the two figures. Whatever the game, the dwarf necessarily conquers the giant 'dont il connaît le point faible' (MMC 39), since it is the dwarf who determines the rules and these often oppose those we might expect. When father and son wrestle, 'c'est le nain toujours qui tombe le mieux et le plus vite, car rien ne le retient de choir sur le sol, ni l'orgueil de la défaite ni la peur de se blesser. À ce jeu, seul le géant triche' (MMC 73).

The infinite freedom of the child is also displayed in the representation of Marin's body. Savitzkaya re-writes the Œdipal myth, or at least stresses the pre-Œdipal stage, in order to re-formulate the child's infantile awareness of his bodily existence as a celebration rather than a prohibition: 'Marin a certaines exigences. Il demande qu'on lui donne son sexe, qu'il trouve joli. Donne mon oreille, donne mon cil. Une fois dans sa main, son oreille, son cil, son sexe lui appartiendraient vraiment' (MMC 53). The child's body is never mapped by the parental figure, but rather, the father is fascinated by the innocent relationship the child has with his body as that which belongs entirely to him.

The father's practice and Savitzkaya's narrative are thus

founded on a logic which opposes that of the traditional father, who initiates and conditions the child into the social world by teaching him regulations, manners and codes of conduct. Savitzkaya creates a relationship between father and son in which it is the child who calls the father forth into his world. The challenge for the adult is to enter this space inhabited by the dwarf without reducing it to the laws of common reality. The adult mind must engage in an arduous yet pleasurable struggle to adapt to this new, less rational environment, and must learn to move in his formerly familiar space. The narrator chronicles the experiences he undergoes in this strange environment, the world of the dwarf. In doing so, he reconstructs the world poetically and embraces a kind of paralogic that might provide a frame of interpretation for Marin's actions and reactions:

> La bave sort d'une fontaine qui semble heureusement intarissable, car le monde est tellement sec qu'il faut sans cesse tout humecter. La bave coule sur son plastron qu'elle lave et amidonne et sur ses vêtements qu'elle rend plus souples et plus doux, lustrés comme la fourrure des loutres, huilés comme le plumage des paons et fumants comme la robe des chevaux. (MMC 18)

The narrator welcomes new forms of thinking that he imagines govern the world of the dwarf and develops outlandish reasons for his son's behaviour. He redefines laws of cause and effect rather than attributing his actions to typical phases of infantile development such as drooling or teething:

> Tout passera par la bouche, Marin s'en fait le serment. Il devra d'abord digérer le monde avec sa salive afin de le rendre visible et limpide. Il devra d'abord réduire en pâte le papier bruissant et sec, faire fondre les surfaces métalliques, émietter les feuilles, les fleurs et le pain, attendrir le bois. (MMC 26)

During his study of this newfound space, the narrator is able to make several observations about its functioning. He notes the particular laws that govern the behaviour of objects. He observes that 'ce qui a disparu par la fenêtre, on le retrouve souvent complètement transformé dans le jardin' (MMC 59). He also learns about the supernatural possibilities that exist in this space. For example, in the world of the dwarf it is possible to transform into a cat and one only needs to alter the angle of one's vision in order to become invisible

(MMC 60). He notes the alternative values and beliefs that underlie this space: 'La transformation vaut mieux que l'inerte possession' and 'le renouvellement vaut mieux que l'inerte possession' (MMC 59). He begins to believe, from watching Marin, that the principle of taking things apart is as heavily weighted as that of construction (MMC 71) and that the most miniscule particles that constitute the world deserve infinite attention (MMC 54).

Savitzkaya's philosophy for approaching the other through writing is characterized by a refusal of the familiar and the homely. There can be no familiar order, no habitual way of seeing things, and the novelist appears to advocate a constant renewal of the *quotidien* and a distortion of the codes of the everyday in order to access and figure a space of original uncertainty.[59] In *Marin mon cœur*, the child is a character who is in some sense excluded from, or not yet apprenticed into, collective reality. It is precisely because of this status that he is a privileged person who can illuminate these corners of strangeness, which might otherwise go unnoticed. In a sense, Savitzkaya reproduces in this novel the strategy of defamiliarization he developed in *En vie*, where he rendered bizarre the most ordinary moments of domestic life by dwelling strangely on the trivial activities and objects of the home. By exploring an obscure dynamic within the most ordinary moments of home and reality, Savitzkaya's writing blends familiar content with poetic practices, locating a discursive space where the ordinary is invested with marvel.

In *Marin mon cœur*, this defamiliarization of the ordinary world is performed through a deformation of the paternal myth and an approach conditioned by wonder. The narrator embraces the supreme alterity of the existence of Marin. Rather than encourage his son to adopt the norms and logic of the collective real and facilitate his entry into the narrator's familiar world, the writer voluntarily un-homes himself in order to imagine an alternative significance for common reality. While traditionally the paternal role is associated with the stabilization of meaning, the father in this novel displays a desire for plurality and play. The unthematizable difference of Marin's world is not represented purely as incoherent, but as the foundation for cre-

---

[59] This idea is reminiscent of the Heideggerian uncanny referenced in the introduction to this book (see p. 82 above). For Heidegger the uncanny suggests a form of primary, pre-phenomenological authenticity from which we are alienated in everyday being. Not being at home in the world is a more primordial state than that of homelessness.

ativity and constant transformation. Savitzkaya's paternal rapport is
one that maintains a more 'maternal' reality.[60] Yet the absence of
maternal characters suggests the transcendence of traditional parental
gender roles. The maternal dimension in *Marin mon cœur* is thus one
which contrasts with that evoked in NDiaye's work. In *Rosie Carpe*,
the maternal space was uncanny in a threatening sense, since the
mother impeded the development of the child. In Savitzkaya's text,
the blurring of strange and familiar is not fear-provoking, but rather a
means to encourage the child's individual development.

In 'The Uncanny', Freud suggests the capacity of the young
child to absorb make-believe with ease into ordinary life. Images of
the uncanny that provoke disconcertedness in the adult mind, such as
the double, or dolls coming to life, are often harmless or amusing
thoughts for the child, who in play will often imagine that such figures
are her companions. In both *La Classe de neige* and *Marin mon cœur*,
the vision of the child is exploited as a narrative mechanism to
imagine a defamiliarized space and to represent a state of exclusion
from the norms of the collective sphere. The child is portrayed as
being closer to a place where reality and fantasy coalesce. For Nicolas,
at a phase when he seeks to cross over from the world of children to
that of adults, this experience is anxious, since uncertainty is what
needs to be overcome in order for him to move forward. In *Marin mon
cœur*, the narrator's regression to a child-like world is experienced as
magical and joyful. This difference may be partially explained by the
different ages of the focalized children. The estranging power of the
pre-symbolic existence of Marin encounters no resistance on the part
of the father and this in some sense removes the anxiety of the
blurring of strange and familiar; without a desire for rationality or
certainty, the effect of repression is absent. For Savitzkaya the uncanny is not a moment of stress or fright where the homely world
dissipates, but rather the desire for an extended return to a primitive

---

[60] Unlike Freud and Lacan, the psychoanalyst D. W. Winnicott privileges the mother
over the father in the development of the subject. His concept of dyadic space refers
to the maternal relationship. Dyadic space is 'characterized by an absence of a sense
of boundaries, a lack of real-world constraints, and a potentially infinite, free flow of
images and ideas'. See Graham Lee, 'Alone Among Three: The Father and the Œdipus Complex', in *Fathers, Families and the Outside World*, Winnicott Studies
Monograph Series, ed. by Val Richards (London: Karnac Books, 1997), pp. 73-87, p.
80. Savitzkaya invents a paternal space which is given over to these more 'maternal'
qualities.

way of thinking as a basis for innovation and writing.

In all three novels explored in this chapter, the uncanny provides a plethora of narrative mechanisms and modes of perception for the representation of subjectivity within the contemporary family. Once again, as seen in the last chapter, the uncanny has become a possible quality of the 'ordinary', familiar world, or the *chez soi*. This time the focus is on the dynamics of family relations, rather than on domestic, everyday environments. Rather than being portrayed as stabilizing and reassuring, ties of kinship and encounters with proximate others are presented as the most likely source of an unsettling of the self. The uncanny is thus a way of re-writing the world of family life and relations of kinship in order to stress the dualism of this domain, its suspension between the familiar, comforting associations we might attach to it and its possible deviation from those associations, as a source of uncertainty or estrangement.

As was the case in the previous chapter, it seems that having an uncanny point of view on certain elements of subjective experience informs a series of strategies which allow these writers to take on current themes in contemporary French writing. Like so many of today's authors who have recently explored the theme of family life,[61] NDiaye, Carrère and Savitzkaya view it as a complex phenolmenon. The uncanny is perhaps one way of perceiving or expressing this complexity and representing its effects on subjective experience.

In the novels by NDiaye and Carrère, a character turns to a parental figure in an attempt to regain certainty and to retrieve a sense of origin, sanctuary or knowledge. However, the family, so desired, instead proves to be a source of further instability and estrangement. For Savitzkaya, however, the character seeks such estrangement, rather than assurance, and willingly places himself in a position where his sense of familiarity may be dissolved.

For NDiaye, the blurring of strange and familiar comes across largely through a tension maintained throughout *Rosie Carpe* between

---

[61] The essays which figure in the recently published work *Affaires de famille: The Family in Contemporary French Culture and Theory* indicate just how prominent this theme is today in French writing, and also how complex. Shirley Ann Jordan suggests that a number of contemporary writers 'place family firmly at the centre of their investigations, focusing with nostalgia upon its desirability but emphasizing overwhelming problems of family construction and maintenance'. Shirley Ann Jordan, 'Figuring out the Family: Family as Everyday Practice in French Women's Writing', pp. 57-8.

the quest for a heartening version of home and its estranging manifestation. While Rosie's dialogue and inner thoughts accentuate the mythical values of family as grounding and familiar, the disconcerting incarnations of family members in the novel, as elusive or even monstrous, often contradict these associations and further uproot Rosie's sense of self.

For both Carrère and Savitzkaya, a blurring of the codes of strange and familiar was achieved through an appeal to the perspective of the child. Yet, the foreignness of the experience of childhood was portrayed in very different ways. As well as contrasting interpretations of fatherhood, they both present opposing versions of the experience of youth. Carrère presented us with a vision of the child's world as a threatening and often hostile space. His portrayal of Nicolas's youth emphasized the lack of access that the child has to the world of adults, and the ways in which this lack renders ordinary environments mysterious. The child's constant uncertainty is not a form of wondering, but results from his exclusion from adulthood. This is experienced as a deprivation and leads to fearsome childhood fantasies. At the same time, for Nicolas, the uncanny world of fantasy is shown to be productive in his development, as his imagination helps him to channel his uncertainty into creativity. In *Marin mon cœur*, the world of the child is not experienced as lacking, but as one which is in some sense richer and superior to that of adults.[62] It is by 'borrowing' the child's perspective that the narrator reinvents ordinary experience as enchanted and renewed.

To return to some of the ideas expressed in the introduction to this chapter, it seems that the portrayals of family life elaborated in the above novels can be seen to reflect the duality of current thought concerning family relations, which address its simultaneously strange and familiar nature. What is well brought out in all three novels is the duality inherent in the family, its responsibility to guide the subject,

---

[62] It is also interesting to compare these representations of childhood with the experience of childhood as represented in *Rosie Carpe*. Throughout most of the novel, Titi, Rosie's son, is deprived of any point of view whatsoever. The reader only encounters him as the object of rejection and criticism on the part of the other characters. For Rosie, Titi must be sacrificed in order for her to continue with her life. At the end of the novel, however, this dynamic shifts. Years later, Lagrand encounters Titi as an adult demonstrating at a strike with other teachers. He is holding a sign which reads 'DES SOUS'. After being a victim of the scorn of others for many years, Titi finally expresses himself, if only to make mercantile demands.

and especially the child, in constituting her subjectivity and its potential to undermine this very process by destabilizing the development of individual identity. In all these novels, a protagonist naturally turns to the family as part of either an identity quest or a desire for understanding, and in all three cases the solicited family members remain elusive and so troubling to the subject's sense of integration into the community and self-certainty. As was the case with the representation of the everyday in the previous chapter, there is a sense in which NDiaye, Carrère and Savitzkaya are presenting 'the other side' of life within the home.

A Narrative Ethics of the Unhomely

In certain accounts of the uncanny, including those of Cixous and Kristeva, the concept moves beyond many of its more immediate phenomenological or imagery-related associations, and is constructed in terms of selfhood. The uncanny is not simply a feeling or theme, but an ethics of or approach to experience, founded on the unsettling of the *chez soi* in order to re-negotiate the strange/familiar dichotomy. Both of these thinkers believe that certain forms of uncanny experience have the potential to generate an estranging mode of perception, which is projected back onto the self. Emphasis is here placed not on the disconcerting nature of external or foreign phenomena, but on the 'otherness' or vulnerability of the self. While for Freud the experience of the *Unheimliche* involves a glimpse of certain repressed remnants of ego development, Kristeva and Cixous suggest that in the uncanny, the perceived stability and mastery of the *je* might be evacuated, so that the self encounters its own uncertainty. This may be a starting point for engaging with the world more ethically, so as to avoid dynamics of repression. While the political or social value of such theories is not under investigation here, I have argued throughout this book that their aesthetic implications are noteworthy; this is particularly the case with respect to the stance of the writing subject.

As we will see in the present chapter, the act of writing creates a site in which the strangeness of the self may be welcomed and reflected upon. In all three of the novels studied in this chapter, stories which, on the surface, appear to be non-fictional exposés of selfhood or descriptions of real events turn out, upon closer examination, to be first and foremost narratives of the uncanny experiences which the writer undergoes during the writing process. In this context, the *Unheimliche* might be understood not only as an array of images and a literary device for the articulation of the strangeness of home and self, but also as a narrative ethos or stance of writing, which is based on the acknowledgement of the vulnerability and uncertainty of the writing subject when faced with the challenge of thematizing or 'domesticating' the elusive realities he or she seeks to portray. The stories which are foregrounded are not those of the alleged non-fictional content, but the writerly adventures generated by the quest to appropriate a *chez soi* from which to write. The privileging of authorial unhomeliness serves to convey a reflection upon both the ostensible object of representation (either the *fait divers* or the self) and upon writing itself, which is portrayed as a voluntary act of uprooting from the *chez soi*.

Finding one's place
The return to non-fictional forms of writing, such as autobiography or the representation of the *fait divers,* is a widespread tendency in French literature today.[1] Yet, rather than complying with the codes conventionally associated with non-fictional genres, such as linearity or supposed objectivity, many writers re-appropriate and modify these frameworks in order to question their ability to portray reality and subjective experience truthfully. In the wake of literary tendencies such as *autofiction,* contemporary novelists are often seeking ways inventively to counterbalance more traditional approaches to the depiction of the self, the event or the other, by employing narrative strategies that embrace representational uncertainty and problematize the distinction between fiction and fact.

It is not uncommon, in certain recent works that fit this des-cription, for a writer to question the legitimacy of his or her own narrating stance, and to confess a sense of disorientation with regard to an object of representation. This is perhaps due, as Dominique Viart implies in his book *La Littérature française au présent,* to the era in which they are writing, which is dominated by new forms of suspicion following the *Nouveau Roman*:

> Que le narrateur en vienne à ne plus savoir comment écrire son récit, ni quelle place se donner dans le texte sinon au prix de changements dans la structure énonciative, paraît très carac-téristique d'une époque en manque de certitudes et de repères, inquiète d'elle-même et de sa pensée. (LFP 240)

---

[1] Many contemporary French novelists have based their works on *faits divers*. For example, Olivier Rolin's *Invention du monde* is based on a selection of *faits divers* from various international newspapers. François Bon's *Un fait divers* (Paris: Minuit, 1994) tells the story of a young woman accused of murder. Danielle Sallenave's *Viol* (Paris: Gallimard, 1997) recounts the legal and psychiatric proceedings which result from the rape of a 13-year old girl. Other well-known examples of this return to the *fait divers* are works by J.M.G. Le Clézio and Patrick Modiano.

In today's writing, the expression of hesitation with regard to representation is not only displayed in techniques of fragmentation, repetition, erasure and *mise en abyme,* but often takes the form of a more personal expression of strangeness, disorientation and homelessness, which the writer shares with the reader in various ways.

For Carrère, NDiaye and Savitzkaya, the question of 'quelle place se donner' may be understood more specifically in terms of home. Emmanuel Levinas tells us that the *je* 'trouve dans le monde un lieu et une maison'.[2] For the philosopher, this idea implies that, in order to dwell in a coherent world, the subject of ontology creates a comfortable location from which to perceive external phenomena, a place of subjective stability. In the narratives under investigation in this chapter, however, an experience of *un*homing is primordial to a perception of the world and the act of writing. None of these authors is able to establish a grounding point, a *chez soi,* from which to carry out the textual appropriation of the literary object. The experience of writing is itself revealed to be uncanny, in the sense that these writers are each confronted with the uninhabitable nature of any single authorial position.

This sense of authorial disorientation seems to be a response to the strangeness that each writer perceives within the familiar. The unhomeliness of the writing subject resonates in harmony with the themes of the narratives. Like the previous texts examined in this book, all three novels studied in the present chapter are stories of the intangible nature of the *chez soi.* For Carrère, the familiar world in question is that of collective reality, which is estranged in light of a *fait divers* which devastates the life of one French family. In his work *L'Adversaire,* he employs heterogeneous, intersecting voices and genres to bring about a tentative reconstruction of the crimes and trial of the real figure Jean-Claude Romand, who murdered his wife and children and then set fire to his home to conceal his crime. In the novels by NDiaye and Savitzkaya, the notion of the *chez soi* is primarily understood as relating to the self. In NDiaye's *Autoportrait en vert, unheimlich* imagery, particularly the image of the double, constantly haunts and interferes with the author's attempts at self-representation. She presents the self as a kind of haunted house and

---

[2] Emmanuel Levinas, *Totalité et infini,* p. 26.

the task of autobiographical writing as an attempt to 'rentrer chez soi'. In Savitzkaya's autobiographical text, *Fou trop poli,* the writer depicts self-representation as the impossible quest to define and locate the place from which one is writing. A conscious displacement of self is inherent in and required for self-representation, and this notion informs his descriptions of both the self and the writing process. By privileging the theme of exile and transposing his autobiographical enunciation into the figure of 'le fou', the author explores moments from his past and his present day-to-day existence to articulate some of the confusion arising between selfhood and authorship.

Approaching Uncertainty: Carrère's *L'Adversaire*

L'Adversaire (2001) unites Carrère's journalistic and fictional fortes in a reconstruction of the story of the criminal Jean-Claude Romand. In 1993, in a suburb near the border between France and Switzerland, this man killed his wife, children and parents before attempting unsuccessfully to end his own life and to destroy the evidence of his act by setting fire to the family home. The investigation conducted after the crime revealed that, prior to the event, Romand had been living a fictitious existence. His persona as a successful doctor, unquestioned by family and friends, was entirely fraudulent. In *L'Adversaire,* intellectual uncertainty, an *unheimlich* presence within the family home and an ethical obligation to acknowledge the intricacy and subjective complexities relating to representation, converge to create a mystifying text, which, like the event itself, blurs the borders between reality and fiction. Guided by principles of uncertainty and empathy, the novelist interweaves factual, journalistic, biographical and autobiographical detail with fragments of invention, sporadically adopting the various roles of journalist, fictional writer, autobiographical narrator and character.[3] It is through this narrative mechanism of a constant unhoming of the authorial voice, observed in constant self-displacement, that Carrère is able to re-create this man's experience as well as produce a parallel story of his own.[4]

---

[3] A similar style of story-telling can also be seen in *Je suis vivant et vous êtes morts, Philip K.Dick, 1928-1982,* Carrère's biography of the science fiction writer, which is both biographical and fictional.

[4] Some of the ideas addressed in this section are also explored in a chapter published

An uncanny tale

The Romand affair, as communicated by police and media, appears quite uncanny, in the sense that a fearsome strangeness appears to have emerged from the heart of the familiar, domestic sphere. On 9 January 1993, firefighters were called to investigate a house fire in a quiet suburban neighborhood on the border between France and Switzerland. The bodies of Romand's wife, two young children and parents were discovered separately. Jean-Claude was taken to the hospital, unconscious. When the autopsies revealed that his wife and children had died before the fire, investigators concluded that there had been an attempted murder of the Romand family and they interrogated neighbours and friends. Perplexed and shocked, each one stressed the unlikelihood of such a scenario. Romand was a successful doctor, a researcher at the World Health Organization, and well-liked by the entire community. When the WHO was unable to identify him as one of their employees it was revealed that he was not, in fact, a doctor and had simply feigned the completion of his medical degree and the subsequent commencement of his practice. He had generated an income by appropriating relatives' financial resources, which he claimed to be investing on their behalf. In 1993, when he had finally exhausted his funds and feared his lie would crumble, he apparently took the decision to end his life and also the lives of his closest relatives, allegedly to prevent the suffering they might endure upon knowing the truth. The bitter denouement of the story is the fact that Romand survived. The use-by date of the bottle of pills he swallowed before starting the fire had expired. Several days later, he awoke in his hospital room, badly burned, to face the consequences of his acts.

Since this occurrence in 1993, French media, film and fiction have attempted to represent this catastrophe, which poses multiple representational challenges.[5] Aside from the sensitivity required on the

---

in another work. See Daisy Connon, 'Dislocation of the Authorial Voice in Emmanuel Carrère's *L'Adversaire* and Eugène Savitzkaya's *Fou trop poli*', in *Aesthetics of Dislocation in French and Francophone Literature and Art: Strategies of Representation*, ed. by Daisy Connon, Gillian Jein and Greg Kerr (Lewiston, Queenston, Lampeter: The Edwin Mellen Press, 2009), pp. 69-86.

[5] Besides the media coverage of the event, there have been two French films. Both were released in 2001. The first, directed by Nicole Garcia, was simply entitled *l'Adversaire* and based on Carrère's text. The second, *L'Emploi du temps*, directed by Laurent Cantet, is only loosely inspired by the Romand affair, and features a character

part of the creator to engage credibly with the theme of family violence, an account of the Romand affair demands a reinterpretation of the past in light of an incident which obfuscates the moral, legal, familial and figurative codes that might inform such a representation. Not only must we digest the fact that a father consciously killed his entire family in a premeditated act, but also the absurd notion of his false standing as a doctor at the WHO. How was he able to construct and maintain such a tight or functional narrative for 18 years surrounding a false career without arousing the suspicion of his family and friends?

Such questions reflect the peculiar significance of the *fait divers,* a phenomenon Roland Barthes described as a moment of social and ideological contravention that points to a place 'où le monde cesse d'être nommé'.[6] This subsidiary journalistic category treats absurd crimes, disasters and marvels emerging from the private sphere, whose essence Barthes characterized as 'étonnement'.[7] While it would seem that the *fait divers* constitutes news in the most concrete form, Barthes stresses its incongruous, literary quality. The *fait divers* does not participate in a political, ideological or other contextual discourse, but has a 'monstrous' nature, and contributes to unsettling such discourses.[8] The significance of such an event is experienced as the absence of sufficient representational means of accounting for it. As scandalous stories, *faits divers* always risk being dismissed or sensationalized in the interest of preserving the harmony of community and home. As David H. Walker suggests in his examination of the history of *faits divers,* these events serve to 'map the sensitive outer edges of public opinion'.[9] Given its unvalued status, yet its capacity for disrupting the status quo by revealing strange realities within the private sphere, the *fait divers* might itself be seen as an uncanny phenomenon. For Michel Foucault, such an event is 'à la fois comme très proche et tout à fait étrang[er]'.[10] Chris-

---

forced to turn to fraudulent financial investments after concealing the loss of his job from his family.

[6] Roland Barthes, 'Structure du fait divers', in *Œuvres complètes, 1962-1967, Tome II* (Paris: Éditions du Seuil, 2002), pp. 442-65 (p. 442).

[7] Ibid, p. 445.

[8] Ibid, p. 442.

[9] David H. Walker, *Outrage and Insight: Modern French Writers and the 'Fait Divers'* (Oxford, Washington: Berg Publishers, 1995), p. 2.

[10] Cited in David H. Walker, *Outrage and Insight: Modern French Writers and the*

tian Vandenorpe suggests that the *fait divers* blurs the boundaries between the familiar, comprehensible world and the grotesque, or the absurd:

> Le fait divers est aux antipodes de la science-fiction, qui exige de la part du lecteur une capacité de décentrement culturel et d'imaginaire que tous ne possèdent pas. Il exploite des schémas correspondant à notre univers quotidien. Il recueille ce qui, dans la banalité ambiante, est élevé à la dimension du tragique ou du cocasse. Aussi reste-t-il facilement compréhensible quand bien même les informations en sont faiblement connectées, bourrées d'ellipses, et l'organisation peu cohérente.[11]

In his analysis of J.M.G. Le Clézio's texts, Bruno Thibault proposes that '[une] force étrange hante l'univers du fait divers et vient miner la relation des causes et des effets'.[12] As well as raising problems of illogicality and definition, resisting absorption into closed categories, the *fait divers* also constitutes a form of social haunting. Our trivializing treatment of such events perhaps points to a larger mechanism of societal repression.

Although the novelist felt compelled to represent this story, its incoherent and shocking qualities presented him with the difficulty of gaining perspective on the event. The strangeness of the occurrence seemed to elude more objective approaches, yet the author felt that a predominantly fictional portrayal would not permit him to engage with the event as a 'true story', nor respond to a self-imposed duty to tell it. He considered several forms and points of view, from fact-based, neutral accounts to dynamic literary creations exploring the philosophical notions of emptiness and lying. He successfully completed another work, the novel *La Classe de neige*, only distantly inspired by Romand's story, but continued to be plagued by it. He encountered numerous moral difficulties, at times feeling repulsed by his own fascination for the event. In an interview he recalls leaving the final manuscript of his novel with his publisher and subsequently

---

'Fait Divers', p. 5.

[11] Christian Vandenorpe, 'La Lecture du fait divers: fonctionnement textuel et effets cognitifs', *Tangence* 37 (1992), pp. 56-69 (p. 60).

[12] Bruno Thibault, 'Du stéréotype au mythe: l'écriture du fait divers dans les nouvelles de J.M.G. Le Clézio', *The French Review*, Vol. 68, No. 6 (May 1995), 964-75 (p. 966).

reclaiming it, regarding it as 'radioactive'.[13] His sense of uncertainty with respect to this event was communicated to Jean-Claude Romand himself in a letter the author sent to him in prison: '[Mon problème] est de trouver ma place face à votre histoire'.[14] It was as if he felt unable to locate himself, as author, in relation to the story he wished to tell. The author is not simply describing a problematic of truth or objectivity, but one of authorial place, or point of view, a feeling of not being *chez soi* in one's authorial function.

The difficulties encountered by the author in 'finding his place' are perceptible in the nature of his reconstruction. There is a significant journalistic component. At times, the reader confronts a seemingly detached collection of facts and figures and can discern a uni-linear reconstruction of the events leading up to the crime and the details of the trial and sentence. In passages such as the following, the author employs Romand's full name and maintains the distant, forthright tone of a *fait diversier*:

> Après cinq heures de délibération, Jean-Claude Romand a été condamné à la réclusion criminelle à perpétuité, assortie d'une peine de sûreté de vingt-deux ans. Si tout se passe bien, il sortira en 2015 âgé de soixante et un ans. (A 204)

This thread of the narrative generates a space for commentary by psychiatrists, lawyers, legal consultants and police, discourses which are simply present in the text, but never stand as the whole interpretation. But elsewhere, these fact-oriented lines of explanation are shifted into the background to make way for a variety of other intersecting perspectives. The author interrupts his journalistic text to assume the role of narrator or biographer. Relying on details confided to him during interviews with Romand, he describes the days leading up to the crimes, inserting anecdotes and recollections from Romand's youth and the early years of his marriage. Here the narrative voice assumes a certain proximity and familiarity with Romand. When describing his curiosity about why he was an only child, the author adopts a more personal tone, which diverges significantly from the distanced quality of the narration above:

---

[13] Jean-Pierre Tison, 'Interview avec Emmanuel Carrère', *Lire* (February 2000) 24-30, p. 27.
[14] Emmanuel Carrère, *L'Adversaire* (Paris: P.O.L., 2000), p. 205. All other references are given in the text, following the abbreviation A.

> Il sentait que cette question recouvrait quelque chose de caché et que sa curiosité mais plus encore sa peine leur faisaient du chagrin. C'était un mot de sa mère, le chagrin, auquel elle donnait un sens curieusement concret, comme s'il s'agissait d'une maladie organique qui la minait. (A 52)

The reader identifies impressions and memories related directly to the author by the character himself. However, in turn, these biographical moments morph into predominantly fictional descriptions. Working with some first-hand indication of the feelings of alienation this man experienced, the author frequently elaborates upon episodes featuring Romand, transforming him into a fictional figure. Imagining the days preceding the crimes, Carrère describes his possible thoughts and feelings of weariness, as a novelist evoking the subjective reality of a fictional protagonist:

> Il s'est senti lourd, fatigué la dernière semaine. Il s'assoupissait sur le canapé, dans la voiture, à n'importe quelle heure. Ses oreilles bourdonnaient comme s'il avait été au fond de la mer. Son cerveau lui faisait mal, il aurait voulu pouvoir le retirer de son crâne et le donner au lavage [...] Florence a fait une lessive et il est resté dans la salle de bain où se trouvait la machine à regarder derrière le hublot le linge qui se tordait mollement dans l'eau très chaude [...] Leurs vêtements mélangés à tous les quatre, leurs souffles mélangés, paisibles, sous le toit bien calfeutré qui les abritait de la nuit d'hiver. (A 151)

Romand emerges as a character, allotted a certain voice and subjecttivity. Yet the author is hesitant to assess his level of guilt or anxiety, and concentrates primarily on impressions, visual imagery and physical sensations. These observations confer a sense of depth on the representtation of this figure, which extracts him momentarily from his role as criminal, without detaching him entirely from the context of his acts.

Focalization through the character of Luc Ladmiral, Romand's best friend, allows the author to approach some of the emotional implications of the event for family and friends. Luc functions as a fictional figure, but, since he is based on a real person, also as a non-fictional source. Details conveyed in passages which feature Luc are often allegedly accurate, but are framed in a fictional discourse, containing dialogue imagined by the author, which unsettles their objectivity. Often, the journalistic and fictional discourses intersect one another. This is the case in the following passage, for example, just after Romand confesses to his friend that he has been having an affair:

> À un feu rouge, Luc s'est tourné vers son ami, cherchant son regard. Il tenait pour acquis que la raison de sa dépression était la rupture avec Florence (ce qui d'une certaine façon était vrai) et venait de faire valoir que les filles sont changeantes, que rien n'était perdu. (A 81)

This description is not entirely fictional, since by inserting the phrase in parentheses, the author himself intervenes on his own portrayal of this interaction, providing background to this scenario.

One observes the novelist at work in Carrère's description of Luc's encounter with Florence's body. The author plays the role of omniscient narrator in the character's mind, familiar with his reflections:

> Florence avait seulement été recouverte d'un manteau. Son visage, noirci par la fumée, était intact. En lissant ses cheveux, dans un geste d'adieu désolé, les doigts de Luc ont rencontré quelque chose de bizarre. Il a tâtonné, fait rouler avec précaution la tête de la jeune femme, puis appelé un pompier pour lui montrer, au-dessus de la nuque une plaie béante. (A 9)

However, the details communicated in this passage are those which were imparted to the author during his interviews with the real Luc Ladmiral. When representing Florence, the author again adopts the voice of an omniscient narrator, presenting the suspicions or concerns she might have had, but kept hidden, concerning her husband: 'Elle avait bien senti que quelque chose n'allait pas ces derniers temps' (A 125). While a certain degree of novelistic embroidery is often tolerated in journalistic and non-fictional writing, Carrère frequently oversteps the boundaries so that the reader has the impression she is reading fictional text.

The interrogative form is often exploited as a cautious bridging of fiction and non-fiction. When imagining the scene where Romand emerges from his coma in the hospital to acknowledge his crimes, the form of a question and the conditional are used to evoke a scenario which is uncertain, but poignant:

Lui, seul, encore dans le coma, ne savait pas qu'il était vivant et que ceux qu'il aimait étaient morts de sa main. Cette absence n'allait pas durer. Il allait sortir des limbes. Que verrait-il en ouvrant les yeux? Une chambre peinte en blanc, des bandages blancs enveloppant son corps. Que se rappelait-il? Quelles images l'accompagnaient pendant qu'il remontait vers la surface? Qui, le premier, allait croiser son regard? (A 31)

The reader often wonders whether she is being exposed to reinterpretations of the reflections Romand confided to the author during their communication, or if these instances are simply imagined moments and affects, inserted into the text at the author's own stylistic discretion. Jean-Claude Romand's identity in the narrative is divided amongst his roles as a journalistic subject, a biographical personality and an invented character. Likewise, Carrère's authorial voice is split into fictional narrator, author, biographer, journalist and autobiographical protagonist.

The expression of the author's sense of disorientaion is not reduced to these textual mechanisms. It is often conveyed in a straightforward manner by the narrator himself, who interrupts the non-fictional and fictional portions of the text with his own reflections concerning his writing project. During such sequences, he recalls conversations he held with Romand during the writing process, includes letters they exchanged and refers to the Romand family photos, which remind him of his own children.[15] The novel begins with a one-page reflection where a chronological parallel is evoked between his own family's activities and the murder of the Romand family on the morning of 9 January 1993. By placing his version of the story in this very subjective framework and drawing his own reality into the text, the novelist casts himself in the role of a character in Romand's story.[16] In assuming various stances of narration, and in speaking from within the act of narration itself, the novelist concomitantly reconstructs Jean-Claude Romand's story and puts forth his own sense of hesitation with respect to its telling.

---

[15] See, for example, his commentary on *Le Progrès* on p. 25 of the novel.

[16] As the writer told Romand at one point, 'Ce n'est évidemment pas moi qui vais dire "je" pour votre compte, mais alors il me reste, à propos de vous, à dire "je" pour moi-même. A dire, en mon nom propre et sans me réfugier derrière un témoin plus ou moins imaginaire ou un patchwork d'informations se voulant objectives, ce qui dans votre histoire me parle et résonne dans la mienne' (A 206).

Aesthetically, Carrère's fractured technique textually re-enacts the disintegrating effect of the *fait divers* on the myths and codes of the communal real, and on any possible authorial perspective from which an 'objective' interpretation might be possible. More than this, the author's project may be viewed as expressing a narrative ethos of uncertainty, one driven by a wish to provide a literary counterbalance to the depictions of Romand presented by the more sensationalist or narrower discourses of media, psychology or law. In alignment with Barthes's analysis of the *fait divers*, journalists often tended to construct Romand as a kind of monster. Much of the journalistic treatment of the affair presents the irony of both trivializing the event, by relegating it to a marginal status in the newspaper, detached from the more pertinent or authentic news, and appealing to a flamboyant language of horror to depict it as a monstrous intrusion on an otherwise harmonious world. Carrère cites one article published in *Le Monde* on the day of the trial, which begins: 'On n'a pas toujours l'occasion de voir le visage du diable' (A 46). Carrère's portrayal of this same event suggests that, while we may condemn Romand's acts and sympathize with his victims, we nonetheless have an obligation not to simplify the affair by employing a one-dimensional logic of scapegoating, turning the criminal into a receptacle for societal ugliness. Following a Kristevan line of thought, one might consider that entirely 'othering' Romand represents a struggle to preserve the integrity and comfort of the *chez soi*, of our own homes and self-unity.[17]

It is perhaps the author's commitment to remaining 'homeless' in his narrative stance, observed in the multi-dimensional and inter-mittent nature of his authorial intervention, which permits him to approach the unapproachable. By turning the incriminating glance towards various possible subjects of enunciation, rather than towards the criminal himself, the author resists easy condemnation or stock categorization of the crimes of Jean-Claude Romand. Rather, he circumvents this question by representing the impact of the event, which, by fracturing the social pact, denies us any firm ground on which to stand in an effort to formulate a clear perception of it. These strategies of fragmentation allow the author to penetrate some of the

---

[17] The title of the work, *L'Adversaire*, might appear to suggest a form of 'othering'. However, Carrère understands this title somewhat differently. See below, pages 219-20.

emotional depths of the event, while engaging with the moral and figurative difficulties of representing the other. The novel thus presents two intertwining tales, and features two main characters. It is both a representation of the *fait divers*, focusing on the real character Jean-Claude Romand, and the story of the emotional, ethical and representational anxieties of Carrère as writer, as he searches for a firm ground to stand on in order to interpret these catastrophic events.

Self and community

The author's voluntary destabilization of his own narrative stance is also a response to the images of selfhood and community that emerge through Romand's story. Depictions of Romand as an imposter who threatens the integrity of the community neglect to account for the haziness of the frontier between the fictional and the real revealed by this man's story. The sudden emergence of an event like the Romand affair out of the domain of the comfortably ordinary is something that demands contemplation precisely because it jostles the codes of realism. An element in this story which harbours great potential for disquiet is what Romand's case reveals about simulacra and their social effects. Romand had successfully engaged in a certain form of performativity which allowed him to participate in the community as the man he claimed to be. This brings to light a fictional element in the presuppositions we might make about domestic space and societal roles. Romand frequently left papers with the WHO logo on coffee tables, debated with other doctors about current medical topics, bought travel guides and brought back souvenirs for his children from airport gift shops as proof of having spent a week in New York or Tokyo. Although empty, these signs of his identity were adequate, enabling him to occupy a certain role in the community. What is perhaps disturbing to realize is that these symbols were enough to create the illusion of normality; they functioned impeccably for eighteen years, interpreted transparently by everyone without the slightest suspicion, without reference to the reality they were believed to indicate. Viewed from a certain perspective, this successful but false inscription into the codes of collective reality raises suspicions about the authenticity of collective meaning itself, a space where we ordinarily feel at home.

The crime that was committed was a transgression of the moral, legal and social codes of the family, and its occurrence unsettles the image we have of home as a fundamental, reassuring structure of collective reality. Romand's acts mark the emergence of a fearsome, incomeprehensible foreignness from the midst of a seemingly ordinary domestic space, a nightmare which ended in the unforgettable image of the Romand house aflame. Neighbours and friends would not only revisit in their minds their previous encounters with the Romand family, doubting their own past perceptions of reality, and their obliviousness to this man's imposture, but perhaps even question the sanctuary and comfort of their own homes. The catastrophe suggests a form of haunting, but one which surfaces from within the familiar itself, and invites us to go back over the image of stability presented by the Romand family as a detective might re-examine the past, seeking a clue, something which was slightly awry, but to no avail. In the novel, the strangeness of the familiar world which is revealed by the Romand affair is reflected in narrative strategies which imply a second glance at the real, a broadening of visions of the everyday from a less rigid point of view. Carrère employs narrative strategies which permit him to 'rethink' everyday reality in an unhomely light.

Strangely, these strategies involve a de-emphasis of the peculiarity of the Romand family in order to accentuate instead its familiarity and banality, so that the codes of strange and familiar enter into a state of tension. The particularity of the Romand story permits the writer to blur the strange/familiar distinction by employing a paradoxical, reconstructive narrative strategy in which the familiar becomes synonymous with the strange. A great part of the novel concentrates on painting a minutely detailed and realistic portrait of the Romand family which, far from accentuating their singularity, places the accent on their predictability, the ways in which they blended into the community and resembled the average suburban family. Carrère gives examples of the pet names they exchanged at home, well-known films they watched together, such as *Le Père Noël est une ordure* or *Le Grand bleu* (A 92), the Renault 'Espace' which transported them to after-school activities and Christmas parties, the involvement of both parents in community organizations, the holidays they took together, the big plates of chips and ketchup that the kids were permitted after skiing, even the breakfast cereals that Jean-Claude served his children and the news magazines he purchased just hours before the murders. Some of these very ordinary details are facts, which were perhaps collected by the author during research and interviews; others appear incidental and do not have a function in the fact-driven discourse. These details participate in the novelistic décor which characterizes Carrère's version of the affair. One example is a passage describing a moment just days before the crime when Romand is in the bath, observing the family laundry spinning in the washing machine:

> Il y avait des chemises et des sous-vêtements à lui, imprégnés de sa sueur mauvaise, il y avait ceux de Florence et des enfants, les tee-shirts, les pyjamas ornés de bestioles de dessins animés, les petites chaussettes d'Antoine et Caroline qu'il était difficile de distinguer au moment du rangement. (A 151)

The more commonplace the details of the narration and the more they coincide with a description of an ordinary family, the more uncanny the reading becomes, given the reader's awareness of the tragic end. As was the case with the portrayal of identity, the most trivial moments appear to stare back at the reader, inviting her to identify with, but subsequently doubt, these indicators of reality. In a similar way to that observed previously in *La Moustache*, negligible details suddenly begin to acquire a capacity to signify, challenging the authenticity of the ordinariness and familiarity we attribute to the everyday.

The author's description of the family before the crimes simultaneously posits the conventional nature of the Romand family and renders strange this extremely conventional image by framing this description in the context of the violent crime that emerged from their seemingly tranquil environment. An entirely wholesome, familiar description of a family's existence then takes on a menacing appearance when viewed in the light of the crime, suggesting that the familiar might be already haunted. This experience of defamiliarization resonates on an extremely personal level, since, in Carrère's text, this also implies the strange aesthetic experience of urging the reader into an identification with Romand, into a perception of his existence, which, on the surface, resembles her own.

This relocation of strangeness to the intimate and the familiar is also felt through the problematization of self which emerges in this story. Although Romand presents a disturbed, criminal psychology, the author attempts to extract from his story a universal instance we might recognize in ourselves, rather than simply dismiss as pathological. In an interview, Carrère elucidates the title of his book, 'L'Adversaire'. Although given the subject of his text, the term could perhaps be seen to evoke a threat to family and community, Carrère suggests another meaning, which he connects to the notion of identity. For the author, *L'Adversaire* points not simply to an external antagonism, but rather to a moment of fraud and deception existing within every individual and sometimes reaching exaggerated proportions.[18]

While the media were inclined to use phrases such as 'double identity' or 'living a lie' to describe this character, Carrère's text reveals the fallacy of these terms given the case of Romand.[19] Such concepts presuppose the existence of a true and coherent self, which was merely masked by Romand's external façade. However, Romand did not have a double identity, where the true and false elements were distinguishable, but a single persona, which may not be simply viewed as either accurate or fabricated. In his interview with the literary magazine *Lire*, the author reveals that what first triggered his interest in the case of Jean-Claude Romand was the desire to represent a certain nothingness brought out by his story, a factor he refers to as a 'vide blanc'. He explains:

> Un mensonge, normalement, sert à recouvrir une vérité, quelque chose de honteux peut-être mais de réel. Le sien ne recouvrait rien. Sous le faux docteur Romand il n'y avait pas de vrai docteur Romand. (A 99)

Underneath the surface identity of an honest professional man, a loving father and husband, there was of course no 'real Romand' to reconstruct, no other, integral person who could provide an account of his societal exclusion or justify his bifurcation into falsehood. While he was allegedly at work, Romand's days were spent alone, in his car, perusing medical text books and magazines, absently roaming the forests of the Jura near the Swiss border or holed up in airport hotels on feigned business trips, watching television. Carrère's story is inspired by this lack, this 'blanc qui n'a cessé de grandir à la place de celui qui en (Romand) doit dire "je"' (A 206), an emptiness held in

---

[18] Jean-Pierre Tison, 'Interview avec Emmanuel Carrère', pp. 24-30.
[19] Several articles published in French newspapers around the time of the crimes used the term 'double vie' to describe Romand's existence. See, for example, the article by journalist David Dufresne, 'La Rage narcissique de Romand', *Libération* (2 July 1996).

check by mimesis and artifice but which ultimately drove Romand to acts of desperation.

This is a theme which recurs throughout Carrère's work. His novels often explore the discepancies between the inner turmoil of subjectivity and the individual as socially constituted through the reality principle and through the socio-symbolic and moral codes of the collective sphere.[20] This view of identity could of course be interpreted as simply a contemporary version of the Proustian *moi social* verses the *moi profond*, but it is also not so different from certain psychoanalytic models of subjectivity which posit a split subject: a model acknowledging a lack or 'white emptiness' in every individual, and open to the possibility that this may be intermittently revealed to the subject, yielding certain forms of uncanny anxiety.[21] Certain branches of psychoanalysis will go so far as to see the 'white emptiness' as a pre-eminent component of the psyche and to regard the subject's inscription in language itself, through the assumption of the signifier 'I', as in some way fictional, necessitating a partial repression of this emptiness in order to maintain adherence to a linguistically and collectively formulated identity.[22] According to this conception, the founding moment of subjectivity is based on a positing of oneself as a kind of character, a falsely total, integral individual whose self-image is dominated by what is actually a form of alterity. This description of identity should serve not to reduce the deceptive practice carried out for eighteen years by Jean-Claude Romand to a universal and unchangeable psychological trait, but rather to locate an instance of imitation and performance present in every individual, which must be identified before we can begin to reflect or moralize upon the conceptually and ethically intricate notions of honesty and falsehood, and assume the responsibility to 'tell the truth'.[23]

---

[20] We might recall *La Moustache*, for example, where a minor cosmetic detail takes on horrendous proportions and eventually causes the character's disintegration into insanity.

[21] See, for example, the Lacanian concept of the gaze as the revelation of the subject's lack in *Le Séminaire XI, Les Quatre concepts fondamentaux de la psychanalyse*.

[22] A classic statement of this position can be found in the Lacanian 'stade du miroir', for example. See Jacques Lacan, *Écrits I*, p. 93.

[23] This view of identity is similar to one put forward in Alison Leigh Brown's book, *Subjects of Deceit: A Phenomenology of Lying* (Albany: State University of New York Press, 1998), p. 114. For Brown, social subjectivity is largely performative, and

Carrère's commitment to accounting for this *vide blanc* meant that one of the challenges the author faced was choosing a point of view, a complication which arose from the ambiguity of the signifier 'je' with respect to this character. Jean-Claude Romand as 'I' – that is, in terms of the face he put forward in communication and his role in society – *was* indeed, in some sense, a doctor and loving father. Carrère chose not to say 'I' for Romand, but neither could he comfortably speak solely as an outsider, from the third person. This further explains his choice to recount the story largely from his own perspective as author. But given the complexities of the self raised by Romand's story, and which already underlie Carrère's understanding of selfhood, the author's 'I' is no more definite or authentic than that of Romand. Perhaps it is this crisis of identity that is reproduced in Carrère's text within the narrative voice, which becomes both subject and object of its own questions. By oscillating between author, narrator and character, Carrère identifies figuratively with Romand, while speaking personally and self-consciously from the first person. This gesture in turn allows him to portray Romand as a figure who eludes a categorical reconstruction and instead wavers between criminal, father and phantom. In *L'Adversaire*, the author battles with the morals of reconstructing the *other*, as an act which must necessarily bring about a re-appraisal of the self.

In his article 'Se construire en écrivant l'autre', Daniel Madelénat examines the merging of biographical and autobiographical genres in approaches to representing the other. He considers various forms of biographical writing which he feels foster a dynamic of 'autohospitalité'.[24] Rather than simply disappearing behind her own text to bring the life of her subject into relief, the biographer foregrounds the obstacles, ambiguities and failings of the biographical undertaking, performing a kind of 'coming out':

> L'entreprise déraille ou s'enlise, et le biographe émerge comme
> figure pleine à mesure que la biographie se vide (en une sorte

---

covers the 'secret skins' we do not reveal in communication with others.

[24] One early example of such a text is Vladimir Nabokov's *The Real Life of Sebastian Knight*, in which the author represents the life story of his half brother, while presenting personal reflections on identity and selfhood which occur to him during the writing process. See Daniel Madelénat, 'Se construire en écrivant l'autre', in *De soi à soi: l'écriture comme autohospitalité*, ed. by Alain Montandon (Clermont-Ferrand: Presses Universitaires Blaise Pascal, 2004), pp. 53-65, pp. 58-9.

d'effet sablier) […] Il entre en dissidence et en hérésie par rapport
à l'évolution linéaire 'normale' de sa tâche, qui programme l'ef-
facement de l'historien. Il se révèle à lui-même au cours des
projections, introjections, interrogations qu'il subit.[25]

In the case of *L'Adversaire*, 'autohospitalité' might imply welcoming
the foreignness and unknowable nature of the other, encountered in
the biographical task, as an incentive to re-write the self. Dominique
Viart notes that this coupling of non-fiction and self-interrogation is
also perceptible in the contemporary representation of the *fait divers*:
'[L]e fait divers est prétexte à un questionnement de soi au moins
d'autant et sinon plus que des enchaînements de causes qui l'ont
permis ou produit' (LFP 234). In Carrère's text, the vulnerability of
the self leads to the creation of a new story, in which the author's
inability to place himself in relation to the event becomes a journey
through the *chez soi*, a tale in which the author is also the main
character. We are reminded of the Derridean conception of hospitality
as a gesture which would ideally imply not only opening up one's
doors to the other, but giving up one's position as host or master of the
house.[26] Hospitality paradoxically requires the renunciation of the
chez soi in Cixous's sense of the term, of the domination and power
over the premises, which constitute one's ability to be a proper host.

This conception of hospitality also resembles Kristeva's view
of the uncanny foreigner as a form of alterity which provokes the
disassembling of the self. In accordance with Kristeva's uncanny,
Carrère engages in a re-assessment and figurative dispersal of the
ordinary, as a response to the unthematizable alterity of his object of
representation. In this way, the strange and familiar enter into dialogue
with one another to generate a meaning for the event, which is
precisely this re-interrogation of the familiar. His tactics of defame-
liarization, in which the ordinary domestic space re-appears to the
reader as strange, constitutes a narrative approach which reminds us of
Kristeva's dynamic of re-directing the perception of otherness inside

---

[25] Ibid, pp. 59-60.
[26] Derrida describes the paradox of hospitality, which opposes '*la* loi de l'hospitalité',
meaning an infinite opening up to the other: 'donner à l'arrivant tout son chez-soi et
son soi', to '*les* lois de l'hospitalité', which regulate and limit hospitality, by requiring
the foreigner to answer to the host according to the laws of the latter. The principle of
hospitality is thus in conflict with its manifestation in reality. See Jacques Derrida, *De
l'hospitalité*, with Anne Dufourmantelle (Paris: Calmann-Lévy, 1997), p. 73.

towards the home, creating a form of meaning which is not reduced to rejection. The *chez soi* in question is not only that of Jean-Claude Romand or the self, but also that of the preconceptions which inform our understanding of the real on a daily basis.

Carrère's fictionalization and fragmentation of the Romand affair resonates in harmony with the *vide blanc* which the writer perceives in his character's identity and the void opened up in meaning by the unsettling *fait divers*. Faced with this destructive, ungraspable event which destroys all the principles upon which the real may be seen to rest, he cannot find an objective perspective, a singular viewpoint. Just as he cannot adopt the 'I' to speak for Romand, Carrère cannot find a stable authorial voice from which he may construct an unwavering truth. By inhabiting and exhausting different positions, pushing them to a breaking-point, metamorphosing them into their other, Carrère constantly enables and disables representation, announcing the uncertainty of both his authorial position and his own implements of reconstruction in the face of this tragedy.

Autobiography and the Uncanny in NDiaye and Savitzkaya

The intricacies and ambiguities of the representation of the *chez soi* have become the object of much contemplation both in contemporary thought and in recent French autobiographical writing. According to the definition proposed by Philippe Lejeune, an autobiography is a 'récit rétrospectif en prose qu'une personne réelle fait de sa propre existence, lorsqu'elle met l'accent sur sa vie individuelle, en particulier sur l'histoire de sa personnalité'.[27] While the French novel has returned to the subject and to selfhood as primary topics of preoccupation, it has done so by contesting or slackening this traditional definition of autobiography. Contemporary life writing often expresses the illusory or superficial quality of conventional, non-fictional self-representation. The above criteria (possessing a retrospective quality, constituting an 'histoire' and taking the form of prose) have been interpreted flexibly in order to suit the representational trends of current writing and revised conceptions of subjectivity. Today's autobiography stresses the inconsistencies and

---

[27] Philippe Lejeune, *Le Pacte autobiographique* (Paris: Édtions du Seuil, 1975), p. 14.

disarray of the self, bringing out the mythical nature of any vision of selfhood that affirms its rationality and unity. This dual return of subjectivity as an object of both interest and suspicion is reflected in Roland Barthes's expression of the paradox of the autobiographical pact. In reference to his own 1975 self-portrait, he stated 'C'est moi et ce n'est pas moi'.[28] The entire first page of *Roland Barthes par Roland Barthes* is dedicated to the decidedly anti-autobiographical declaration: 'Tout ceci doit être considéré comme dit par un personnage de roman'.

In accordance with this Barthesian vision of autobiography, the practitioners of *autofiction*[29] seek to obscure the boundaries between reality and fiction in the representation of their life stories. This is performed in the interests of portraying the subject not in a straightforward way as coherent and knowable, and therefore inscribable in the codes of non-fiction, but as a product of fantasy and desire and a victim of obsession, lack, uncertainty and the ambiguity of memory. In *Enfance,* for example, Nathalie Sarraute presents a dialogue between two voices, those of a narrator and an interlocutor, which are parts of the 'same' self. In other works of *autofiction,* by writers such as Alain Robbe-Grillet, Serge Doubrovsky or Marguerite Duras, distortions of temporality, appeals to fantasy and the presence of literary figures such as *mise en abyme* express the ultimate elusiveness of the self and its inability to be seized in a cohesive narrative.

With *autofiction,* there comes a temptation to present these less certain approaches to life narrative as being more 'real' or authentic than more traditional forms. Dominique Viart explains the need for *autofiction* by evoking the potential superiority of this genre over non-fictional self-representation:

> Nul en effet ne saurait produire directement, *ex abrupto,* de représentation objective de lui-même. Aussi l'autofiction en dit-elle sans doute plus long, y compris dans les interstices du non-dit et de l'implicite, que le plus soigné et le plus 'sincère' des récits

---

[28] Roland Barthes, *Roland Barthes* (Paris: Éditions du Seuil, 1975), p. 123-4.

[29] Although this term has become generic, it was originally coined by the writer Serge Doubrovsky, who used it to describe his novel *Fils*. Other terms which designate similar forms of self-representation include 'automythobiographie', 'nouvelle autobiographie' and 'égolittérature', according to the list proposed by Dominique Viart (LFP 27).

rétrospectifs. (LFP 39)

For Viart, contemporary variations on autobiography are just as concerned with 'truth' as more traditional forms, creating texts which relate 'non pas l'histoire mais l'essence' of a life (LFP 48). Viart distinguishes between 'fiction existentielle' and 'fiction littéraire', the latter's presence in an autobiography reflecting the role of the former in the construction of identity in new visions of the subject (LFP 42).[30] Mounir Laouyen suggests that the rationale behind the fictional innovations of contemporary autobiographical writing is still connected to a concern for realism: 'S'ils refusent d'adhérer à la *mimésis* traditionnelle, c'est précisément au nom d'une *mimésis* d'ordre supérieur. Ce qui relève du vécu n'a pas accès à l'intelligence'.[31] Again, the renunciation of traditional faith in the realism of the linear, lucid life story is performed in a quest to gesture to a real which is revealed through rupture, dissonance and silence, and which resists interpretation. There is a tendency simply to re-locate the real, by designating it as opaque, dispersed or unknowable. If the texts of *autofiction* and, more particularly, those examined in this chapter, are indeed more 'realistic' than traditional autobiographies, this is perhaps according to a more recent definition of realism proposed by Lawrence R. Schehr in his work *Figures of Alterity: French Realism and its Others*: realism is 'the literary practice that most clearly shows the artifice of literature'.[32]

Broadly speaking, the narrative strategies employed by NDiaye and Savitzkaya and the visions of the self that they present permit us to classify their novels as *autofictions*. In their texts, the task of portraying the self implies coming to terms with its ultimate instability and uncertainty. These writers combine elements of autobiography and fiction in order to account for the problematics of self-representation, and these issues are encountered and reflected upon within the act of representation. Whereas Emmanuel Carrère in

---

[30] Viart is perhaps thinking of the Lacanian conception of the subject as based 'dans une ligne de fiction', which has become a catch phrase in criticism on *autofiction*. See Jacques Lacan, *Écrits I*, p. 94.

[31] Mounir Laouyen, 'Le Texte autobiographique: une demeure à soi ?', in *De soi à soi: l'écriture comme autohospitalité*, ed. by Alain Montandon (Clermont-Ferrand: Presses Universitaires Blaise Pascal, 2004), pp. 125-43, p. 129.

[32] Schehr, Lawrence, *Figures of Alterity: French Realism and its Others* (Stanford: Stanford University Press, 2003), p.7.

L'Adversaire moved between different positions of narration, these two novelists are writing about their own lives from an *unheimlich* place, which can never become a basis for coherent understanding. For both writers, the attempt to locate the *chez soi*, to pin down the self and demarcate its borders, leads to an uncanny experience which is expressed through doubling and displacement. In the work by NDiaye, this comes across through the representation of a subtly dispersed haunting, which intervenes in her attempts at self-portrayal. In the case of Savitzkaya, the text displays the writer's repeated and failed efforts to locate a firm ground from which he might begin his self-representation. However, the writer rejoices in this disorientation, which drives and invigorates his narrative. Again, the theme of dislocation, seen either through dreamscapes or textual distortion, provides a means for these authors to express their views on writing and contemplate the role of the artist in society as a person not quite at home in the community.

Criticism has already directed attention to the imagery of the home that is apparent in some *autofiction* and discourses of self-representation. In her article, 'Le texte autobiographique: une demeure à soi?', Mounir Laouyen describes autobiography as a quest to define the *chez soi*. Laouyen employs spatial metaphors to describe autobiography, and seems to understand this form of writing as a process of mapping the frontier between self and other. Self-representation involves carving out a home for oneself, delineating the boundaries of the self: 'Écrire sur soi, c'est marquer sa différence, s'octroyer une identité, délimiter son territoire, fonder sa propre demeure'.[33] Such a vision of writing as a search for home is well exemplified in NDiaye's and Savitzkaya's works through an emphasis on the difficulties of achieving comfort and certainty within the *chez soi*, understood as the represented self.

Laouyen's use of a vocabulary of home, foundation and location, leads her to view new forms of self-representation, such as Robbe-Grillet's *Nouvelle Autobiographie* or Doubrovsky's *Auto-fiction,* as essentially deconstructionist: 'Le lecteur assiste à la mise en place d'une poétique de la ruine, du délabrement, du démembrement, de la déconstruction généralisée du sujet autobiographique'.[34]

---

[33] Mounir Laouyen, 'Le Texte autobiographique: une demeure à soi?', p. 125.
[34] Ibid, p. 126.

However, regardless of whether or not we can say that their texts are more or less 'authentic' than traditional autobiographical forms, there is no doubt that for Savitzkaya and NDiaye, the disorientation and dispersal generated in attempting to represent their own existences is not simply a taking apart, but also productive, since it is in the midst of this destruction of home that they are able to generate meaningful stories of the self.

The Haunted House: Uncanny *Autofiction* in NDiaye's *Autoportrait en vert*

Marie NDiaye is one of many contemporary French women writers to re-appropriate classic fantastic imagery within an ordinary, present-day context. As already stated, in her novels we find abundant incarnations of the supernatural, including the themes of sorcery, metamorphosis, vampirism or the omnipotence of thoughts; and leitmotifs of the uncanny, such as spectrality, or the double. Yet, rather than conveying a quest for the otherworldly, these images are often brought into proximity with a representation of familiar, everyday relationships and environments in today's society. One of the most disconcerting and uniquely reinterpreted fantastic images in NDiaye's work is that of the haunted house. In her writing, the home is portrayed as an uncertain, often unwelcoming location, which harbours all the strangeness of the traditional Gothic mansion; yet in NDiaye's fiction this strangeness assumes a very modern form. *Rosie Carpe* (2001), *La Sorcière* (1996) and *En famille* (1991) are set in dismal suburban flats or malodorous family homes, in which we find numerous unloving or monstrous parents, dispersed or quasi-incestuous families, siblings with fluctuating identities and prota-gonists who, for different reasons, cannot feel at home. In her 2004, semi-autobiographical text, *Autoportrait en vert*, NDiaye presents us with yet another take on this theme of homelessness that recurs throughout her œuvre. This time, however, the story explores not only the disconcerting elements of home and family, but also the problematics of selfhood and self-representation. This combination of themes evokes the dual meaning of the French *chez soi*, a term referring simultaneously to home and self. In *Autoportrait en vert*, we encounter a narrator who, struggling with the uncertainties of self which surface during the autobiographical act, discovers she is not 'master of her own house'. In this section, I would like to suggest that, for Marie NDiaye, the haunted house is not only a thematic element, as observed in her portrayal of the family home, but also serves as a motif to illuminate the author's understanding of selfhood and writing, and that this observation can also elucidate tendencies in NDiaye's representation of subjectivity throughout her work.[35]

Autoportrait en vert was published in 2005 as part of a collection entitled 'Traits et portraits'. According to Colette Fellous, its initiator, the aim of this ongoing project is to produce a series of self-portraits which contain a visual component. Selected images, whether sketches, photographs or tableaux, are to inhabit the books like an echoing voice, themselves providing an autonomous undercurrent to the text, a secret story of their own. With the aid of this visual supplement, the participating artists are asked to create a textual space 'où se révèle la face cachée, pudique de l'auteur'.[36]

At first glance, NDiaye's positive response to this invitation to expose her 'face cachée' in a text with autobiographical resonances seems surprising, given the reticence that critics have come to associate with the author. As NDiaye's readers are well aware, until very recently, she avoided discussing her work publicly and has gained a reputation for evading interviews and television appearances. However, the dynamics generated by Colette Fellous's proposed project might have appealed to the author, since they reflect very well NDiaye's approach to the representation of selfhood in her other novels. The collection requires that each author produce a self-portrait, which is itself 'inhabited' by a foreign, echoing presence: that of the images. Likewise, in NDiaye's novels we often encounter characters who are haunted by various forms of hidden echoes. Her protagonists are often inhabited by 'other voices', which seem to multiply and

---

[35] Some of the ideas addressed in this section are also explored in a chapter published in another work. See Daisy Connon, 'Marie NDiaye's Haunted House: Uncanny Autofiction in *Autoportrait en vert*', in *Redefining the Real: The Fantastic in Contemporary French Women's Writing*, ed. by Margaret-Anne Hutton (Bern: Peter Lang, 2009), pp. 245-60.

[36] Tirthankar Chanda, 'L'Essentiel d'un livre: portrait de l'écrivain en vert', *MFI HEBDO* (April 2005), http://www.rfi.fr/Fichiers/Mfi/CultureSociete /1455.asp (accessed 10 March 2007). As was specified by Fellous, the texts were to be 'ponctués de dessins, d'images, de tableaux ou de photos, qui habitent les livres comme une autre voix en écho, formant presque un récit souterrain'. Ibid.

become intensified when the individual begins to question her identity or seek to attain self-awareness within day-to-day life. Perhaps the 'autres voix' that may be heard in *Autoportrait en vert* – incarnated by the mysterious 'femmes en vert' that pursue the narrator – represent an amplification of this condition of selfhood that is omnipresent in the author's work. For Marie NDiaye, writing one's 'face cachée' involves a willingness to enter into dialogue with the figures and the echoes that haunt the *chez soi*.

In *Autoportrait en vert*, the author thus provides us with a fascinating and enigmatic interpretation of the criteria guiding the collection 'Traits et Portraits'. Against a backdrop of familiar landscapes and autobiographical details, NDiaye undertakes her self-representation through imagery of the uncanny: the double, haunting, disconcerting configurations of the family and the *chez soi* under threat. Incongruous, sinuous and dream-like, the story is presented as a patchwork of images and spurts of narration.

This fragmented form is well suited to the expression of the anxieties of a befuddled narrator, unable to separate the real from the imaginary, the strange from the familiar. Marie NDiaye herself figures in the story as character, narrator and author, and the text does contain some factual content being set, for example, in contemporary southwest France where the author resides. There are numerous evocative and detailed descriptions of the landscape and vegetation surrounding Bordeaux, although these reach a point of exaggeration with continuous allusions to copious tropical fruit trees. We recognize the narrator as a mother of five, a writer, who engages in conventional tasks of motherhood such as driving her children to and fro or mingling with other parents in the schoolyard. She alludes to details we know to be true of Marie NDiaye's life, such as the name of her husband. She cites the dates and locations of literary conferences she in fact attended and she shares what appear to be genuine memories from her youth. But this realism is subordinated to an agenda of discord and confusion as the author foregrounds a different story, one of subtle haunting. Uncanny apparitions, eruptions of daydream, characters who transform into others, feelings of illegitimacy and a perpetual sense of unhomeliness dominate the otherwise banal realm of the narrator, her half-hearted interactions with other somewhat dislikeable characters, her daily rituals of family life and troubled parental relations.

The author's particular approach to self-representation is partially orchestrated through descriptive tactics of uncertainty. This first becomes apparent near the beginning of the narrative, as the author converses with Cristina, an acquaintance, in the schoolyard after dropping off the children. Suddenly in mid-conversation it becomes evident to the narrator that this woman is not in fact Cristina, but a complete stranger: 'Il m'apparaît alors évident que je ne connais pas ce visage. Sur le trottoir d'en face, une jeune femme m'adresse un salut de la main. C'est Cristina, dans un petit short rose'.[37]

The text displays a series of such seemingly innocuous and often humorous ambiguities. Characters frequently appear to morph into others and identities fluctuate. The aesthetic is one of dream, where extremely ordinary elements coalesce effortlessly with the improbable. These ambiguities contribute to the anxiety that reigns in the inner world of the narrator and appears to alienate her from the rest of the community, with which she does not identify symbolically. A friendly village is thus transformed into an obscure, foreign land, inhabited by a character who cannot learn the rules or feel at home. Uncertainty dominates in this vision of the ordinary in which the uncanny becomes a prolonged gaze which is projected onto the moments of daily life, thereby coming to express a mild *décalage* between the subject and the collective real.

While Emmanuel Carrère approached the representation of real events through fragmentation and numerous self-conscious statements relating his authorial doubt, NDiaye employs fictional, often fantastic forms to convey similar hesitation. Near the beginning of the text, and then again at the very end, we find another salient symbol of the uncertainty that separates the writer from her community. During the narrator's conversation with Cristina, preceding her realization that she is in fact speaking to a different woman, her interlocutor is relating the news of a formless, inexplicable, presumably harmful 'thing', which has been found in the schoolyard. This entity has been brought to the attention of the mayor and the village. Cristina refers to this presence as '[q]uelque chose de noir, de rapide' (AV 20). When the narrator expresses her own ignorance of this object, 'Cristina' appears surprised, exclaiming: 'Tu

---

[37] Marie NDiaye, *Autoportrait en vert* (Paris: Mercure de France, 2005), p. 20. All other references are given in the text, following the abbreviation AV.

n'as rien vu?' (AV 20-1). Near the end of the narrative this indescribable form is evoked again, this time brought to the narrator's attention by exclamatory remarks from her children who are gathered around the object: 'Il était tout noir! Il s'est enfui, il est rapide!' (AV 93). Here, however, the author first believes to perceive a 'forme sombre, mouvante, nerveuse', but later admits that in truth she saw nothing. She is unable to account for the existence of this phenomenon: 'Je crois, dis-je, que ça n'a pas de nom dans notre langue' (AV 93). Readers familiar with interviews given by Marie NDiaye will know that, in December 2003, a pedophilia charge was brought against one of the teachers in the school her children attend. This affair greatly troubled the entire community. One wonders whether the shapeless, black form might not be the literary embodiment of anxieties the author experienced with respect to the event. At no point in the text, however, does the author affirm such a possibility. The strange black form also introduces a contrast which persists throughout the text between phenomena perceived by the community and unseen by the author, and those perceived by the author but which escape the awareness of other characters. We will see that this is also the case for the *femmes en vert*.

Uncanny family

Like nearly all of NDiaye's characters, the protagonist of *Autoportrait en vert* encounters the problem of the dislocation of the family and the impossibility of going home. As we saw in the previous chapter, Marie NDiaye's most pronounced narrative theme is the dualism of the family. While she constantly affirms its inability to foster a sense of identity, or function hospitably as a place of refuge and comfort, she also appears to view the site of home as the source and measurement of selfhood. The individual dwells in a place of struggle and suspension between the inability to survive without the family, and the elusive and disagreeable nature of the family, which can never provide the sense of origin and unity she seeks in it.

Although the narrator's own children are depicted as loving, obedient, smelling of honeysuckle, angelic, endowed as they are with golden halos (AV 10), other family members of *Autoportrait en vert* are portrayed unpleasantly. Her sisters are 'deux très grosses femmes', by whom the narrator is simultaneously revolted and charmed when she embraces them reluctantly at her mother's house. In a daydream, she compares them to 'Les sœurs Papin', two infamous French cleaning women who savagely murdered their employers (AV 75).

The narrator wishes to reassemble her scattered family, but is unable to find her place within its configuration. Due to a confusion of roles and cross-generational blurring, characters are unable to occupy their proper places within the familial structure. Her divorced parents have both remarried and founded new homes, from which she feels excluded. The narrator's father refuses to look any of her children in the eye or to acknowledge his role as their grandfather. Her mother, remarried later in life to a young man named Rocco, gives birth to a baby during the course of the narrative, although we can assume she is of retirement age. This anxiety-provoking dispersal of home leads the narrator both to indulge in reveries of reuniting with her family, and to contemplate the woeful impossibility of such a prospect:

> Ma mère, Rocco et Bella, où sont-ils à présent? Je n'écrirai pas, eux non plus, jusqu'au jour où, peut-être, une lettre m'arrivera d'un lieu inconnu, accompagnée de photos d'inconnus, qui se trouveront être mes proches à divers degrés – lettre dont, même si elle est signée 'Maman' je contesterai l'authenticité, puis j'enfouirai quelque part où elle ne sera pas dénichée. (AV 72)

In these reflections, the family passes from a familiar site of intimacy and comfort to a source of strangeness which will return in a form of haunting. The word 'Maman' fails to encompass the myth of motherhood, or, as the narrator states, of functioning with enough 'authenticity' to guarantee the mother-daughter rapport. Descriptions of the narrator's mother show her to be both familiar and entirely foreign. Although the narrator wishes or expects her to be grounding and identity-confirming, she always appears cold, fluctuating and alarming:

> Comme il est curieux, après qu'on a côtoyé sa propre mère pendant une quarantaine d'années [...] que cette femme qu'on ne supportait plus de connaître aussi bien tout d'un coup se métamorphose d'elle-même en femme verte et en devienne une des figures les plus troublantes, les plus étrangères. (AV 64)

However, despite the recurrence in *Autportrait en vert* of the theme of family dislocation and the presence of uncanny parents, in this novel the difficulty of feeling *chez soi* manifests itself primarily in perturbbations of selfhood. The notion of the *'rentrée chez soi'* might be seen to refer to the mastery of the self in autobiographical representation. As Serge Doubrovoksy tells us: 'l'autobiographie suppose un sujet qui peut avoir accès à soi-même par le retour sur soi, le regard intérieur, l'introspection véridique'.[38] However, we will see that, to use Mounir Laouyen's metaphor, cited above, for Marie NDiaye this return home cannot occur since the character encounters significant difficulties in her attempt to 'fonder sa demeure'. If it is indeed founded, the home reveals itself to be haunted by echoes and spectres.

This haunting declares itself in the ghostly *femmes en vert* who plague the narrator and seem both to trouble and to enrich the narrative act. Throughout the novel, she is pursued by a series of ethereal presences, women dressed in green, who resurface throughout the text, eluding the gaze of other characters. The first *femme en vert* is introduced in the opening scene of the text. The narrator alludes to a green-clad figure, standing next to a banana tree, in front of a particular house in her neighbourhood. We learn that she routinely observes this strange woman on the way to the school, but that her children, from the backseat of the car, do not perceive her. Although this figure unexpectedly intrudes on the ordinary by an elusive, ghostly form, she is also capable of assuming the concreteness of an ordinary character, conversing with the narrator 'dans une voix flegmatique' and in 'phrases monotones', rambling on about her trivial domestic problems and alcoholic husband (AV 27). More strangely, her identity is shared among numerous female characters. The author's mother, the first wife of a friend's husband, and the *maîtresse* remembered from her primary school days are all at one point or another, however abstractly, associated with this *femme en vert*, or designated as such.[39] Given the aim of the collection, the title of the text 'Autoportrait en vert' and the strange ontological status of the *femme en vert*, who reveals herself only to the narrator, it seems the reader is urged to view the *femmes en vert* as maintaining a connection to the self, as ethereal embodiments through which the

---

[38] Serge Doubrovsky, 'Textes en main', *RITM* 6 'Autofiction et cie' (1993), p. 210.

[39] For example, on page 15, the narrator is watching the children in the schoolyard after driving her own to school: 'Me revient alors l'inquiétant souvenir d'une femme en vert, au temps de l'école maternelle. Cette grande femme brutale et carrée nous promet à tous la prison si nous mangeons trop lentement, si nous salissons nos vêtements, si nous ne levons pas les yeux vers les siens'.

author has chosen to depict herself. Although they bear no physical resemblance to the narrator, they appear to be a multiplied form of autofictional double.

As we saw in the first chapter of this book, the recognition of one's double is, for Freud, an exemplary uncanny experience, which he linked to a regression to a more primitive phase in the development of the psyche. In the fantastic literature of romanticism, the double often takes the form of a malicious counterpart, who represents one's sinister side and foreshadows death.[40] However, as will become evident further on, the narrator views the woman in green not just as a disconcerting figure, but also as a companion.

The double has also been known to represent the splitting of the self and indecision. *Autofiction* has often employed this figure and its textual avatars to represent autobiographical uncertainty. At the beginning of Sarraute's *Enfance*, for example, the narrator's second voice functions to prohibit a sense of self-unity, by criticizing the author's decision to recount her childhood memories. Likewise, for NDiaye, the strange and familiar figure of the woman in green in the context of her autobiography could be interpreted as a critical commentary on the autobiographical act. The attempt to make the self an object of representation necessarily becomes the story of someone else. The women in green persistently perturb the narrator's efforts at self-portraiture. The following extract, in which the identities of the narrator, character and author are intertwined, lends itself to such an interpretation. Concerning the *femme en vert*, the narrator tells us:

> Il me semble qu'elle a revêtu les qualités de quelqu'un d'autre, sans le savoir elle-même. Ce n'est pas très clair. Je dois m'expliquer plus exactement. Je crois que la femme en vert, qui m'a dit s'appeler Katia Depetiteville, n'est pas Katia Depetite-ville, et je crois que si je demandais au village une description de Katia Depetiteville, on ne me décrirait pas cette femme-là, la femme en vert. On me décrirait quelqu'un de très différent. Mais la femme en vert ne le sait pas. Elle pense sincèrement et naturellement être Katia Depetiteville. (AV 27)

---

[40] According to John Herman, Hoffmann was influenced by the psychological works of G. H. Schubert, who developed the idea of a 'shadow-self', a 'dark and hidden counterpart of, or supplement to, the daytime consciousness'. See John Herman, *The Double in Nineteenth-century Fiction* (Houndmills, Basingstoke, Hampshire, London: MacMillan, 1990), p. 153.

At the moment when the *femme en vert*'s identity might possibly be pinned down through the proper name, it escapes the mastery of the narrator, refusing to adhere to it, having 'revêtu les qualités de quelqu'un d'autre'. Despite the repeated references to Katia Depetiteville in this extract, the name itself, while obsessing the narrator, remains foreign to the story; it does not relate to any of the figures of the auto-fictional triangle, thereby evoking the suspicion of autobiography we often find in contemporary writing.[41] This passage also raises a more universal identity-related uncertainty. The *femme en vert* herself (who is, in a sense, also the narrator) does not know who she is, since the name she claims to possess is brought into doubt by the author, unless it is simply that the narrator is lacking in reliability. By privileging an element of doubt with regard to this figure's identity in her self-portrait, the author generates a form of self-representation which consciously undermines the act itself by putting forth a vision of subjectivity as plural and ultimately unknowable. In engaging in dialogue with the *femme en vert*, in distrusting the name she puts forth as her own, Marie NDiaye suggests that the self, as an object of representation, is only approachable within a literary space of interrogation or crisis. Magdalena Silvia Mancas comments on the use of the double in Nathalie Sarraute's autobiographical writing, highlighting the creative role of this uncanny image in representations of self. For her, such a displacement of self 'engendr[e] de nouvelles structures et assur[e] la mobilité permanente des idées, leur contradiction, leur dépassement'.[42] Similarly, NDiaye's *femme en vert* generates a space of dialogue and creativity in which the self appears to exist in contradiction, thereby articulating an exchange between its different facets. This ungraspable quality of the self perhaps explains the author's choice of visual component in her self-portrait. Interspersed throughout the text are photographs by Julie Ganzin, displaying the elusive landscape of the Montagne Sainte Victoire. This

---

[41] Philippe Lejeune defines an *autofiction* as: 'un récit dont auteur, narrateur et protagoniste partagent la même identité nominale et dont l'intitulé générique indique qu'il s'agit d'un roman'. Cited in Jacques Lecarme, 'L'Autofiction: un mauvais genre?', in *Autofictions et Cie*, ed. by Serge Doubrovsky, Jacques Lecarme and Philippe Lejeune (Paris: Université Paris X, 1993), pp. 227-48, p. 227.

[42] Magdalena Silvia Mancas, 'Le Retour à soi dans la Nouvelle Autobiographie: sur le rapport entre (auto)hospitalité et mensonge', in *De soi à soi: l'écriture comme autohospitalité,* ed. by Alain Montandon (Clermont-Ferrand: Presses Universitaires Blaise Pascal, 2004), pp. 107-25, p. 117.

choice of image is particularly striking with respect to the plurality of the self embodied by the *femmes en vert*, since this landscape has become a symbol for uncertainty, known for its indefinable nature, its capacity to undergo transformations of colour and form depending on light and season, and its ability to lend itself to various reinterpretations. This is reflected, for example, in Cézanne's plethora of paintings of this mountain.

However, the significance of the figure of the double for NDiaye appears to surpass the expression of the self's resistance to autobiographical representation. This figure, which, for Sarraute, reflects a problematic arising from writing and memory, seems for NDiaye to be a day-to-day reality, a fundamental aspect of subjective experience, which grows stronger in the autobiographical act insofar as it may be viewed as an attempt to *rentrer chez soi*. In order to better appreciate the proliferation of this haunting figure, it is helpful to situate this problem in the more global context of the representation of subjectivity in the writer's work.

The objectives of the 'Traits et portraits' collection are in fact well aligned with the representation of subjective experience found throughout Marie NDiaye's writing. Each of her protagonists has 'une face cachée et pudique' and appears to be inhabited by 'une autre voix' that disturbs her attempts to confirm her sense of identity or to come to terms with herself. This tormenting voice often emerges from inside the self, and is experienced as banal, occurring in fleeting moments of self-perception. An example of this phenomenon may be observed in the haunting that troubles the protagonist of NDiaye's short story 'Une journée de Brulard'. In this text, which plays on the narcissistic uncertainties linked to self-image in the eyes of the other, Ève Brulard regularly receives visits from a younger version of herself. This scantily dressed figure watches over her with 'une bienveillance inquiète',[43] while emitting squawks, yelps and teasing noises.

In *Rosie Carpe*, a more discrete voice appears within the narrative language itself, expressing a lack of unity between the character's proper name and her being. For Rosie, engaged in an identity and family quest which is destined to fail, attempting to return

---

[43] Marie NDiaye, 'Une journée de Brulard', in *Tous mes amis* (Paris: Éditions de Minuit, 2004), p. 114.

to her family origins and attain self-knowledge sparks a kind of tautological, subjective confusion. This uncertainty manifests itself in a superfluous, circular textual voice. In the passage studied in the third chapter of this book, in which Rosie is strolling in her Parisian suburb, the more she pronounces her name, the more the description relates a doubling of self and affirms the precariousness of her identification with this signifier, and with the Carpe family, affirming the impossibility for Rosie to feel *chez elle*:

> Rosie était cette toute jeune femme, nommée Rosie Carpe, qui marchait le long des haies de fusains en laissant courir sa main sur les grillages, les treilles. Elle savait qu'elle était Rosie Carpe et que c'était bien elle, à la fois Rosie et Rosie Carpe, qui marchait en ce moment d'un pas tranquille longeant les haies bien taillées de ce quartier résidentiel, silencieux, d'Antony. (RC 127)

The identity-related instability of these two characters manifests itself in symbolic echoes, which oblige them to observe or listen to themselves. Ève Brulard hears her own words which 'flott[ent] devant ses lèvres comme si quelqu'un d'autre les avait soufflés à côté d'elle, d'une comique voix de tête'.[44] For Rosie Carpe, it is often not her own voice that appears foreign, but her smile, which seems to 'flotter juste devant ses lèvres indécises' (RC 82). Based on these examples, it seems that, as soon as the subject engages further in an identity quest or in any form of self-interrogation, this haunting only worsens. Rosie is striving to reconnect with her family origins to cure herself of her ontological insecurity. Likewise, the mediocre actress Ève Brulard engages in egocentric self-contemplation when no one in the hotel recognizes her from the film in which she played the heroine's sister. For Marie NDiaye, some of the most authentic moments of subjectivity involve the recognition of one's own alterity or duality. At the most intimate level of the self, but in the midst of ordinary experience, a silent monologue is constantly unfolding, contradicting the outward impressions of unity and stability that the individual would like to present to the external world.

The intimate echoes that inhabit each of NDiaye's characters are intensified in *Autoportrait en vert*, where the act of self-interrogation is rooted in a more explicitly autobiographical agenda.

---

[44] Marie NDiaye, 'Une journée de Brulard', p. 154.

Unlike Rosie Carpe and Ève Brulard, who hardly recognize the existence of this other voice, and seem to accept it or casually cast it aside, the narrator in *Autoportrait en vert* actively listens to it. She expresses her willingness to enter into dialogue with this hidden side of the self. At one point the narrator, tortured by the uncertainty of the existence of the *femme en vert*, takes it upon herself to visit the house where she routinely perceives her. She glances up at the balcony, from which the *femme en vert* then proceeds to jump, landing on the ground in front of the narrator. This occurrence introduces an extraordinary scene where she confronts the *femme en vert* and enters into a discourse with her 'autre voix':

> – Vous vouliez me voir ? me demande-t-elle une fois assise devant moi, de l'autre côté de la table. Ses yeux sont d'un vert très clair, comme ceux de l'ogresse de la maternelle lorsque j'étais enfant. Je ne réponds pas à sa question. Nous tenons chacune sa tasse des deux mains à hauteur de la bouche et par-dessus les tasses nous nous regardons avec un peu de suspicion. La vérité commanderait que je lui dise : 'Il me fallait vérifier que vous existiez'. Aussi, ne pouvant dire cela, je me tais. Elle se présente, très courtoise, obligeante, me dit son prénom, et son nom que je savais déjà. Sa parole reste suspendue. Elle attend que je me fasse connaître comme elle vient de le faire. Je suis prudente, je ne dis rien. Malgré les objets qui nous entourent dans cette triste cuisine tout aménagée dans les années soixante-dix et jamais remaniée depuis, malgré le visage de la femme en vert si proche que je pourrais avancer les doigts et le toucher, quelque chose d'impalpable, un voile, une lueur d'irréalité me rendent réticente à lui livrer qui je suis. Je ne crois pas tout à fait à ce qu'elle est. (AV 26)

The *femme en vert* poses a challenge to interpretation, which is evident in the narrator's hesitations, which echo and encourage the uncertainty of the reader: 'Il me fallait vérifier que vous existiez' and 'Je ne crois pas tout à fait à ce qu'elle est'. On the one hand we perceive the triteness of this woman; she is an ordinary and tangible being, someone to be addressed conventionally. But she is also evoked through codes of the fantastic, surrounded by 'une lueur d'irréalité'. While the act of composing her self-portrait allows the author to approach this second voice more closely than ever before, she nonetheless remains unable to understand or thematize it. However, the attention she pays to the dialogue with the *femme en vert* constitutes the most effective revelation that the author can elaborate of her 'face cachée'. The self is grasped only in its perpetual doubt, in its attempt to come to terms with this uncertain voice that inhabits it.

Catastrophe
In the background of *Autoportrait en vert* there lie images of flooding and catastrophe, which pose a challenge to the *chez soi* as home. NDiaye situates her self-representation within an atmosphere of anxiety, evoking the sinister waters of the Garonne, that are constantly rising and threatening to flood the village on the edge of the river, to 'envahir le rez-de-chaussée des maisons, parfois l'étage, parfois la maison entière' (AV 7). This theme materializes through a series of dream-like sequences in which the narrator contemplates the villagers' reaction to the threat of flooding, and questions their attachment to their homes, their refusal to leave them despite the rising water:

> Pourquoi, puisque nous prenons garde à protéger nos voitures, puisque nous passons un certain temps à les emmener à l'abri de l'eau, pourquoi cette chose faite, revenons-nous en hâte vers les maisons menacées d'inondation, comme si ces maisons étaient des êtres qu'il ne saurait être question d'abandonner à la crue? Pourquoi, une fois montés les meubles du rez-de-chaussée, ne nous sauvons-nous pas, pourquoi préférons-nous la perspective de nous retrouver prisonniers de la maison environnée, sinon remplie, d'eau limoneuse et glaciale, et là, coincé à l'étage, d'attendre, dans l'inaction, dans l'ennui et l'inconfort, la baisse des eaux ? (AV 29)

The villagers' denial of the invasion of their homes and their reluctance to abandon them are associated with the self: 'comme si ces maisons étaient des êtres'. The home is here portrayed as a form of being, an affirmation of the integrity of the self and a resistance to chaos and splitting. Within this figure, the author discerns the community's dislike of anything that disturbs the order of home or unsettles the foundations of the familiar. Strangely, the narrator perceives this reaction on the part of the inhabitants as irrational, a suicidal thought, which is disturbing in its own right. In the self-portrait, the dispersing of the self and the impossible task of self-portrayal constantly bring the author back to the metaphor of the riverside house threatened by the murky, sinister waters of the Garonne. However, as in the depiction of the *femmes en vert*, the

Unheimliche is not simply feared but also desired. Why, the narrator asks, this resolute refusal of the others to abandon their homes, constantly threatened by chaos? Why this unwavering devotion to a place where we remain prisoners?

There is reason to think that, for the narrator, the invasion of the *chez soi* suggested by the muddy waters of the Garonne is, in a certain sense, fruitful and welcomed. The same is true for the *femme en vert*, who perhaps incarnates this same crisis, given the last line of the text: 'la Garonne est-elle une...est-elle une femme en vert' (AV 94)? Although the narrator suffers from discomfort when she sees the *femme en vert*, she also regards her with fascination: 'Toutes [s]es histoires m'intéressent' (AV 27). She in fact pursues her own double and welcomes this strangeness by accepting an invitation for coffee.

Thus, when the river specifically threatens to flood Katia Depetiteville's house, the narrator invites her to come and stay with her and her husband, Jean-Yves. While the Garonne *invades* the village, the *femme en vert* is in fact *welcomed* into the narrator's home, while she composes her self-portrait. Near the end of the narrative, the narrator shares with the reader a thought that suggests the fertility of the *femme en vert* as an unhoming figure:

> Je redoute de me considérer moi-même comme un être insensé si toutes les femmes en vert disparaissent l'une après l'autre, me laissant dans l'impossibilité de prouver leur existence, ma propre originalité. Je me demande alors, dans la cuisine proprette de mes sœurs, comment trouver supportable une vie dénuée de femmes en vert découpant en arrière-plan leur silhouette équivoque. Il me faut, pour traverser calmement ces moments d'hébétude, d'ennui profond, de langueur désemparante, me rappeler qu'elles ornent mes pensées, ma vie souterraine, qu'elles sont là, à la fois êtres réels et figures littéraires sans lesquelles l'âpreté de l'existence me semble râcler peau et chair jusqu'à l'os. (AV 77)

The uncanny figures of the double and the haunted house are not so much dark foreshadowings of death, as they are the essential condition for life and indeed the foundation of her originality as a writer. The writer is she who welcomes the *femmes en vert*, contradictory figures that lurk within the everyday, often ignored. They are the expression of what haunts the author, but seemingly, without which she could not write.

The photographic images interspersed throughout the text also serve to reinforce this strangeness. Just as the *femmes en vert* paradoxically both interfere with the narration of the story and constitute its very essence, so the visual support accompanying *Autoportrait en vert* both heightens the reader's sense of the insecurities created by the plurality of the self presented in the text, and impedes interpretation, by distracting or perplexing us.

The inclusion of a visual component was one of the requirements for this collection of self-portraits. The images were to maintain a unique rapport with the text, by inhabiting it like an echo, forming their own autonomous narrative. *Autoportrait en vert* successfully incorporates these two criteria: that of an echoing voice and that of a secret, nearly independent story, which unfolds alongside the textual content.

Autoportrait en vert contains two types of photograph[45]: first, a series of anonymous black and white family portraits from an unknown collection. Some of these pictures feature entire families and others individuals. We see a female figure standing in front of a house, a woman writing at a desk, a mother with a small child, two adolescent girls dressed as angels. In several of the photos, all the subjects are looking at the camera, while in others the gaze is directed away from the viewer, or subjects are exchanging looks. There is a blurring of strange and familiar at work, both because we see people who are unknown to us in familiar poses and because the photos are often repeated, doubled up on the page, but often with a slight discrepancy between the two images. This may be due to content, as on page 63, in a photo of mother and child, where one subject's facial expression is different in the two images.[46] At other times, this dissimilarity concerns the borders of the print, so that the same image is framed differently, thus altering its content. On page 29 for

---

[45] In an interview with Shirley Ann Jordan and Andrew Asibong at the conference 'Autour de Marie NDiaye', held at the London Institute of Germanic and Romance Studies (28-29 April 2007), Marie NDiaye stated that she herself found the black and white photographs and also selected the landscape photographs.

[46] In her analysis of *Autoportrait en vert,* Shirley Ann Jordan proposes that the family photographs in this text perhaps exemplify Marie NDiaye's tendency to 'turn the family photograph against its own familial purposes'. Shirley Ann Jordan, 'Figuring Out the Family: Family as Everyday Practice in French Women's Writing', p. 55. For Jordan, rather than evoking a sense of unity or familiarity, these family portraits act as 'enigmatic signifiers'. Ibid, p. 56.

instance, we see two side-by-side images of a woman seated at a desk, writing. In the first, the borders frame the photo in such as way as to include a piece of white fabric, a garment or curtain, to the far left of the photograph. This garment does not feature in the second photo, yet the viewer makes out what appears to be a bulletin board on the wall to the far right, which is absent from the first image. This same image resurfaces alongside another series of photographs on page 41. Doubling these images is perhaps a meta-photographic gesture on the part of the author, since the realism of the photographs is undermined by the changeable nature of their content. The viewer is invited to look several times at the same photograph, to go back and forth from one to the other, producing a disconcerting effect through repetition. This also challenges the concept of the portrait as a visual guarantee of the self, reflecting, like the *femmes en vert*, the multiple essences of self which the author has presented in her self-portrait. This contrasts with a more conventional use of the photograph in the autobio-graphical text. One might expect to find a series of images of the same individual across a period of time, in which case the differences observed in various photographs would be attributed by the viewer to the passage of time. The use of the image in NDiaye's self-portrait undermines such a cumulative view of selfhood, by suggesting the different possible ways of perceiving the same individual in any given moment.

The second series of photographs is a collection of landscape images from the 1990s by the photographer Julie Ganzin. These primarily feature various images of the Montagne Sainte Victoire in Provence, taken from various angles, often incorporating a female figure into the image, either in the foreground or off to the side. Again, there appears to be a challenge posed to the transparency of the photographic image. In the image on page 80, for example, a woman appears to be throwing something at the camera, as if obscuring the spectator's view. As was mentioned previously, the choice of the Montagne Sainte Victoire is particularly striking with respect to the plurality of the self embodied by the *femmes en vert*, since this particular landscape has become a symbol for uncertainty.

Yet while we may connect the imagery of the photos to our reading of the textual component of *Autoportrait en vert*, there is also a lack of correspondence between the textual and visual stories. For the most part, these photographs are arbitrarily placed. They are, in a sense, an echoing or haunting presence, rather than an illuminating one, since they appear to be superfluous and the text does not require them in order to be complete. Although the photos raise similar themes to those of the family, the home and the fluidity of identity presented in the text, they maintain no *direct* correlation with the passages they accompany. Like a ghostly presence, these images appear to be other-worldly, and are trapped in the wrong place in this text that ignores their existence. The text does not acknowledge the photographs and the images do not appear to acknowledge the text. Nevertheless, there is a sense that they perhaps have something to tell us about our own world. Due to their seemingly random insertion, the images interrupt, fragment and haunt the text. They draw the reader's attention away from the story, thereby impeding its flow.

In an attempt to reconcile the self with what haunts it, the writer is brought to interrogate the *chez soi* from various angles. The home, the self and the authorial stance become entangled in the autobiographical gesture. In this text, the *Unheimliche* is not reduced to the expression of a crumbling or a dispersing of the narrative subject. Nor are we confronting a simple incarnation of the formula 'je est un autre', which is often associated with contemporary autobiographical writing. The author proposes rather, an *unheimlich* representation of the self, a portrait of the subject as a haunted house, inhabited by uncertainty and spectral presences. Yet she also suggests that this haunting follows a logic of hospitality or cohabitation. Self-representation may be viewed as a quest to summon these ghosts and to welcome them *chez soi.*

In *Autoportrait en vert*, we rediscover some of the themes which surfaced in *L'Adversaire*. While representing the self is a project that, in this case, appears to be less ethically engaged than that of portraying the criminal, NDiaye too arrives at the elusiveness of her object of representation. Rather than appealing primarily to fragmentation and changing points of view to capture this uncertainty, NDiaye employs the uncanny imagery of the double and haunting. This imagery enables the author to tell her story, while affirming her attentiveness to the intervention of an outside voice, one which constantly undermines the initial gesture of representation. Marie NDiaye's portrayal of the self as vulnerable to haunting and exile, her subtle deployment of the forms and leitmotivs of the uncanny, particularly her self-dispersal through the *femmes en vert*, present once more a text which abandons the vision of the individual as a rational, chronologically constituted, self-knowing subjecttivity and instead introduces an element of fantasy into non-fiction, responding to some of the preoccupations of *autofiction*. However, in *Autoportrait en vert*, the crisis of subjectivity is not simply to be understood as the expression of the challenges of self-representation. These figures both interfere in the author's attempt to represent herself as artist, and enrich her *autoportrait*, by assuming significance as the means through which she portrays subjective experience.

The Self in Exile: Savitzkaya's *Fou trop poli*

> Je suis propriétaire d'une maison qui, d'un moment à l'autre, dans l'instant peut-être, va s'écrouler avec un bruit de falaise qui s'abat, de falaise de craie qui tombe dans l'eau et s'y dissout [...][47]

Written just before the novelist's fiftieth birthday, *Fou trop poli* (2005) is Savitzkaya's most recent novel and a text which exemplifies the merging of the autobiographical, fictional and poetic modes that characterizes his œuvre. More consciously geared towards an exploration of self than many of his other novels, this fragmented work exploits some of the semantic liberties of poetry to confer a hesitant tone on the autobiographical. This uncertainty both perturbs and enriches the writer's contemplation of his own existence.

In *Fou trop poli*, the writer appears to embark on a pathway to self-representation, but the text subsequently transforms into the bewildered monologue of a writer who seems to have been distracted from this primary task by the need to assert his own sense of unhomeliness and of the strangeness of the self. Although Savitzkaya's reflection on writing is less plain-spoken and ethical than Carrère's, his predicament resembles that of the author of *L'Adversaire*. He cannot 'find his place', and the novel is dominated by the desire to contemplate and figure this hindrance to his own expression. However, what is dislocated is not the self's relationship to the other, but the self in its entirety. This disorientation both troubles and enriches

---

[47] Eugène Savitzkaya, *La Disparition de Maman*, p. 8.

the writer's contemplation of his own existence, allowing him to articulate his vision of the self as non-locatable.[48]

Homeland

Despite the author's renunciation of narrative conventions such as temporality, plot and unified point of view, *Fou trop poli* is ostensibly autobiographical, presenting an array of childhood memories interspersed with present reflections and experiences. There are images of the writer's family home in suburban Liège, anecdotes of playing in the schoolyard and stealing sweets from the local shop in his village with his brothers and sisters, recollections of times of illness and hardship and memories of his mother's death. These recollections often take the form of child-like moments interwoven with fragments of the author's interpretation of these events from an adult perspective:

> Pour se rendre en ville, il y avait un bois à longer, très touffu, très sombre et nous demandions à notre mère si des loups habitaient ce bois: elle n'avait garde de répondre, toujours encline à jouer de ses silences et de ses mots, comme elle était je le devine, elle viendra peu à peu comme viennent les choses quand on tire sur le fil. Parfois, le soir, les vitrines étaient des aquariums.[49]

At other times, these memories are listed less contemplatively as a series of succinct, candid sentences: 'Je me souviens de tout. Je courais sur les toits, j'escaladais des murs. Un jour, j'ai tué une poule' (FTP 108).

However, these autobiographical sequences only appear in fragments, as they are frequently pushed aside by the narrator's affirmations of his dislocated position, which interferes with the process of memory and with his sense of self-unity. The question 'Who am I?' is expressed as 'Where am I?', since composing an autobiographical narrative is essentially the task of defining the point from which one is writing, that is, identifying and representing the origin of one's own text. For Savitzkaya, this questioning of location

---

[48] As was evoked in the second chapter of this book, Savitzkaya's novels often gesture towards a non-locatable reality, one inaccessible from within the *chez soi*, thereby suggesting a yearning for a more primitive, pre-subjective state.

[49] Eugène Savitzkaya, *Fou trop poli* (Paris: Éditions de Minuit, 2005), p. 20. All other references are given in the text, following the abbreviation FTP.

is primary, but can lead to no concrete answers, since the self exists in a state of constant fluctuation and deviation from the concept of a fixed *chez soi*. This elusiveness is expressed in spatial terms: 'Où serais-je demain? Là où j'étais ou là où je voulais? [...] Si vous me touchez, que rencontrez-vous?' (FTP 77-8).

There is a constant tension in the novel between the quest for location or origin, which defines the autobiographical task, understood as the creation of a tangible text which defines the self, and the evasiveness of selfhood as that which can never be 'pinned down'. As was the case in NDiaye's autobiographical text, the expression of this problematic as a quest for an authorial home reflects a tendency to evoke autobiographical writing as the task of forging or carving out a location for oneself. Savitzkaya undermines this objective by insisting instead on the self's resistance to such attempts at localization, stressing the aspects of his life and subjectivity that elude place.

Savitzkaya's predicament, unlike that of Carrère, does not emerge retrospectively, in the aftermath of catastrophe. Rather it is an aporia of beginning. An appropriate starting point for his autobiography would have been to express his identification with an original family home, or a national or cultural identity, which might act as guarantor for the writer's sense of who he is. The narrator's reminiscences often return to the house where the writer grew up, which he describes as a 'petite maison d'exilés', since his mother and father were Russian and Polish respectively, living in Belgium. As we saw in the second chapter of this book, Savitzkaya privileges the home in many of his novels as a fecund, poetic site of transformation and metaphor, sometimes portraying it as haunted, at other times as peaceful and heartening. This dualism is again perceptible in *Fou trop poli*:

> La porte d'entrée de la maison donnait directement dans le séjour. Des monstres vinrent, en tous genres, laitiers, rémouleurs, passants curieux, et je ne pouvais me mouvoir, ma tendre mère seule les chassait [...] (FTP 20-21)

In this passage we find the duplicitous, contradictory image of home, which is to premise the entire novel. The home is portrayed as a vulnerable space, threatened by the intrusion of the unknown outside world. From the point of view of the young boy, visitors to the home are suspect and unwelcome, since they trouble the frontiers of the home, calling on the inhabitants to expand to welcome the foreign element. But the home is also a haven of comfort, where the child can take refuge in the solace of the family and maternal protection. The home as constituted in the text is represented much like the authorial position, in that it is an object of quest on the part of the writer yet always eludes the stability he would like it to display in his memories. The geographic imagery of homelessness that arises in the author's ponderings over his own mixed national identity further troubles the writing process and the search for an authorial *chez soi*. The home is both familiar and strange, simultaneously a goal to be sought and a pure illusion. The writer's inability to feel truly *chez lui* comes across in the home's constantly shifting representation; the home is never quite a point of origin, or an identity-ascribing location, but neither is it entirely lacking, since it is the object of an incessant quest. While a certain nostalgia for origin envelops the story, as if it were something once possessed and now missing, the borders of the *chez soi* are also represented as those of an arbitrary structure, implying that home is an illusory notion:

> Mon père et ma mère ont vécu en exil sur une terre dont la composition chimique variait à peine de la composition chimique de leur terre natale. Un lieu de naissance n'implique ni la nécessité de ne jamais le quitter ni l'obligation de le fuir. (FTP 15)

The home has no inherent qualities of comfort or stability; there is nothing which authentically differentiates it from any other place, obliging us to remain there.

Due to the status of his parents as immigrants, Savitzkaya was himself 'born in exile' and the idea of the origin as a place where one is already not-at-home serves to reinforce the author's inability to write about himself, to identify the point from which he is writing: 'Le plus drôle, d'un point de vue de simple logique, c'est de naître en exil' (FTP 16). The notion of exile, which ordinarily evokes a state of distance from an original home, is presented in this text as a paradoxical starting point in itself, since the quest is one, not for an existing origin, but for an origin which the writer feels never did exist.

This logic is again perceptible in the representation of linguistic alienation. Striving to anchor his identity in an original point of familiarity, such as a maternal language, the narrator can only arrive at something missing or forgotten: the languages of his parents, which he spoke when he was young but has now lost: 'J'ai désappris deux langues. J'ai désappris des lieux et j'ai peut-être perdu quelques privilèges. Mais, par ailleurs, j'ai su qu'aucun privilège ne m'importe. Est-ce parce que je suis un privilégié ou le contraire?' (FTP 14).

It is therefore not through a rediscovery of his own Belgian identity, native language, family history, or birthplace that the narrator can hope to define himself, to produce a narrative which will represent his existence: 'Ce n'est pas le droit au sol qui me sauvera de l'anéantissement' (FTP 14).

The theme of exile resurfaces in many forms throughout the text, in various descriptions which often appear to begin from memory of personal unhomeliness and then transform into imagined, dreamlike sequences such as the following:

> Pendant que les bombes, vendues par les grossistes, secouent le sol, les ours partent en exil. Informés par la mort de l'un d'eux explosé sur une mine, les ours partent en exil. Les serpents les ont procédés et les populations humaines ont suivi. (FTP 75)

Here, the writer explores an imagery of being forced to take exile, of having to migrate or abandon the home when its vulnerability is revealed. While NDiaye invoked the natural catastrophe of the flood to suggest this thought, Savitzkaya refers to bombing and the disasters of war, which command the departure of beings from their homes. In both texts, the quest for home appears destined to fail.

Consequently, like the character himself, this autobiographical text seems to have been 'born in exile'. *Fou trop poli* is written in a space which appears somehow prior to the intelligibility required for a unified and legible narrative account. The indefinable origins of the writer, underscored by the theme of exile, are echoed in the versatile, oscillating point of view. The narrating voice is continually relocated, with respect to the self, amongst the third, second and first persons.

Le fou

Fou trop poli highlights the strangeness of autobiography as an act which renders other the intimacy of the self, exteriorizing the inside, an act through which the writer generates his or her textual double. The novel begins in the third, rather than the first person. Savitzkaya chooses to represent himself not only as other, but as a self-proclaimed 'fou'. When we are introduced to 'le fou', he is going about his everyday gardening activities and 'se prépare à fêter cinquante années de folie' (FTP 7). The reader perceives the repetitive, commonplace activities of unloading mounds of dirt and manure from a wheelbarrow as the strange, unsystematic performance of a madman: 'Le fou revient à la charge, il décharge ici devant vous trente-sept brouettes de bonne bouse, dix-neuf de terre de taupinière, dix de crottin d'ânesse, quatre de diverses variétés de pommes de terre' (FTP 7). Descriptions of the 'fou' in *Fou trop poli* display this child-like quality, lending something of the tone we saw in the evocation of the writer's son in *Marin mon cœur*. This time, however, this atmosphere is exploited to portray the author himself and to convey detail about his own dwelling in the ordinary.

In an earlier novel, Savitzkaya proposed the image of himself as a 'fou civil'.[50] *Fou trop poli* is a variant of this title, which again evokes the narrator's suspension between adherence to the rules and expectations of the community and a certain distance from it, since as a writer he is occasionally subject to feelings of marginality and an awareness of his own eccentricity. Yet, although he may be 'mad' in one sense, as 'trop poli', he is inoffensive. If madness implies the inability to integrate into the community, politeness implies just the opposite: the capacity to identify symbolically on a collective level with others. The writer is thus a polite dissident. While the 'fou trop poli' might refer specifically to the writer, there is a sense in which, for Savitzkaya, every individual is a kind of madman whose idiosyncrasies must comply with the expectations of the collective sphere.[51]

Like the *femmes en vert* for Marie NDiaye, the 'fou trop poli' thus appears to designate a peculiar character in the text, but also serves as a device for the articulation of the vulnerability and foreignness of the self and the uncertainty of the autobiographical endeavour. The authority of everything he says is questionable, coming as it does from the mouth of his double, the 'fou', who is

---

[50] Eugène Savitzkaya, *Fou civil* (Paris: Flohic Éditions, 1999).

[51] This quality of the writer as marginal, or as a kind of 'jester', is an idea which has been previously evoked by Savitzkaya. He has a vision of the writer as a 'bouffon', a peculiar, child-like character who is treated differently by the community. As he says in an interview: 'J'ai l'impression que dans le monde culturel et pour les institutions, les artistes sont toujours des bouffons, ils sont pris pour des enfants.' Aurélie Dijon, 'Interview avec Eugène Savitzkaya: le regard du fou', *Chronic' Art: Le Webmag Culturel*, (21 December 2005), p. 2. http://www.chronicart.com (accessed 8 June 2006).

displaced, *décalé*: 'Le fou se remet au mensonge. Il songe. Le fou se remet au roman. Et remet ça par pur plaisir' (FTP 17). The idea that self-representation necessarily implies lying is prominent in criticism on autobiography. We might cite, for example, Philippe Lejeune's warning about the genre: 'Attention: autobiographie, danger: Mentir, mourir. Être dépossédé de soi'.[52] Yet by following the term 'mensonge' with 'il songe', Savitzkaya suggests the possible redemption of prose by poetry, insisting on the joy of writing. In his text, the displacement of the writing self into 'le fou' functions to frame the author's statements in a suspect context, and further suggests a loss of self in the act of self-portraiture. The image of the madman also allows the author to counterbalance autobiographical narcissism with a more modest approach, and to explore certain humorous or fragile moments of subjecttivity, and the ways in which these might be amplified and celebrated, rather than superseded, in the act of self-representation (as was the case for Marie NDiaye's use of the double). Of course, this reference to the 'fou' might also evoke the insight of the madman, as he who sees more clearly than the rest of society and who, as a writer, brings an outlandish brilliance to the ordinary.

The 'fou trop poli' resurfaces frequently throughout the narrative, 'un citadin devenu jardinier' (FTP 49) who writes and carries out inconsequential domestic chores. The reader follows 'le fou' on a journey through his habitual environment, his garden, and his everyday life, observing him while he 'se remet au sport' and 'fait la fête' (FTP 30-31). The reader always retains the impression, not of complete madness, but of a slight disparity between this 'fou trop poli' and the communal real.

Descriptions of the 'fou trop poli' in the third person only constitute one thread of the narrative. At times, the writer adopts the 'nous' for the voice of the members of the community, who regard the madman as an unconventional character leading a strange marginal existence in his garden, while still belonging partially to society: 'Le fou trop poli vit parmi nous. C'est une espèce de fou civil parfois amer et parfois pas. Il vit vertement sa vie' (FTP 49). Here we have an image of the writer who, although he participates in the community, is

---

[52] Philippe Lejeune, 'Nouveau Roman et retour à l'autobiographie', in *L'Auteur et le manuscrit*, ed. by Michel Contat (Paris: Presses Universitaires de France, 1991), pp. 51-70, p. 56.

somehow not entirely at home within it, reflecting the position Eugène Savitzkaya perhaps occupies in his own neighbourhood, living somewhat in retreat.

The second and third persons are also frequently employed to make short, affirmative statements describing the routine activities of the madman or addressing the reader or readers as 'vous': The words 'Je vous écris' (FTP 41) introduce several passages. However, in the majority of fragments where the 'I' is adopted, it is in displacement, or the object of a circular, rambling line of questioning, which asks 'where?' The 'je' seems to be undergoing extreme disorientation:

> Je ne sais pas d'où je suis parti ni où on m'a relégué. Je ne sais rien et ne veux rien savoir de pareil. J'ai d'autres questions qui me trottent dans la tête. Mais je suis bien parti de quelque part et je suis bien sorti de quelqu'un. (FTP 13)

While the 'je' seems certain about coming from 'quelque part' and 'quelqu'un', the question of precise origin cannot be answered. The certainties put forth in the narration remain within the domain of language itself; the 'je' only leads to other pronouns. The pronoun 'je' appears as a part of speech, rather than as a designator of selfhood or origin, becoming an obstacle to self-understanding. The narrator expresses immense doubt about where he *truly* comes from and about the place from which he is essentially writing. There is a sense that the truths which might alleviate the narrator's uncertainty really lie further away – or perhaps closer – than the 'je' will allow him to reach. As Jean-Baptiste Harang suggests, *Fou trop poli* is a text which is suspended in a place of self-doubt, 'entre le je et le il',[53] between the self as intimate and knowable and the self as foreign and unknowable. The irony is that only by displacing himself, and viewing himself as an other, as a madman, is the writer capable of formulating coherent statements about his own existence.

At times the author appears to address his reader directly from another strange and transitory place, that of a section of the dictionary: 'Je vous écris aujourd'hui de canitie à canoéiste, de la tablette d'un petit secrétaire [...]' (FTP 54). Here the narrator evokes a state of suspension between two places of writing: firstly an intellectual or

---

[53]   Jean-Baptiste Harang, 'À quoi songe le fou sur son futon?', *Libération* (10 November 2005).

linguistic position, and secondly a physical support, with which he writes ('la tablette d'un petit secrétaire').

Through techniques of repetition and the dislocation of terms from their usual context, language is often turned into a device of estrangement rather than reference. Part of the writer's inspiration for *Fou trop poli* appears to have been the desire to celebrate the strange resonances of certain words he discovered in an old dictionary. He inserts these words into the text in the form of intermittent exclamations: 'Ecballium! Ecballium!' These sporadic expletives may at first interrupt or obscure the reading, but as Jean-Baptiste Harang suggests, this is not entirely a divergence from the autobiographical project, since 'Ecballium' is perhaps being presented as an alternative name for the human being. The definition of the word 'Ecballium' in the 1960 edition of the Larousse is: 'nom masculin, plante glauque, hérissée de poils raides, à fruits pendants lorsqu'il est à maturité, s'ouvrant en lançant au loin ses graines [...] pousse dans les décombres, synonyme du momordique'.[54] Like the 'fou', the ecballium is perhaps a device of personification, with which the author forges an eccentric, humbling identification.

The vision of the self that Savitzkaya puts forth is one which is never quite *chez soi*, one which resists localization and thus representation. Although he continually seeks to identify this point from which he is writing, the description produced during the writing experience insists that his subjectivity is situated in a place which is 'out of place', dispersed amongst various feelings, states and experiences: 'Je ne suis plus ici, mais déjà là de l'autre côté. Voyez-vous où je suis sans presque bouger, vais-je me transformer en rhinocéros?[55] Comment serais-je transformé demain métamorphosé' (FTP 77)? This ethereal quality of self may also be expressed in spatio-temporal terms. The self is the transitory product of the combination of different temporalities: 'Le temps ne passe pas, il monte rejoindre le grand fluide, le 'tout-temps' qui se dilate et ne peut qu'accueillir le courant des objets, des êtres et des mots lâchés comme buée dans le feu du soleil' (FTP 64). Yet this impossibility for the self to be located and for the writing subject to domesticate his or her own self-image is what makes the writing process an adventure or quest.

---

[54] Cited in Jean-Baptiste Hareng, 'À quoi songe le fou sur son futon?', p. 4.

[55] This could well be a reference to Ionesco's play, *Rhinocéros*, and perhaps also to Kafka's 'Metamorphosis'.

The novel generates a dialogue between the narrator's attempts to locate himself physically, geographically and historically and the refusal of his object of representation to adhere to any possible place or understanding of his origins.

The writer-gardener

The predominance of autobiographical content in Savitzkaya's novels is perhaps due to the fact that, for him, writing is inextricably connected with his day-to-day experience and to his immediate perception of his surroundings. Creativity is inseparable from the writer's way of being. As we saw in *En vie,* the logic of the uncanny provides a gentle, defamiliarizing perspective which allows him to continually re-acquaint himself with the most banal or familiar phenomena, and is not simply an instance of breakdown or anxiety. Through literary creation, the writer projects a strange, constantly renewed gaze onto his own domestic existence as a writer and gardener in Belgium. *Fou trop poli* displays this uncanny way of dwelling in the real, whereby the subject accepts a more humble, less 'domesticating' role within his or her everyday environment. Besides memories from his past, the narrator also recounts his own current day-to-day activities, such as tending his garden, a theme which frequently figures in the author's work.

The garden is represented as an enthralling space, where the individual can regain a harmonious, primordial rapport with nature by participating in its evolution. There is both familiarity and exoticism to be experienced in the individual's quest to 'cultiver son jardin'. The writer often describes at length the repeated movements of planting, filtration, collecting, sorting, digging, trimming and depositing which contribute to the constant modification and renovation of the garden, in much the same way as in *En vie* he poetically exhibits the commonplace tasks which are undertaken within the home. The home and garden are in constant movement, repeatedly opening, closing and transforming through processes of incorporation, rejection and renewal.

The garden is an in-between space, both belonging to the home and external to it, since it is on view for the community. As the author once stated in an interview: 'Je taille mes arbres et cultive mon potager. C'est ma manière d'appartenir à ma ville, je lui donne quelques arbres et disperse au-dessus d'elle l'odeur des fleurs du jardin.'[56] The garden is perhaps a location, like the text, which exists as a transitional space between the self and the rest of the world. Like writing, which for Savitzkaya defamiliarizes and revitalizes the *chez soi*, the garden is a domain which is concerned with the evolving borders of the home.[57] In several passages, the narrator's literary and gardening activities are evoked side-by-side:

> Mais quand le jardinier se repose, ses mains sont libres et les pieds, nus sous la tablette du secrétaire. La main gauche ouvre le dictionnaire. La main droite joue au gribouri de la vigne en écrivant à ses amis, faisant précéder sa lettre de ces deux mots, de ces deux signes: ecballium ! ecballium ![58]

In the above passage, the narrator establishes an analogy between the writer and the insect called 'gribouri'. This insect is a fearful creature which lives on the stems of certain plants, feeding on their buds and frequently drawing itself into a ball and falling away from its home when threatened. Throughout the text, writing itself is portrayed as an act which extracts the individual from home, an act performed in a space of dislodgment. But this unhomeliness is not a negative experience. On the contrary, although the home is constantly sought in the novel, Savitzkaya's writing encourages a celebration of this state of unhomeliness. As we saw in *Marin mon cœur* and *En vie*, the uncanny, in Savitzkaya's writing, maintains its defamiliarizing, absurd and disorienting connotations, but loses its sense of 'dis-ease'.[59] The capacity for the self and the ordinary world to evade the writer's understanding, containing only the most singular of meanings, generates feelings of vulnerability and disorientation which are again represented as constructive, since they give rise to poetry. Savitzkaya's authorial unhomeliness appears to seek resolution, but is also itself the voice with which the writer chooses to speak. A similar observation is made by Guillaume Fayard in his review of the novel:

> Aussi frêle et instable que puisse être dans *Fou trop poli* l'embarcation du roman, sa grande pauvreté de moyens lui donne

---

[56] Antoine de Gaudemar, 'Interview avec Eugène Savitzkaya'.
[57] As the writer himself states: 'Le jardin, c'est comme l'écriture. C'est un travail de patience'. Antoine de Gaudemar, 'Interview avec Eugène Savitzkaya'.
[58] Eugène Savitzkaya, *Fou trop poli*, p. 41.
[59] This is Lucie Armitt's term, cited in the introduction to this book.

son cap: roman sur l'enfance et l'amour filial tout en sauts
disjonctifs et petits chapitres, poème en prose délirant célébrant le
monde comme patate, et patate désirable qui plus est.[60]

It is the absence of a secure, immobile *chez soi* that propels
the text; the story appears to circulate around its own missing origin,
consumed by feelings of disarticulation which are never surmounted.
Representing this state of prolonged uncanniness is a way for the
writer to express his experience of selfhood. As in the previous novels
reviewed in this chapter, the confused relationship that the author
maintains with his own text appears to reflect an *unheimlich* feeling
experienced by the writer during his quest to represent his own being.
In a manner similar to that found in the texts by Carrère and NDiaye,
the construction of a text involves the deconstruction of the *chez soi,*
as the narrator dwells on moments where it is impossible to locate the
self, or which appear to elude representation. This uncertainty is
creative, since it allows the author to reflect upon the transitory nature
of the self and to display its hesitation between strangeness and
familiarity.

The narrative ends on a note of haunting. Although less
prominent than the *femmes en vert* who feature in NDiaye's self-
representation, ghostly presences also occur in some of the childhood
memories recounted in the very last fragment of *Fou trop poli*. Savitzkaya concludes his self-portrait with a passage relating a recurring
uncanny experience from the writer's youth. He speaks of repeated
sightings of a threatening, phantom-like figure, 'la haute silhouette
d'un homme hirsute à trois bras' who would regularly appear in the
courtyard of the family home, the vividness of his appearance varying
depending on the light, from 'très présent' to 'invisible' (FTP 124-25).
Like the narrator in *Autoportrait en vert*, the writer wonders whether
or not such haunting presences are perceptible to others: 'Les autres
avaient-ils ce genre d'individu dans leur cour?' This question contains
a reference to home. The author asks whether other homes are equally
troubled by such invasions. But the phrasing of the question lends
itself to a more figurative interpretation, as an inquiry about the self.
The narrator wonders whether or not others experience similar forms

---

[60] Guillaume Fayard, 'Eugène Savitzkaya, Fou trop poli: en nous il vibre',
Peauneuve.net, http://peauneuve.net/article.php3?id_article=104 (accessed on 8 June
2006).

of haunting. Again, he sets himself apart as a writer, or simply as an individual, from the rest of the community.

While in NDiaye's autobiographical text, feelings of displacement sometimes do give rise to anxiety, for Savizkaya they appear to fuel a mechanism of curiosity. Both authors ultimately stress the potential fruitfulness of uncertainty and unhomeliness for literary creation, and portray the writer as a person who transforms strangeness into something significant. In both novels, autobiography is depicted as an uncanny act, one which brings its own paradoxes; it both obscures the subject-object relation and reinforces it. Autobiography might be viewed as a narcissistic, self-affirming experience. Depicting the self as a foreign object strengthens the perceived integrity of the self and presupposes a state of self-domestication. In this way, traditional autobiography is perhaps premised on the fantasy of the unified *chez soi*, vigorously rejected by thinkers such as Cixous. However, self-representation is also always an experience of doubling, an act in which one acknowledes one's own splitting and ultimate vulnerability and 'mourns one's own loss' (LFP 50), as Viart puts it. Nicolas Royle underlines this duality in his reflection on the uncanny:

> It is impossible to think about the uncanny without involving a sense of what is autobiographical, self-centred, based in one's own experience. But it is also impossible to conceive of the uncanny without a sense of ghostliness, a sense of strangeness given to dissolving all assurances about the identity of a self. (UN 16)

Autobiography raises the question of self-annihilation evoked by the uncanny double. For Freud, it is the subject's capacity to conceive of itself from an external point of view which makes the uncanny possible. In uncanny experience, not only do we encounter the crumbling of the world around us, but also of the ego. The texts presented in this chapter rather inventively, and even playfully, display these autobiographical ambiguities and reveal the multi-layered connotations of the *Unheimliche*. As well as bringing out the process of the doubling of self implied by the autobiographical undertaking, they render more vivid some of the preoccupations of *autofiction,* by addressing the *chez soi* as a form of home.

Although only two of the texts studied in this chapter are explicitly autobiographical, all three are to some degree stories of the self. They are also stories of home. Each novel recounts the destruction or ambiguity of various forms of the *chez soi.* The elusiveness of home provides the disquieting background for a thorough questioning of the self, the event or the other, and acts as a metaphor for authorial uncertainty. In *L'Adversaire* we confront the haunting image of the fire that destroyed a family home. In *Autoportrait en vert* we find a disagreeable portrayal of family members and experience the susceptibility of the home to the threat of natural disaster. In *Fou trop poli,* a description of home as transitory and simultaneously troublesome and comforting is conveyed through the narrator's childhood memories.

In every case, unhomely contents appear to reproduce themselves on a performative textual level as the expression of an estranging experience which emerges in the act of writing. In all three novels, the author reflects upon the unfamiliarity of the previously familiar domains of home, fact or selfhood and vocalizes this strangeness by causing it to resonate in the textual composition and in the dislocation of the authorial voice.

The notion of home might thus be extended to encompass an authorial *chez soi.* The uncanny is what prevents one from finding one's place, from forging a comfortable stance from which to express oneself. Each of the authors mobilizes figures of the uncanny to convey the instability of the *chez soi.* While NDiaye borrows from a repertoire of typically uncanny imagery, such as the double and the theme of haunting, Carrère's and Savitzkaya's texts display fewer or more subtly deployed uncanny motifs, thereby bringing into relief the uncanny's more seconddary connotations of disorientation and intellectual uncertainty. The texts of these last two writers therefore entertain rapports with some of the more theoretical, less literary incarnations of the concept of the uncanny, which were addressed in the first chapter of this book. Carrère's approach, for instance, suggests some of the reflections on the uncanny set out by James Donald or Nicolas Royle, who posit its broader value as a de-dogmatizing tool and a perspective for re-writing the real.

Each novel also explores simultaneously the themes of representational uncertainty and authorship, incorporating the expression of the hesitations and complexities of the task of narration into their stories. While, for Carrère, the challenges of writing are more directly asserted and become the object of frustration and immediate reflection on the part of the author, NDiaye and Savitzkaya appear to take this doubt for granted, as necessarily constitutive of literary creation.

All three authors have developed forms of story-telling which locate an instance of invention where the *chez soi* – understood as reality, the self or the home – refuses to be domesticated. In order to represent this resistance, all three authors appeal to techniques of fragmentation. For Carrère and NDiaye in particular, this is not a strategy that is seen in their fictional works, but one which emerges uniquely in response to the introduction of a non-fictional element. This tactic reflects the notion of contemporary 'realism' presented in the second chapter of this book, characterized by Viart and Rabaté as seeking to represent the 'fissures' in the real.

However, despite this tendency towards destruction and breakage, each author finds the estrangement he or she experiences with respect to his or her object of representation to be fruitful, leading not only to silence and erasure, but to creativity. Despite the continued emphasis in French writing on the unknowable nature of the real, the reader is here very conscious of what the author *does* say and of his or her commitment to re-engage, however tentatively, with non-fictional representation, despite the precariousness which accompanies this act. Narrative uncertainty and the impossibility of objectivity in all three texts are often very consciously communicated on a personal level. The expression of these personal writing experiences might be seen to foster a shift in the focus of representation-related suspicion towards the potential productivity of such ambiguity, its capacity to become a story in itself, creating a fascinating contemporary context for *unheimlich* imagery such as the double, ghostly presences and haunted homes.

Given the self-alienating gestures made by NDiaye, Carrère and Savitzkaya in order to represent uncertain realities, it is pertinent to turn to Kristeva's and Cixous's ethical analyses of the uncanny as theoretical frameworks capable of enriching an understanding of this approach to narration as a destabilization of the *chez soi*. In inviting the uncanny into their diverse styles of non-fictional writing, what all three writers appear to share is an ethos of representation based on self-estrangement. Each writer accepts the crumbling of the stability of the self as a pre-requisite for articulating a vision of reality and presents his or her own unhomeliness as a force which disrupts and challenges any fixed account of the content being represented.

The strategies displayed in these texts might thus be seen to reflect Cixous's 'aesthethics' of approaching the unthematizable real through a destabilization of self. Carrère, NDiaye and Savitzkaya privilege the strangeness of the authorial voice over the cohesion of their texts, writing from a disorientated moment which appears to precede the impulse to concretize, to determine a final meaning. However, these writers are not so much abandoning the *chez soi,* as was recommended by Cixous, as subjecting it to profound revision, highlighting its ambiguities, its simultaneous lures and dangers and challenging a view of the *chez soi* as a totalizing, prescriptive domain.

Following Kristeva's vision of the uncanny, these writers' portrayals of self lead them to encounter themselves as strangers. The intimate, 'familiar' corners of the subject are revealed to be equally capable of embodying the alterity of disintegration, illogic and the unconscious. Their descriptions of the ordinary perhaps correspond to Kristeva's ethical analysis, in which the foreigner should be welcomed as an incitement to re-write the national narrative, revealing it and the *chez soi* to be foreign, as perceived through the eyes of the newcomer. Like the foreigner in Kristeva's account, writing should provoke a form of exile within the familiar.

In all three narratives the story is constructed at the cost of the firm location of the authorial voice. These novels which, on the surface, appear to be exposés of selfhood or descriptions of real events are, upon closer examination, first and foremost stories of the disorienting experiences which accompany the writing process. The quest for realism seems to have been replaced by textual strategies that are geared towards the representation of the ethical, aesthetic and realist complexities that arise from within this process itself. However, these representations have not entirely missed their targets, since the experience of self-questioning that results from dislocation illuminates the object of representation from an innovative angle and founds an uncanny ethos of representation.[61]

---

[61] Viart suggests: 'Si l'autobiographie recèle quelque vérité, c'est dans la manière de

In all three works, unhomeliness is more than a literary device for the articulation of uncertainty. It is also an ethos or tentative stance, as opposed to a place, from which to write, founded on the recognition and privileging of the vulnerability of the writing subject. Carrère's inability to inhabit any singular viewpoint discourages the inscription of the *fait divers* in closed moral or historical categories, while still addressing some of its implications for selfhood and community. NDiaye's and Savitzkaya's dispersals of the narrative voice and portrayal of the self as fleeting and un-homed tempers such autobiographical notions as self-unity, foundation and narcissism with visions of the self and the writer as intangible, lost and vulnerable.

---

le dire, pas dans ce qu'elle dit' (LFP 29).

General Conclusion

Strategies of the Uncanny?

The aim of this book was to explore the ways in which the uncanny provides a repertoire of narrative tactics, and also an interpretative framework, for the portrayal of the *chez soi* in the writing of Marie NDiaye, Emmanuel Carrère and Eugène Savitzkaya. With reference to a corpus of theoretical literature on the uncanny, this study has assembled a series of observations concerning a tendency in French writing to depict the disharmony that often exists between the subject and certain spaces we tend to conceive of as familiar, such as the home, the self and the family.

I have argued that, although the term 'uncanny' has always served to evoke the collapse of the borders between strange and familiar, the manifestation of this collapse has begun to take on a new form in contemporary French fiction. In the novels of the writers studied in this book, the forms and dynamics of the uncanny are now exploited to express the strangeness of the subject's experience *chez lui* rather than primarily to characterize an encounter with alterity. Through the uncanny, NDiaye, Carrère and Savitzkaya reinterpret domestic space, family relations and selfhood, proposing new codes for the representation of the subject's negotiation of everyday life. The reader is encouraged to re-evaluate these domains and to perceive their foreignness, a stance of reading which enters into contradiction with a vision of the *chez soi* as reassuring, harmonious and stable.

One key contextual element of this study is that formed by recent developments in the interpretation of the Freudian uncanny within contemporary thought. Just as the French novel has arrived at a re-appraisal of familiar spaces, the concept of the uncanny has followed a somewhat similar course within contemporary cultural, literary and psychoanalytic theory. Although in the past the term has appeared mainly in discussions of fantastic literature and in the context of explicitly otherworldly forms, the uncanny is now often viewed as a concept which imposes a reinterpretation of the self-same in the light of its perceived strangeness. It is currently viewed as a conceptual device which reveals the foreignness of familiar locations, ways of thinking and understandings of subjectivity. The uncanny allows us to glimpse the potential to break down that exists within rigid systems of thought and is symptomatic of the impossibility of 'domesticating' concepts. As a term which points to the impossibility of demarcating boundaries between ideas, the uncanny is now seen to express the necessity of recognizing the strangeness in any familiar structure or conceptual 'home' we might have. Based on the readings various thinkers have proposed, Freud's 1919 essay, 'Das Unheimliche', might retrospectively be viewed as an unwitting allegory of this very configuration of uncanniness, insofar as the psychoanalyst is unable to pin down the concept according to his psychoanalytic methodology.

However, although many thinkers have indicated the potential value of the uncanny as a destabilizing intellectual tool, they all seem rather uncertain as to what 'uncanny thinking' might entail. How can a concept which is based on uncertainty and the disintegration of common reality have tangible, collective meaning? In this book I have suggested that the contemporary French novel offers a site in which some of these questions gain significance in a literary context. I have argued that the depictions of the home, the self, the everyday and the family in the work of NDiaye, Carrère and Savitzkaya reflect, and also challenge, the theories of the uncanny expounded by thinkers such as Julia Kristeva and Hélène Cixous. These theorists link the notion to the productive dissipation or abandonment of a fixed *chez soi*, employing it in their elaborations of ethical ways of writing and negotiating relationships with the other.

The uncanny in contemporary French writing
Throughout this study I have argued that, as well as informing and expressing these novelists' personal conceptions of subjective experience, the uncanny provides a way of situating their narrative approaches with respect to some of the key problematics of contemporary French writing. Today's novelists often inscribe their narratives in the personal spaces of home, family and self. As Christian Michel suggests: 'Le roman contemporain jouerait la carte du *domus*

contre celle de la *polis* ou du *cosmos*'.[1] Without wishing to reduce the content of NDiaye's, Carrère's and Savitzkaya's novels to a series of literary fashions, I have, throughout this book, attempted to place my comments about their writing within the context of current tendencies in French writing relating to the representation of the *chez soi*. The uncanny provides these writers with a way of articulating some of these current literary preoccupations. Like many contemporary novelists, they tend to accentuate the foreignness and intangibility of these domains of the *intime*, rather than their familiarity. Through their appeal to the uncanny, they portray the individual as being in an ambiguous relationship with home, and explore the repercussions of familial and domestic complexities for subjectivity. To put it differently, the writing of the three authors studied in this study provides a context in which the current incarnations of the uncanny may illuminate modalities of the representation of the *chez soi* within contemporary French writing.

We first saw that, in different ways, the uncanny provides each writer with an approach to the present-day tendency to write about the *quotidien*, and to represent a perturbed relationship between the subject and everyday domestic phenomena. NDiaye, Carrère and Savitzkaya reconfigure and problematize the subject's relationship to everyday, domestic spaces and phenomena. Through a distortion of the narrative and cultural codes of the everyday, each writer re-creates this environment as a foreign world, challenging the myths and imagery that underlie the notions of home and everyday space as they are constructed in certain theoretical frameworks or in the collective imagination.[2] Without necessarily resorting to traditional fantastic motifs, all three writers evoke the unsettling, monstrous or surreal nature of certain household objects, experiences, tasks and occurrences, and of relationships within the family home. A sense of defamiliarization is conveyed through the attribution of figures of alterity, such as the theme of metamorphosis in *La Sorcière*, or the poetics of the poltergeist in *En vie*, to environments of the *chez soi*. In rethinking the ordinary through codes of the strange, each author reveals an uncanny side of the banal and locates a form of adventure in the subject's negotiation of domestic or family space. If, as was

---

[1] Christian Michel, '"Le Réel dort aussi": un panorama du jeune roman français', p. 44.

[2] See, for example, Eiguer, Bachelard and Bégout.

suggested, this approach may be viewed as generating a form of 'uncanny realism', it is perhaps in the sense that the world of realism itself (in which the everyday world remains quietly in the background and functions smoothly) appears uncannily perfect, when contrasted with the visions of everyday life presented by these writers.

The ambiguity of strange and familiar is also present in the representations of family relations proposed by each author. The representations of family life and subjectivity within the home that emerge from the texts studied may be considered in the context of contemporary writing on the family, such as the *récit de filiation*. In this genre, we often find a narrator who is engaged in a quest to come to terms with a relative, but this quest often results in uncertainty, perturbing identity and narrative expression. All three authors found their narratives on the potential foreignness of 'l'autre proche'. 'Familiar' people are shown to be the strangest possible figures, and those most capable of unsettling the subject and challenging her sense of self and integration into the community. The family home is presented as a source of uncertainty and alterity, rather than grounding. This tension between strange and familiar was found to undermine or obfuscate certain myths of family life, through counter-intuitive or surprising representations of family roles and relation-ships. We witness, for example, the reversal of the *rapport de force* in the father-son relationship in *Marin mon cœur* and in the repre-sentations of uncanny mothers or fathers in *Rosie Carpe* and *La Classe de neige*. A sense of the *Unheimliche* is also conveyed through the depiction of unexpected or negative incarnations of family structure and family qualities. We encounter, for example, quasi-incestuous and unloving families in *Rosie Carpe* and the family as a source of unknown danger in *La Classe de neige*.

Finally, the concept of the uncanny was seen to characterize a narrative ethos of non-fiction in the writing of NDiaye, Carrère and Savitzkaya and to describe the modes of expression adopted by all three novelists in order to engage in autobiographical writing and the representation of the *fait divers*. We observed the writerly disori-entation enacted by each author, and the gestures used to display the strangeness of their own narrating voices in light of the ungraspable or destabilizing nature of the phenomena they seek to represent. Viewing the authorial stance as a form of 'home' from which the narrator might 'domesticate' his or her object of representation, I suggested that the writing tactics of these novelists are founded on the haunting or dislocation of that home. In order to figure the uncertainty of the narrative position, and to approach the self or the other ethically or non-reductively, each writer refuses the foundation of a fixed *chez soi* from which to write. This tendency to privilege their own experiences of self-estrangement suggests that all three novelists view the writing process itself as something *unheimlich*. Savitzkaya and NDiaye come face to face with their own doubles during their autobiographical endeavors, while Carrère experiences the fragmentation of his point of view, and struggles to 'find his place' with respect to strangeness of the familiar brought to light by the unsettling *fait divers*.

Subjects not-at-home
For NDiaye, Carrère and Savitzkaya, the uncanny is a possibility at the heart of the familiar, one which qualifies subjective experience. The stability of the subject's dwelling in his or her day-to-day world is constantly threatened by eruptions of the strange, and there is no facet of human experience that is excluded from this sense of fragility. While the home itself is often quite literally depicted as uninhabitable in the selected texts, the disharmonies and incoherencies of the *chez soi* extend, in a figurative sense, to descriptions of an unsettled mode of inhabiting day-to-day spaces, to intellectual uncertainty, or even to positions of narration.

However, the feeling of distance from collective reality generated by the uncanny may be enriching and even enlightening. Freud held that the uncanny was a return of the repressed, but for these three writers the strangeness of the familiar is a foundation for literary creation and for refreshing our gaze on everyday life. In this way, there are certainly thematic and structural parallels between the representation of the familiar in the writing of NDiaye, Carrère and Savitzkaya and the more political versions of the uncanny advanced by thinkers such as Cixous and Kristeva. In her work *Étrangers à nous-mêmes*, Kristeva exploits the example of the foreigner's potential to reveal the strangeness of the national myth and advances the idea that the acknowledgement of the strangeness of the self and the familiar is a starting point for an ethics of perceiving the other. In *Prénoms de personne*, Hélène Cixous reinterprets the concept of the uncanny to illuminate her politics of writing, which is based on the idea that the myth of the unified, totalizing refuge of the *chez soi* should be abandoned, since the affirmation of the integrity of the home contributes to the marginalization and oppression of the other, which is designated as 'strange'. Both thinkers base their theories of representation upon the acknowledgement of the vulnerability and strangeness of the *chez soi*, and propose forms of self-hospitality, involving the welcoming of *oneself* as other, in order to approach the external world more ethically. While, for the authors studied in this book, it may not be entirely relevant to speak of a 'politics of writing', the representations of the *chez soi* that they elaborate reflect this dynamic in which the foreign is projected inwards, towards the familiar itself.

However, while these theoretical configurations of the *Unheimliche* do shed light on the narrative projects and representations of subjectivity developed by the selected authors, there are also noteworthy differences. Hélène Cixous's theories appear to posit a need for a form of subjectivity which is entirely divorced from the notion of the *chez soi*, a position which is reflected in her own writing. It is the objective of the literary text to 's'attaquer au chez-soi, au pour-soi, au revenu; montrer la fragilité du centre des cloisons du moi' (PP 6). The familiar is sacrificed in favour of the strange. In the writing of the authors under investigation in this study, the *chez soi* is in no way abandoned; on the contrary, it is strikingly present. The codes of strangeness and familiarity remain in constant tension so as to provide an on-going reinterpretation of this space, suggesting its perpetual oscillation between comfort and alienation.

While less relevant to the literary text, Julia Kristeva's elaboration of the uncanny perhaps better embodies this assertion of the concomitancy of strange and familiar. Although it is unclear to what extent Kristeva's ethics of perceiving the other might function on a societal or even individual level, her call for a projection of an estranging glance back onto the subject and the self-same, and her suggestion that the self might be viewed as a foreign object while remaining intact and responsible, perhaps resemble the tendencies of these writers to paint estranged portraits of the everyday world and its inhabitants. Just as Kristeva emphasizes the foreigner's potential to reveal the strangeness of the host land to the home-dweller, all three novelists re-write familiar environments and phenomena, generating the effect of a foreign realm at the heart of the familiar. The parallels between Kristeva's thought and these writing strategies were especially striking in the discussion of the portrayals of the writing subject in the final chapter, in which the narratives were based on a form of self-exile or self-estrangement. However, although Kristeva often adopts the vocabulary of the self *in process*, her analysis, like Cixous's, risks simply exchanging the codes of strange and familiar, so that the foreignness of the self dominates over its tendency towards anchoring and feelings of familiarity. For NDiaye, Carrère and Savitz-kaya, the *chez soi* is never inscribed on either side of the strange and familiar dichotomy. Rather, the subject's experience remains in constant tension between competing codes of *heimlich* and *unheim-lich*.

Writer by Writer

Although in light of this study, the uncanny remains an elusive notion, it is possible to identify, for each writer under investigation, certain tendencies in the representation of this porosity between strange and familiar. Studying these works in the context of the uncanny has brought into relief certain elements of each writer's particular narrative approach.

Marie NDiaye - too close for comfort
NDiaye's œuvre is largely founded on a tension between the subject's constant quest for the comfort and certainty of home and the illusory nature of such a home, one which finds itself affirmed in experience. A feature that runs throughout her work is the representation of the *chez soi* as a phenomenon which appears more and more intangible, the more it is desired or approached. For each of NDiaye's characters, retrieving the *chez soi*, which is often understood as a place within a harmonious, unified home, is viewed as the key to resolving the subject's identity-related confusions. Yet in all three of the novels by NDiaye examined here, a character's movement towards home results in her perception of its otherness. The protagonists of *La Sorcière* and *Autoportrait en vert*, for example, desperately strive to re-unite their dispersed family in the hopes of finding their proper place within its configuration. Yet the family's hostility and impenetrability result in the exclusion or dislocation of the subject. In *La Sorcière*, Lucie is abandoned by her entire family to the isolation and banality of her

suburban existence. For the narrator of *Autportrait en vert*, interactions with family members and encounters with home only further
disturb her uncertain sense of self and reinforce the challenges of self-
portraiture and self-knowledge. Likewise, we saw that the novel *Rosie
Carpe* relates a young woman's quest to come to terms with the
family that deserted her, in order to regain a feeling of rootedness and
certainty about her own identity. Yet home can never provide her with
the comfort she seeks, and Rosie's encounters with various unloving,
often menacing family members further trouble her inscription in the
community and her identity-related questioning. Home is portrayed as
an absent or insufficient structure, which is often very detached from
any positive emotional associations the term might otherwise evoke.

With their contemporary landscapes and commonplace figures
and environments, NDiaye's novels present the reader with a
convincing portrait of relationships in present-day France, while at the
same time asserting the 'unhomely' nature of the depicted realm, so
that it appears 'other'. This disconcerting representation of modern
life is founded on a distortion of the codes of realism and collective
reality through the author's use of subtly fantastic imagery and her
privileging of obscure subjective realities. Just as the subject in
uncanny experience hovers between a world of fantasy and one of
reality, NDiaye's narratives deny us firm footing in a fictional world
that we nonetheless cannot help but identify as familiar, thus renewing
the reader's perception of everyday life.

Emmanuel Carrère - fiction is fact
In Carrère's narrative realm, the strange and familiar dynamic is
configured somewhat differently. Uncanniness, for Carrère, often
involves the realization that the familiar, everyday world is just as
strange, if not stranger, than fantasy. This is often expressed through
blurred boundaries between fiction and reality, two realms which tend
to exchange roles in Carrère's novels. In *La Moustache*, for example,
the protagonist's inability to distinguish his own madness from that of
the people around him leads him to contemplate the limits of his own
identity. Trapped in the drama of the cruel joke he believes others to
have concocted concerning the missing moustache, he is unable to
distinguish the familiar from the strange, fact from fiction. In *La
Classe de neige*, the anxiety evoked by Nicolas's gruesome childhood
fantasies pales in comparison with the true dangers which emerge

from the heart of his own family home. In the end, the uncanny images of metamorphosis and being buried alive, which colour his inner experience, are portrayed as a cathartic escape world, in which the young protagonist evades the oppressive authority of his omnipresent parents and postpones the more terrifying reality of his own father's malevolence.

L'Adversaire, however, is the text which most explicitly reveals this fine line between realism and fantasy that forms the foundation for Carrère's aesthetic. The modalities of Carrère's representation of the *fait divers* echo the impact of the Romand affair as an event which problematizes the boundaries between strange and familiar, and fiction and fact. The success of Romand's identity-related fiction, which went undiscovered for many years, brings the author to observe the 'fictional' quality already present in community logic and common reality. His narrative, like that of Romand, stresses the strangeness that can be found in the most familiar, domestic locations and within the self. In Carrère's writing, there is a sense that the most 'familiar' spaces are also the most fragile, always threatening to collapse into a world of nightmare. The uncanny expresses a fleeting sense of such a world, and a confrontation with the borders between reality and fiction which may emerge from within ordinary life.

Savitzkaya - un cas limite?

Throughout this book it has been suggested that the uncanny as incarnated in Eugène Savitzkaya's novels may be viewed as a *cas limite*. Can we employ the uncanny as a literary term to describe an aesthetic which is fundamentally detached from anxiety or discomfort? In many accounts of the uncanny, the term implies a negative affect, a perceived threat to subjectivity. If all forms of uncanniness do indeed have a unifying thread, could this thread not be understood as a form of fear, which the subject wishes to expel? In Savitzkaya's novels, however, the uncanny is often portrayed not as threatening but as an object of desire. If one considers the theories of the uncanny presented by thinkers such as Cixous and Kristeva, and also the passing comments made by various twenty-first century theorists (Royle, Donald, Masschelein), it becomes clear that in the contemporary period, the uncanny is indeed constructed as something desirable, since, for many, it points to a moment of authenticity within

ordinary experience. The dissolution of the laws of common reality in
the uncanny is an incentive for constant revision of our perceptions of
the everyday world, for beholding the familiar from strange new
angles. The uncanny is now regarded as a foundation for ethics, knowledge and aesthetics, rather than simply as an anxiety-provoking
disintegration of meaning.

I would argue that, although the unease conventionally
associated with the uncanny is not present to the same degree in
Savitzkaya's texts as it is in NDiaye's and Carrère's, his writing
project considered as a whole may be seen as the most exemplary of
the three of the contemporary *Unheimliche*, in that it escapes
mechanisms of repression. If the uncanny is something to be sought
and celebrated, Saviztkaya's texts are very relevant indeed. Many of
his novels manifest a quest for a primitive *chez soi*, which figuratively
returns the subject to a more fluid space that appears to precede
collective meaning. The blurring of the strange/ familiar dichotomy is
a way for the author to represent a sense of such primitiveness within
everyday experience. In *En vie*, this is achieved through a revelation
of the surrealism of the domestic environment. The author employs
narrative tactics which disengage the everyday from the banality
associated with habit and dwelling. Without leaving the *chez soi,* the
narrator is a traveller on a journey through the domestic realm. The
subject's willingness to embrace the alterity of his or her own
familiarity prevents the uncanny from being represented as a fear-
provoking invasion of the refuge of home. In *Marin mon cœur*, the
author exploits the point of view of the child to regenerate this sense
of innovation and foreignness within the familiar. In *Fou trop poli*, it
is the figure of the madman that creates a similar effect. In all three
cases, what the author produces is, once again, a kind of adjacent
reality, which, while it remains in proximity to the familiar world,
undergoes a distortion of its conventional narrative codes. This is a
way of reviving the reader's perception of that familiar world; the
breakdown of the borders between strange and familiar provides a
poetic experience within the ordinary.

While the forms, configurations and thematics of the uncanny
are very different in the work of each author, what they all have in
common is the quest for a reality which is 'in-between' fantasy and
realism. All three authors rely on the reader's sense of familiarity with
the depicted world to distort and unravel some of the comfortable

codes through which common reality is perceived. The uncanniness featured in these novels does not take the form of fleeting instances, but, paradoxically, constitutes the starting point for each of these narratives of home.

Final thoughts

Through an analysis of nine novels by Marie NDiaye, Emmanuel Carrère and Eugène Savitzkaya, this study has sought to delineate certain tendencies observed in contemporary French writing. In my readings of these uncanny texts, I have shown the ways in which, through contending codes of strangeness and familiarity, each author represents the contemporary subject as never entirely *chez lui* or *chez elle* in his or her 'familiar' world. Further reflection in this area might consider the phenomenon of the uncanny within a larger corpus of contemporary texts, including authors of the fantastic, such as Marie Darrieussecq, René Belletto or Linda Lê, for example. Another avenue for further contemplation could involve an analysis of literary texts which, like Savitzkaya's works, cannot be classified as 'fantastic', but express the strangeness of the *quotidien* in other ways. I am thinking of authors such as François Bon or Christian Oster, who place the everyday at the heart of their narrative projects. It may also be valuable to extend the scope of such an investigation to include contemporary art, poetry or film, since these offer alternative textual and visual possibilities for the representation of the strangeness of home.[3] However, for the purposes of the present analysis, I have simply attempted to pose a certain number of questions concerning the forms of uncanniness that are present in the work of the selected writers. What is the motivation behind the de-familiarization of diverse aspects of familiar, everyday life? Is the representation of an uncanny relationship between the subject and his or her immediate surroundings primarily part of a narrative ethos, as was suggested in the fourth chapter, or is it, as was implied in chapter three, sympto-

---

[3] The uncanniness of home is now a prominent theme in French cinema. As well as Emmanuel Carrère's *La Moustache*, films such as Michael Haneke's *Caché* (2005) or Dominik Moll's *Lemming* (2005) present rather chilling depictions of everyday life. All three films feature young to middle-aged couples whose comfortable domestic environments are de-familiarized by uncanny events. In *Caché* this effect is achieved through the theme of surveillance; in the quasi-fantastic film, *Lemming*, a couple's tranquil suburban existence is thrown off course from the moment they discover a dead rodent in their kitchen drainpipe.

matic of certain unhomely aspects of modern society, such as the dispersal of conventional family structures, or evolving parent-child relations in the post-Freudian era? As well as being an indefinable feeling, which emanates from the literary text, how is the uncanny expressed on thematic and textual levels? While I have appealed to various theories of the uncanny in order to address some of these questions, and to suggest possible personal, societal, philosophical and representational factors that come into play in interpreting these novels, they are certainly open for further investtigation. The uncanny remains an elusive quality of literature, which, as has been stressed throughout this book, cannot be attributed to any one motif, motivation or textual mechanism. The nature of the chosen theoretical context then, requires that this analysis conclude with a sense of uncertainty which is equal to, if not greater than, that which inspired it to begin with.

Bibliography

Primary Texts

Carrère, Emmanuel, *Un roman russe* (Paris: P.O.L., 2007)
-----, *L'Adversaire* (Paris: P.O.L., 2000)
-----, *La Classe de neige* (Paris: P.O.L., 1995)
-----, *Je suis vivant et vous êtes morts: Philip K.Dick, 1928-1982* (Paris: Éditions du Seuil, 1993)
-----, *Hors d'atteinte?* (Paris: P.O.L., 1988)
-----, *Le Détroit de Behring* (Paris: P.O.L., 1987)
-----, *La Moustache* (Paris: P.O.L., 1986)
-----, *Bravoure* (Paris: P.O.L., 1984)
-----, *L'Amie du jaguar* (Paris: Flammarian, 1983)
-----, *Werner Herzog* (Paris: Edilig, 1982)

NDiaye, Marie, *Trois femmes puissantes* (Paris: Gallimard, 2009)
----, *Mon cœur à l'étroit* (Paris: Gallimard, 2007)
-----, *Autoportrait en vert* (Paris: Mercure de France, 2005)
-----, *Tous mes amis* (Paris: Éditions de Minuit, 2004)
-----, *Les Serpents* (Paris: Éditions de Minuit, 2004)
-----, *Papa doit manger* (Paris: Éditions de Minuit, 2003)
-----, *Les Paradis de Prunelle*, illustrated by Pierre Mornet (Paris: Albin Michel, 2003)
-----, *Providence* (Chambéry: Éditions Comp'Act, 2001)
-----, *Rosie Carpe* (Paris: Éditions de Minuit, 2001)
-----, *La Diablesse et son enfant*, illustrated by Nadja (Paris: Mouche de l'école des loisirs, 2000)
-----, *Hilda* (Paris: Éditions de Minuit, 1999)
-----, *La Sorcière* (Paris: Éditions de Minuit, 1996)
-----, *Un Temps de saison* (Paris: Éditions de Minuit, 1994)
-----, *En famille* (Paris: Éditions de Minuit, 1991)
-----, *La Femme changée en bûche* (Paris: Éditions de Minuit, 1989)
-----, *Comédie classique* (Paris: Éditions P.O.L., 1987)
-----, *Quant au riche avenir* (Paris: Éditions de Minuit, 1985)

Savitzkaya, Eugène, *Fou trop poli* (Paris: Éditions de Minuit, 2005)
-----, *Célébration d'un mariage improbable et illimité* (Paris: Éditions de Minuit, 2002)
-----, *Cochon farci* (Paris: Éditions de Minuit, 1996)
-----, *En vie* (Paris: Éditions de Minuit, 1995)
-----, *Jérôme Bosch, Musées secrets* (Paris: Flohic Éditions, 1994)
-----, *Marin mon cœur* (Paris: Éditions de Minuit, 1992)
-----, *La Folie originelle* (Paris: Éditions de Minuit, 1991)
-----, *Portrait de famille* (Paris: Tropismes, 1992)
-----, *L'Été: papillons, ortie, citrons et mouches* (Paris: La Cécilia, 1991)
-----, *Sang de chien* (Paris: Éditions de Minuit, 1989)
-----, *Capolican, un secret de fabrication* (Paris: Arcane 17, 1987)
-----, *Bufo, Bufo, Bufo* (Paris: Éditions de Minuit, 1986)
-----, *Quatorze cataclysmes*, illustrated by Alain Le Bras (Paris: Le Temps qu'il fait, 1985).
-----, *Les Morts sentent bon* (Paris: Éditions de Minuit, 1984)
-----, *La Disparition de maman* (Paris: Éditions de Minuit, 1982)
-----, *Les Couleurs de boucherie* (Paris: Christian Bourgois, 1980)
-----, *La Traversée de l'Afrique* (Paris: Éditions de Minuit, 1979)
-----, *Un jeune homme trop gros* (Paris: Éditions de Minuit, 1978)
-----, *Mentir* (Paris: Éditions de Minuit, 1977)
-----, *Mongolie, plaine sale* (Paris: Seghers, 1976)

Interviews

Argand, Catherine, 'Entretien avec Marie NDiaye', *Lire* 294 (1 April 2001), pp. 32-7

Dijon, Aurélie, 'Interview avec Eugène Savitzkaya: le regard du fou', in *Chronic' Art: Le Webmag Culturel* (21 December 2005), p. 2, http://www.chronicart.com (accessed 6 April 2007)

de Gaudemar, Antoine 'Interview avec Eugène Savitzkaya', *Libération* (April 1992), http://www.lesÉditionsdeminuit.fr/extraits/2003/interview_savitzkaya.pdf (9 December 2007)

Tison, Jean-Pierre, 'Entretien avec Emmanuel Carrère', in *Lire*

(February 2000), pp. 24-30

Newspaper, Magazine and Webmag Articles

Bonnet, Véronique, 'Où situer Marie NDiaye', *Africultures* 45 (February 2002) http://www.africultures.com/index.asp?menu=revue_affiche_article& no=2102 (accessed 9 January 2008)

Braudeau, Michel, 'Le Coefficient d'inconfort', *Le Monde* (11 January 1991)

Chanda, Tirthankar 'L'Essentiel d'un livre: portrait de l'écrivain en vert', *MFI HEBDO* (April 2005), http://www.rfi.fr/Fichiers/Mfi/CultureSociete/1455.asp (accesssed 10 May 2007)

Crépu, Michel, 'NDiaye, secousse majeure', *l'Express* (5 April 2001), pp. 78-9

Delorme, Marie-Laure, 'La Discrète', *Livres Hebdo* 416 (9 March 2001), p. 122
-----, 'Marie NDiaye l'ensorceleuse', *Magazine Littéraire* (October 1996), pp. 80-1

Devarrieux, Claire, 'Romand vrai. Le récit de l'affaire Romand par Emmanuel Carrère', *Le Monde* (6 January 2000)

Dufresne, David, 'La Rage narcissique de Romand', *Libération* (2 July 1996)

Fayard, Guillaume, 'Eugène Savitzkaya, Fou trop poli: en nous il vibre', *Peauneuve.net*, http://peauneuve.net/article.php3?id_article=104 (accessed 8 June 2006)

Gazier, Michèle, 'La Sorcière mal aimée', *Télérama* 2436 (18 September 1996), p. 52

Harang, Jean-Baptiste, 'Marie NDiaye, drôle de trame', *Libération* (1 February 2007)

-----, 'À quoi songe le fou sur son futon', *Libération* (10 November 2005)

-----, 'Notre sorcière bien aimée', *Libération* (12 February 2004)

-----, 'Marie Darrieussecq a-t-elle "singé" Marie NDiaye?', *Le Monde* (4 March 1998)

Kéchichian, Patrick, 'Marie NDiaye, hasard et fatalité', *Le Monde* (12 March 2004)

Kossi, Efoui, 'Un repas insipide', *L'Intelligent* 2201 (16-22 March 2003), pp. 112-3

Lepape, Pierre, 'Meurtre au paradis', *Le Monde* (9 March 2001)

Lequeret, Elisabeth, 'Le Phénomène NDiaye', *Jeune Afrique* (20-26 March 1991), p. 64

Mpoyi-Buatu, Thomas, '*Comédie classique* de Marie NDiaye', *Présence Africaine, nouvelle série bilingue: revue culturelle du Monde noir* (1988), pp. 205-6

Nicolas, Alain 'Le Cœur dans le labyrinthe,' *Humanité* (February 1, 2007),
http://www.humanite.fr/2007-02-01_Cultures_Le-coeur-dans-le-labyrinthe (accessed 5 February 2007)

Noiville, Florence, 'Emmanuel Carrère, "J'avais l'impression d'être enfermé"', *Le Monde* (2 March 2007)

Pierre, Jean-Louis, 'Zabou, mégère au service de Marie NDiaye', *Le Monde* (February 2002)

Savane, Sy Ibrahim, 'La Seconde nature de Marie NDiaye', *Jeune Afrique* (8 April 1987) 54.

-----, 'Un imaginaire déroutant: *La Femme changée en bûche* de Marie NDiaye', *La Presse* (7 October 1989)

Vaquin, Agnès, 'Une aliénation permanente', *Quinzaine Littéraire* 806 (April 2000), pp. 5-6.

Books, Chapters and Articles

Aristotle, *Poetics,* trans. by Kenneth A. Telford (Chicago: Henry Regnery Company, 1967; first published in 1961)

Armitt, Lucie, 'The Magical Realism of the Contemporary Gothic', in *A Companion to the Gothic,* ed. by David Punter (Oxford: Blackwell, 2000), pp. 305-16
-----, *Theorising the Fantastic* (London, New York, Sydney, Auckland: Arnold, 1996)

Bachelard, Gaston, *La Poétique de l'espace* (Paris: Presses Universitaires de France, 2001; first published in 1957)

Baldick, Chris, *In Frankenstein's Shadow: Myth, Monstrosity, and Nineteenth-century Writing* (Oxford: Clarendon Press, 1987)

Barthes, Roland, 'Structure du fait divers', in *Œuvres compètes, 1962-1967, Tome II* (Paris: Éditions du Seuil, 2002), pp. 442-65
-----, 'L'Effet de réel', in *Littérature et réalité* (Paris: Éditions du Seuil, 1982), pp. 81-90
-----, *S/Z* (Paris: Éditions du Seuil, 1970)
-----, Roland Barthes, *Roland Barthes* (Paris: Éditions du Seuil, 1975)

Barron, James W. et al., 'Sigmund Freud: The Secrets of Nature and the Nature of Secrets', *International Review of Psychoanalysis*, Vol. 18 (1991), pp. 144-63

Becker-Leckrone, Megan, *Julia Kristeva and Literary Theory* (Basingstoke: Palgrave Macmillan, 2005)

Bégout, Bruce, *La Découverte du quotidien* (Paris: Éditions Allia, 2005)

Bellemin-Noël, Jean, *Psychanalyse et littérature*, coll. 'Que sais-je' (Paris: Presses Universitaires de France, 1978)

Bergler, Edmond, 'The Psychoanalysis of the Uncanny', *International Journal of Psychoanalysis* 15 (1934), pp. 215-44

Bersani, Leo, 'Le Réalisme et la peur du désir', in *Littérature et réalité*, ed. by Gérard Genette and Tzvetan Todorov (Paris: Éditions du Seuil, 1982), pp. 47-80.

Bhahba, Homi, *The Location of Culture* (London: Routledge, 1994)

Biron, Michel, 'Fils de personne', *Voix et images* 81, pp. 566-71

Blanckeman, Bruno, *Les Fictions singulières* (Paris: Prétexte, 2002)

Blanchot, Maurice, *L'Entretien infini* (Paris: Gallimard, 1969)
-----, *La Part du feu* (Paris: Gallimard, 1949)

Bonomo, Sara, 'La Mise en œuvre de la peur dans le roman d'aujourd'hui: *Rosie Carpe* de Marie NDiaye', *Travaux de littérature* 17, pp. 218-25

Bordas, Eric, 'Le Secret du petit Nicolas', in *Modernités* 14, 'Dire le secret', ed. by
Dominique Rabaté (Bordeaux: Presses Universitaires de Bordeaux, 2000), pp.171-82

Bouchy, Florence, '"Mais au diable la peinture sociale": les objets quotidiens dans quelques romans de Christian Oster', in *Christian Oster et cie, retour du romanesque*, ed. by Aline Mura-Brunel (Amsterdam, NewYork: Rodopi, 2006), pp. 83-92.

Bourdieu, Pierre, *Les Structures sociales de l'économie* (Paris: Éditions du Seuil, 2000)

Brown, Alison Leigh, *Subjects of Deceit: A Phenomenology of Lying* (Albany: State University of NewYork Press, 1998)

Bruhm, Steven, 'The Contemporary Gothic: Why We Need it', in *The Cambridge Companion to Gothic Fiction*, ed. by Jerrold E. Hogle (Cambridge: Cambridge University Press, 2002), pp. 259-276

Busch, Akiko, *Geography of Home: Writings on Where We Live* (New York: Princeton Architectural Press, 1999)

Caillois, Roger, *Anthologie du fantastique* (Paris: Gallimard, 1966)

Calle-Gruber, Mireille, *Du café à l'éternité, Hélène Cixous à l'œuvre* (Paris: Galilée, 2002)

Calle-Gruber, Mireille and Cixous, Hélène, 'Entre Tiens', in *Hélène Cixous, photos de racines* (Paris: Des Femmes, 1994), pp. 13-121

Canal, Bernard, *Paysage et Nouveau Roman*, Le Français dans tous ses états 33, 'Le paysage', http://www.crdpmontpellier.fr/ressources/frdtse/frdtse33e.html (accessed 25 November 2007)

Carroll, Noël, *The Philosophy of Horror, or Paradoxes of the Heart* (New York and London: Routledge, 1990)

Castex, Pierre-Georges, *Le Conte fantastique en France de Nodier à Maupassant* (Paris: José Corti, 1951)

Castle, Terry, *The Female Thermometer: Eighteenth-century Culture and the Invention of the Uncanny* (New York and Oxford: Oxford University Press, 1995)

de Certeau, Michel, *L'Invention du quotidien*, 2 Vols, Vol. I, *Arts de faire*, coll. 'Folio essais' (Paris: Folio, 1994)

Chambers, Deborah, *Representing the Family* (London, Thousand Oaks, New Delhi: Sage Publications, 2001)

Chanady, Amaryll Beatrice, *Magical Realism and the Fantastic: Resolved Versus Unresolved Antimony* (New York: Garland, 1985)

Cixous, Hélène, *Jours de l'an* (Paris: Des femmes Antoinette Fouque, 1990)
-----, *La* (Paris: Gallimard, Des femmes, 1979)
-----, *La Venue à l'écriture,* with Madeleine Gagnon and Annie Leclerc (Paris: Union Générale des Éditions, 1977)
-----, *La Jeune Née,* with Catherine B. Clément (Paris: Inédit (Union Générale d'Éditions, 1975)
-----, 'Le Rire de la Méduse', *L'Arc* 61 (1975), pp. 39-54
-----, *Souffles* (Paris: Des femmes, 1975)
-----, *Prénoms de personne,* coll. 'Poétique' (Paris: Éditions du Seuil, 1974)
-----, *Prénoms de personne* (Paris: Éditions du Seuil, 1974)
-----, *Neutre* (Paris: Grasset, 1972)
-----, *Dedans* (Paris: Grasset, 1969)

Collings, David, 'The Monster and the Maternal Thing: Mary Shelley's Critique of Ideology, in *Frankenstein: The Complete Text in Cultural Context*, 2nd Edition, ed. by Johanna M. Smith (Boston and New York: Bedford/St. Martin's, 2000), pp. 280-95

Connon, Daisy, 'Marie NDiaye's Haunted House: Uncanny Autofiction in *Autoportrait en vert*', in *Redefining the Real: The Fantastic in Contemporary French Women's Writing*, ed. by Margaret-Anne Hutton (Bern: Peter Lang, 2009), pp. 245-60.
-----, 'Dislocation of the Authorial Voice in Emmanuel Carrère's *L'Adversaire* and Eugène Savitzkaya's *Fou trop poli*', in *Aesthetics of Dislocation in French and Francophone Literature and Art: Strategies of Representation*, ed. by Daisy Connon, Gillian Jein and Greg Kerr (Lewiston, Queenston, Lampeter: The Edwin Mellen Press, 2009), pp. 69-86.

Copjec, Joan, *Read My Desire: Lacan against the Historicists* (Cambridge, London: MIT Press, 1994)

Creed, Barbara, *Phallic Panic: Film, Horror and the Primal Uncanny* (Melbourne: Melbourne University Press, 2005)

Davis, Colin, 'Hauntology, Spectres and Phantoms', *French Studies* LIX, No. 3 (2005), 373-79

De Man, Paul, *Allegories of Reading* (London, New Haven: Yale University Press, 1979)

Demoulin, Laurent, 'Eugène Savitzkaya à la croisée des chemins,' *Écritures contemporaines* 2, (1999), 41-56

Derrida, Jacques, *De l'hospitalité*, with Anne Dufourmantelle (Paris: Calmann-Lévy, 1997)
-----, *Spectres de Marx* (Paris: Galilée, 1993)

De Rubercy, Eric, 'Rosie ou la désespérance', *L'Atelier du roman* 35 (September 2003), 37-41

Diatkine, Gilbert, *Jacques Lacan* (Paris: Presses Universitaires de France, 1997)

Dolar, Mladen, 'I Shall be with you on your Wedding Night, Lacan and the Uncanny', *October* 58 (1991), 5-23

Donald, James, 'The Fantastic, the Sublime and the Popular, Or, What's at Stake in Vampire Films', in *Fantasy and the Cinema* (London: bfi publishing, 1989)

Doubrovsky, Serge, 'Textes en main', *RITM* 6 'Autofiction et cie' (1993)

D'haen, Theo L., 'Magic Realism and Postmodernism: Decentering Privileged Centres', in *Magical Realism: Theory, History, Community*, ed. by Lois Parkinson Zamora and Wendy B. Faris (Durham and London: Duke University Press, 1995), pp. 191-208

Dubois, Jacques, *Les Romanciers du réel* (Paris: Éditions du Seuil, 2000)

Dufour, Philippe, *Le Réalisme de Balzac à Proust* (Paris: Presses Universitaires de France, 1998)

Eiguer, Alberto, *L'Inconscient de la maison*, coll. 'Psychismes', ed. by Didier Anzieu (Paris: Dunod, 2004)

Ellison, David, *Ethics and Aesthetics in European Modernist Literature: From the Sublime to the Uncanny* (Cambridge: Cambridge University Press, 2001)

Faris, Wendy B., *Ordinary Enchantments: Magical Realism and the Remystification of Narrative* (Nashville: Vanderbilt University Press, 2004)

Flieder, Laurent, *Le Roman français contemporain* (Paris: Éditions du Seuil, 1998)

Fortin, Jutta, 'Brides of the Fantastic: Gautier's *Le Pied de momie* and Hoffmann's *Der Sandmann*', *Comparative Literature Studies* 41, No. 2 (2004), 257-75

Fourton, Maud, 'Marie NDiaye, *Rosie Carpe*: du tant bien que mal au malgré tout', in *Christian Oster et cie, retour du romanesque*, ed. by Aline Mura-Brunel (Rodopi: Amsterdam, NewYork, 2006), pp. 49-63

Frank, Manfred, *The Subject and the Text: Essays on Literary Theory and Philosophy*, ed. by Andrew Bowie, trans. by Helen Atkins (Cambridge: Cambridge University Press, 1989)

Freud, Sigmund, 'Creative Writers and Day-dreaming', in *The Complete Psychological Works of Sigmund Freud*, Volume IX (1906-1908): 'Jensen's "Gradiva" and Other Works', trans. and ed. by James Strachey (London: Hogarth Press, 1959), pp. 141-53

-----, 'The Uncanny', in *The Complete Psychological Works of Sigmund Freud*, Vol. XVII, 'An Infantile Neurosis and Other Works', trans. and ed. by James Strachey, (London: Hogarth Press, 1955), pp. 219-56
-----, 'Beyond the Pleasure Principle', in *The Complete Psychological Works of Sigmund Freud*, Vol. XVIII, 'Beyond the Pleasure Principle, Group Psychology and Other Works', trans. and ed. James Strachey (London: Hogarth Press, 1955), pp. 7-64

Garnier, Xavier, *L'Éclat de la figure: Étude sur l'antipersonnage de roman*, coll. 'Nouvelle poétique comparatiste' (Bruxelles, Bern and Berlin: P. Lang, 2001)
-----, 'Métamorphoses réalistes dans les romans de Marie NDiaye, le réalisme merveilleux', *Itinéraires et Contacts de Cultures* (1982), 79-89

Giorgio, Adalgisa, 'Mothers and Daughters in Western Europe: Mapping the Territory,' in *Writing Mothers and Daughters*, ed. by Adalgisa Giorgio (New York, Oxford: Berghahn Books, 2002), pp. 1-9

Gratton, Johnnie, 'Postmodern French Fiction: Practice and Theory', in *The Cambridge Companion to the French Novel, From 1800 to the Present*, ed. by Timothy Unwin (Cambridge: Cambridge University Press, 1997), pp. 242-260

Grotjahn, Martin, 'Some Clinical Illustrations of Freud's Analysis of the Uncanny', *Bulletin of the Menninger Clinic* 12 (1948), 57-60

Hammond, Ray, *The Modern Frankenstein, Fiction Becomes Fact* (Poole, New York, Sydney: Blandford Press, 1986)

Hansen, Elaine Tuttle, *Mother Without Child: Contemporary Fiction and the Crisis of Motherhood* (Berkely, Los Angeles and London: University of California Press, 1997)

Harwood, Sarah, *Family Fictions: Representations of the Family in 1980s Hollywood Cinema* (London: MacMillan Press Ltd, 1997)

Heidegger, Martin, *Being and Time*, trans. by J. Macquarrie and E. Robinson (Oxford: Basil Blackwell, 1962)

Herman, John, *The Double in Nineteenth-century Fiction* (Houndmills, Basingstoke, Hampshire, London: MacMillan, 1990)

Hertz, Neil, *The End of the Line: Essays on Psychoanalysis and the Sublime* (New York: Columbia University Press, 1985)

Hoft-March, Eileen, 'En famille de Marie NDiaye' *The French Review* 67 (February. 1994), 557-8

Hoquet, Thierry, 'Adieu les monstres, vivent les mutants', *Critique* 709-710 (June-July 2006), 479-81

Igboemeke, Adeze, 'Le Père silencieux: la métaphore paternelle chez Eugène Savitzkaya', *Neophilologus*, Vol. 85, No. 4 (October 2001), 519-27

Jay, Martin, 'Forcefields: The Uncanny Nineties', *Salmagundi* 108, Saratoga Springs (Fall 1995), 20-9

Jentsch, Ernst, 'On the Psychology of the Uncanny', trans. by Roy Sellers, *Angelaki* 2, 7-16

Johnson, Barbara, *Mother Tongues* (Cambridge, Massachusetts and London: Harvard University Press, 2003)

Johnson, Erica L., *Home, Maison, Casa: The Politics of Location in Works by Jean Rhys, Marguerite Duras and Ermina Dell'Oro* (Madison, Teaneck: Fairleigh Dickinson University Press/Rosemont Publishing & Printing Corp, 2003)

Jordan, Shirley Ann, 'Figuring out the Family: Family as Everyday Practice in French Women's Writing', in *Affaires de famille: The Family in Contemporary French Culture and Theory* (Amsterdam, New York: Rodopi, 2007), pp. 39-58

Justice Gentile, Kathy, 'Anxious Supernaturalism: An Analytic of the Uncanny', *Gothic Studies* 2 (April 2000), 23-38

Kaplan, E. Ann, *Motherhood and Representation: The Mother in Popular Culture and Media* (London and New York: Routledge, 1992)

Kofman, Sarah, *L'Enfance de l'art, une interprétation de l'esthétique freudienne* (Paris: Payot, 1970)

Kristeva, Julia, *Étrangers à nous-mêmes*, (Paris: Fayard, 1988)
-----, *Pouvoirs de l'horreur: essai sur l'abjection*, coll. 'Tel Quel'
(Paris: Seuil, 1980)
-----, *La Révolution du langage poétique*, coll. 'Tel Quel' (Paris:
Éditions du Seuil, 1974)

Lacan, Jacques, *Le Séminaire V, Les Formations de l'inconscient*,
coll. 'Champ Freudien', ed. by Jacques Alain and Judith Miller (Paris:
Éditions du Seuil, 1998)
-----, *Le Séminaire XVII, l'Envers de la psychanalyse*, ed. by Jacques-
Alain Miller (Paris: Éditions du Seuil, 1991)
-----, *Le Séminaire XI, Les Quatre concepts fondamentaux de la
psychanalyse*, ed. by Jacques-Alain Miller (Paris: Éditions du Seuil,
1973)
-----, *Écrits II* (Paris: Éditions du Seuil, 1971)
-----, *Écrits I* (Paris: Éditions du Seuil, 1966)
-----, 'Some Reflections on the Ego', *The International Journal of
Psychoanalysis* XXXIV(1953), 11-17

Laouyen, Mounir, 'Le Texte autobiographique: une demeure à soi ?',
in *De soi à soi: l'écriture comme autohospitalité*, ed. by Alain
Montandon (Clermont-Ferrand: Presses Universitaires Blaise Pascal,
2004) pp. 125-43

Laplanche, J. and Pontalis, J. B., *Vocabulaire de la psychanalyse*
(Paris: Presses Universitaires de France, 1967)

Lardreau, Fabrice, 'Au sein de familles éclatées', *L'Atelier du roman*
35 (September 2003), 60-7

Lecarme, Jacques, 'L'Autofiction: un mauvais genre?', in *Autofictions
et Cie*, ed. by Serge Doubrovsky, Jacques Lecarme and Philippe
Lejeune (Paris: Université Paris X, 1993), 227-48

Lefebvre, Henri, *La Vie quotidienne dans le monde moderne*, coll.
'Idées' (Paris: Gallimard, 1968)

Lejeune, Philippe, 'Nouveau Roman et retour à l'autobiographie', in *L'Auteur et le manuscrit*, ed. by Michel Contat (Paris: Presses Universitaires de France, 1991), pp. 51-70

Lee, Graham, 'Alone Among Three: The father and the Œdipus complex', in *Fathers, Families and the Outside World*, Winnicott Studies Monograph Series, ed. by Val Richards (London: Karnac Books, 1997), pp. 73-87

Lejeune, Philippe, *Le Pacte autobiographique* (Paris: Édtions du Seuil, 1975)

Lepape, Pierre, 'En panne de famille', *L'Atelier du roman* 35 (September 2003), 42-7

Levinas, Emmanuel, *Totalité et infini: Essai sur l'extériorité* (Paris: Kluwer Academic, 1971)

MacGregor Wise, J., 'Home: Territory and Identity', in *Cultural Studies* 14, No. 2, ed. by Andrea L. Press and Bruce A. Williams (April 2000), 295-310

Madelénat, Daniel, 'Se construire en écrivant l'autre', in *De soi à soi: l'écriture comme autohospitalité*, ed. by Alain Montandon (Clermont-Ferrand: Presses Universitaires Blaise Pascal, 2004), pp. 53-65

Mancas, Magdalena Silvia, 'Le Retour à soi dans la Nouvelle Autobiographie: sur le rapport entre (auto)hospitalité et mensonge', in *De soi à soi: l'écriture comme autohospitalité*, ed. by Alain Montandon (Clermont-Ferrand: Presses Universitaires Blaise Pascal, 2004), pp. 107-25

Marcotte, Gilles, 'Symptômes de l'insignifiance', in *L'Atelier du roman* 35 (September 2003), 56-9

Masschelein, Anneleen, 'A Homeless Concept, Shapes of the Uncanny in Twentieth-Century Theory and Culture,' in *Online Magazine of the Visual Narrative* 5, 'The Uncanny', ed. by Anneleen Masschelein (January 2003)

http://www.imageandnarrative.be/uncanny/anneleenmasschelein.htm
(accessed 20 November 2006)
-----, 'The Concept as Ghost: Conceptualization of the Uncanny in
Late-Twentieth-Century Theory', *Mosaic* 35 (March 2002), 53-68

Memmi, Germaine, *Freud et la création littéraire* (Paris:
L'Harmattan, 1996)

Mérigot, Bernard, 'L'Inquiétante étrangeté, note sur *l'Unheimliche*',
Littérature 8 (1972), 100-6

Michel, Christian, '"Le Réel dort aussi": un panorama du jeune roman
français', *Esprit* 225 (October 1996), pp. 43-67

de Mijolla, Alain, *Préhistoires de famille* (Paris: Presses
Universitaires de France, 2004)

Millet, Gilbert and Labbé, Denis, *Le Fantastique* (Paris: Belin, 2005)

Milner, Max, *Freud et l'interprétation de la littérature*, coll. 'Les
livres et les hommes', ed. by Gabriel Conesa, 2nd Edition (Paris:
Sedes, 1997)

Mose, Kenrick, *Defamiliarization in the Work of Gabriel Garcia
Marquez From 1947-1967*, 'Studies in Hispanic Literature' Vol. 1
(Lewiston, Queenston, Lampeter: Edwin Mellen Press, 1989)

Motte, Warren, 'Marie NDiaye's Sorcery', in *Fables of the Novel,
French Fiction Since 1990* (Normal, Illinois: Dalkey Archive Press,
2003)

Patterson Thornburg, Mary K., *The Monster in the Mirror: Gender
and the Sentimental/Gothic Myth in Frankenstein*, 'Studies in
Speculative Fiction', Vol. 14, ed. by Robert Scholes (Ann Arbor: UMI
Research Press, 1984, 1987)

Prendergast, Christopher, *The Order of Mimesis: Balzac, Stendhal,
Nerval, Flaubert* (Cambridge: Cambridge University Press, 1986)

Proguidis, Lakis, 'Les Enfants de la bourse', in *L'Atelier du roman* 35 (September 2003), 76

Punter, David, *A Companion to the Gothic* (Oxford: Blackwell, 2000)

Punter, David and Byron, Glennis, *The Gothic* (Oxford: Blackwell, 2004)

Rabaté, Dominique, *Marie NDiaye* (Paris: Textuel, Culturesfrance, 2008)
-----,'Résistances et disparitions', in *Le Roman français contemporain*, ed. by Thierry Guichard, Christine Jérusalem, Boniface Mongo-Mboussa, Delphine Peras and Dominique Rabaté (Paris: Panoramas, 2007), pp. 9-46
-----, 'L'Exaltation du quotidien', in *Modernités 16: Enchantements, mélanges offerts à Yves Vadé* (Bordeaux: Presses Universitaires de Bordeaux, 2003), pp. 229-37
-----, 'L'Éternelle tentation de l'hébétude, le nom de Rosie Carpe', *L'Atelier du roman* 35 (September 2003), 48-55
-----, *Le Roman français depuis 1900*, coll. 'Que sais-je' (Paris: PUF, 1998)

Rand, Nicolas and Torok, Maria, 'The Sandman looks at 'The Uncanny', in *Speculations after Freud, Psychoanalysis, Philosophy and Culture*, ed. by Sonu Shamdasani and Michael Münchow (London and New York: Routledge, 1994), pp. 185-203

Rank, Otto, *The Double: A Psychoanalytic Study* (London: Karnac Books, 1971)

Ricardou, Jean, *Problèmes du nouveau roman* (Paris: Éditions du Seuil, 1967)

Richard, Jean-Pierre, *Terrains de lecture* (Paris: Gallimard)

Ricœur, Paul, *La Mémoire, l'histoire, l'oubli* (Paris: Éditions du Seuil, 2000)

Robbe-Grillet, Alain, *Pour un nouveau roman* (Paris: Éditions de

Minuit, 1963)

Robert, Marthe, *Roman des origines et origines du roman* (Paris: Gallimard, 1981; first published in 1976)

Ropars-Wuilleumier, Marie-Claire, *Écrire l'espace* (Paris: Presses universitaires de Vincennes, 2002)

Roudinesco, Elisabeth *La Famille en désordre* (Paris: Fayard, 2002)

Royle, Nicolas, *The Uncanny* (Manchester: Manchester University Press, 2003)

Sarrey-Strack, Colette, *Fictions contemporaines au féminin: Marie Darrieussecq, Marie NDiaye, Marie Nimier, Marie Redonnet* (Paris: L'Harmattan, 2002)

Scepi, Henri, 'Eugène Savitzkaya: une poétique du continu', *Critique* 576 (May 1995), 399-416
-----, 'Eugène Savitzkaya et le souci de l'origine', *Critique* 550-551 (March-April 1993), 140-66

Schehr, Lawrence, *Figures of Alterity: French Realism and its Others* (Stanford: Stanford University Press, 2003)

Schneider, Monique, 'Les Ambiguïtés de Freud aux prises avec le fantastique' in *La Littérature fantastique*, Colloque de Cerisy (Paris: Albin Michel, 1991), pp. 221-33

Schneider, Steven, 'Monsters as (Uncanny) Metaphors: Freud, Lakoff, and the Representation of Monstrosity in Cinematic Horror', *Other Voices*, V.1, No.3 (January 1999), http://www.othervoices.org/1.3/sschneider/monsters.htm (accessed March 20 2007)

Segal, Naomi, *The Banal Object: Theme and Thematics in Proust, Rilke, Hofmannsthal and Sartre* (London: Institute of Germanic Studies, 1981)

Sellers, Susan, *Hélène Cixous: Authorship, Autobiography and Love* (Oxford, Cambridge: Blackwell Publishers in association with Polity Press, 1996)
-----, *The Hélène Cixous Reader*, ed. by Susan Sellers (London: Routledge, 1994)

Shapiro, Michael J., *For Moral Ambiguity, National Culture and the Politics of the Family* (Minneapolis, London: University of Minnesota Press, 2001)

Sheringham, Michael, 'The Law of Sacrifice: Race and the Family in Marie NDiaye's *En famille* and *Papa doit manger*', in *Affaires de famille, The Family in Contemporary French Culture and Theory* (Amsterdam, New York: Rodopi, 2007), pp 23-37
-----, *Everyday Life, Theories and Practices from Surrealism to the Present* (Oxford: Oxford University Press, 2006)
-----, 'Le Romanesque du quotidien', in *Le Romanesque*, ed. by Michel Murat and Gilles Declercq (Paris: Presses Sorbonne Nouvelle, 2004), pp. 255-66

Shiach, Morach, *Hélène Cixous: A Politics of Writing* (London and New York: Routledge, 1991)

Shklovsky, Victor, 'Art as Technique', in *Russian Formalist Criticism: Four Essays*, trans. by Lee T. Lemon and Marion J. Reiss, ed. by Paul A. Olson (Lincoln: University of Nebraska Press, 1965), pp. 3-57

Simon, Bennett, *Tragic Drama and the Family: Psychoanalytic Studies from Aeschylus to Beckett* (New Haven and London: Yale University Press, 1988)

Smith, Anna, *Julia Kristeva: Readings of Exile and Estrangement* (Houndmills, Basingstoke, Hampshire, London: Macmillan Press, 1996)

Spadoni, Robert, *Uncanny Bodies, The Coming of Sound Film and the Origins of the Horror Genre* (Berkeley: University of California Press, 2007)

Stoloff, Jean-Claude, *La Fonction paternelle* (Paris: In Press Éditions, 2007)

Tatar, Maria M., 'The Houses of Fiction: Toward a Definition of the Uncanny,' in *Comparative Literature* 33, No. 2 (Spring 1981), 167-82

Têko-Agbo, Ambroise, '*En famille* de Marie NDiaye ou l'insupportable étrangeté de "l'étrangère"', in *Littératures et sociétés africaines: regards comparatistes et perspectives interculturelles, mélanges offerts à János Riesz à l'occasion de son soixantième anniversaire* (Tübingen: G. Narr, 2001), pp. 533-43

Thibault, Bruno, 'Du stéréotype au mythe: l'écriture du fait divers dans les nouvelles de J.M.G. Le Clézio', in *The French Review*, Vol. 68, No. 6 (May 1995), pp. 964-75

Thomas, A., 'Marie NDiaye. Renaissance de la littérature française', *Amina* 253 (May 1991), 81

Todorov, Tzvetan, *Introduction à la littérature fantastique*, coll. 'Poétique' (Paris: Éditions du Seuil, 1970)

Tulinius, Torfi H., 'Relations proches', *L'Atelier du roman* 35 (September 2003), 68-75

Vandenorpe, Christian, 'La Lecture du fait divers: fonctionnement textuel et effets cognitifs', *Tangence* 37 (1992), 56-69

Vercier, Bruno and Dominique, Viart, *La Littérature française au présent: Héritage, modernité, mutations* (Paris: Bordas, 2005)

Viart, Dominique, *Le Roman français au XXe siècle* (Paris: Hachette, 1999)

Vidler, Anthony, *The Architectural Uncanny: Essays on the Modern Unhomely* (Cambridge, London: MIT Press, 1992)

Walker, David H, *Outrage and Insight: Modern French Writers and the 'Fait Divers'* (Oxford, Washington: Berg Publishers, 1995)

Wearing, Betsy, *The Ideology of Motherhood: A Study of Sydney Suburban Mothers* (London and Boston: George Allen & Unwin, 1984)

Webber, von Andrew, *The Doppelganger: Double Visions in German Literature* (Oxford: Oxford University Press, 1996)

Weber, Samuel, *The Legend of Freud*, expanded edition (Stanford: Stanford University Press, 2000)

Whitehead, Claire, *The Fantastic in France and Russia in the Nineteenth Century. In Pursuit of Hesitation* (London: Legenda, 2006)

Wilson, Emma, *Cinema's Missing Children* (London: Wallflower Press, 2003)

Ziarek, Ewa 'The Uncanny Style of Kristeva's Critique of Nationalism,' in *Postmodern Culture* 5 (January 1995), http://www3.iath.virginia.edu/pmc/text-only/issue.195/ziarek.195 (accessed 10 november 2004)

Žižek, Slavoj, *Looking Awry: An Introduction to Jacques Lacan through Popular Culture* (Cambridge, London: MIT Press, 1992)
------, *The Sublime Object of Ideology* (London and New York: Verso, 1989)

Literary Texts

de Balzac, Honoré, *Le Père Goriot*, ed. by Charles Gould (London: University of London Press, 1967)

Belletto, René, *La Machine*, (Paris: J'ai Lu, 1990)
-----, *Sur la terre comme au ciel* (Paris: Hachette, 1982)

Darrieussecq, Marie, *Truismes* (Paris: P.O.L., 1996)

Hoffmann, E.T.A., *The Best Tales of Hoffmann*, ed. by E.F. Bleiler (New York: Dover Publications, 1967)

Kristeva, Julia, *Meurtre à Byzance* (Paris: Fayard, 2004)

Vigouroux, François, *Le Secret de famille* (Paris: Presses Universitaires de France, 1993)

Lightning Source UK Ltd.
Milton Keynes UK
05 August 2010

157913UK00001B/21/P